To Grace — with much affection and gratitude for your grace to me in so many ways — understanding, empathy, concern, and buying this book!

Lots of love
Dec 15, 05
(Dec 11, 03)

Learning to Fulfill the Needs of Your Self

It's an Inside Job!

Faith H. Charles, PhD

Copyright © 2003, Faith H. Charles, PhD

All rights reserved. No part of this book may be used or reproduced, in any manner whatsoever, without the written permission of the Publisher.

Printed in United States of America

For information address:
INFINITY
2325 North 52nd Street
Philadelphia, PA 19131
phone: 215.878.9887   fax: 215.878.6196

Library of Congress Cataloging-in-Publication Data
Faith H. Charles, 1939

Learning to Fullfill the Needs of Your Self: It's an Inside Job!
by Faith H. Charles, PhD

p. cm.

ISBN 0-7414-1446-5

First Edition

10 9 8 7 6 5 4 3 2 1

Visit our Web site at
http://www.URL.com

E mail: OCharles@aol.com

Book design by:
www.madhof.com

This book is dedicated with much love and gratitude to
the seven most important people in my life:

My beloved and ever present mentor and guide
Lloyd Butler (1917-1996)
who brought me from darkness to light

My beloved husband
Oscar Charles, Jr.
who walks with me in the light

My beloved daughter & son-in-law
Jocelyn & Christopher McMahon
&
My beloved daughter
Christina Kaissi
who—thanks to the force that guides us all—have
discovered their own light, and are so generous
as to share it with me

And to **Aidan & Fiona McMahon**, the next generation:

"Behold the child among his newborn blisses,
A six-years' Darling of a pygmy size!
See, where 'mid work of his own hand he lies,
Fretted by sallies of his mother's kisses,
With light upon him from his father's eyes!
See, at his feet, some little plan or chart,
Some fragment from his dream of human life…"
William Wordsworth
*Intimations of Immortality from
Recollections of Early Childhood* st. VII

Acknowledgements

This book has its roots in the theories and practice of many outstanding teachers and therapists. The ones to whom I owe the greatest debt, in order of acquaintance with them or their work, are Emilie Cady, Abraham Maslow, Aldous Huxley, Satya Sai Baba, Sogyal Rinpoche, Alexander Lowen, Deepak Chopra, Anne Wilson Schaef, and Peter Breggin. The first five are major lifetime scholarly and spiritual teachers of my personal and professional life. From the work of the last four, I have absorbed particular therapeutic practices plus scientific themes and information that have both enlightened me and also verified some of my own insights and theories.

Therapists I have learned from in person include Jackie Small, Anne Wilson Schaef, Doris Amaya, Mary Whipple, and Sharon Wegscheider-Cruse. Ms. Small's presentation of Maslow's hierarchy of needs was a life-changing experience for me, providing both the foundation for the Chart presented in this book, and also revealing to me the source of my own pain. Anne Wilson Schaef's iconoclastic approach and forthright presentation said out loud concepts I was able only to whisper. The theory described in her workshops and detailed in her books, especially *Beyond Therapy, Beyond Science,* validated and helped expand the process I had been developing for several years that evolved into the Process presented in this book.

The Process also owes much to workshops with Sharon Wegscheider-Cruse and extended co-counseling with Mary Whipple, with whom I worked in Houston in 1979-80 in my first job. A compassionate therapist, so subtly insightful she seemed at times psychic, she modeled for me the art of sensing and caring for (not *taking care of*) the client's feelings, while allowing him to do his own work. She called this procedure "tracking the psychic flow." Doris Amaya's profound understanding of family dynamics, and her compassion for the recovery of the family as a whole, taught me empathy and strategy. These five brilliant, courageous, inspiring women demonstrated in their counseling the qualities of character I admired and wanted, and the path of healing which made sense to me.

Elements from these wonderful models that rang true to me were incorporated into the developing process I offered to my clients. At the same time, I was awakening to the realization of how much my clients were teaching me. I can say with pleasure that I have learned something about human nature and about the healing process from every client I've worked with. Some were things I didn't want to know—in particular, about myself!—but of course those are the very learnings that have benefitted me the most, both professionally and personally. I owe a lifetime of gratitude to all the many clients who, during the twenty-three years of my practice, have allowed me into their lives and psyches so freely.

On a personal level, it is a joy to me to acknowledge the help and support of my husband Oscar Charles, first for the insight, interest, patience, love, and computer training he gave me throughout the entire project, even at times when he was pressed with his own work. He came up with wonderfully helpful suggestions when I couldn't see my way clearly. But most important, his amazing technical expertise enabled him to find a way to construct all my weird charts and diagrams and somehow make the computer accept them (though none two willingly!). My gratitude, respect, and love for him are boundless; to put it simply, I couldn't have done it without him.

My staff also deserves my heartfelt thanks. Their willing and enthusiastic performance of their own jobs freed me to use the time not occupied by counseling to write. Mary Jean Wagenhoffer kept my house and office in beautiful shape with unfailing zeal and expertise; Evelin Fields took care of the business and insurance end of my practice with patience, good humor, and expert skills; and Nina Kochel, my secretary and girl Friday, word-processed draft upon draft upon draft, as many times as I needed—and how many times that was, we both lost count! She was meticulous, insightful, swift, cheerful, enthusiastic, and clever beyond belief in deciphering my over-written, labyrinthine manuscripts. The generous help of these three wonderful friends allowed me to make the most of my time.

Two more people deserve extra special thanks. First, to Madeline Hoefer, book designer extraordinaire, for her painstaking ingenuity and skill in arranging all my charts. Her helpful guidance made the whole project come together. The second is my "author support rep," Ed Pratowski. Available apparently around the clock, he invariably pulled me up when I was sinking, and left me singing. He also contributed a beautiful piece in the Appendices—#5.

My final tribute is the most important. This book would not have been possible without the presence in my life of Lloyd Butler. I met him early in my life and immediately knew him to be my mentor. His effect on my life—my growth, work, and spiritual development—is inestimable. To all who entered his orbit, Lloyd radiated unfailing loving-kindness, understanding, and profound connectedness with spirit and with truth. "Just standing next to Lloyd makes you feel good," a friend of mine once said. Through spiritual practice he had evolved to the stage of loving everyone, unconditionally, all the time, *for real*—an accomplishment light-years above any of the other people I know, but especially myself. His style of mentoring was unique: he healed by surrounding one with love. Once, in a phone conversation, when I had been talking for about twenty minutes (he never interrupted me), and he had been as usual completely silent, I asked him, "Papa, what do you do while I babble on like this?" (Sometimes I suspected that he dozed off). His reply blew me away: "I am beholding the Christ in you." *Wow! What* Christ? in *me?* His teaching made me see that I had been walking in darkness all my life, and showed me a great light, which lights my path still, from then till forever. *Sine quo non.*

His passing in 1996 has not diminished that light or love. In his last talk, he acknowledged the influence his mentors had on him: "Doc Hobbs and ol' Buddy Stokes be alive in me today because of the gifts they gave me." So I say of him: his Spirit lives today in all of us who knew him—and all who knew him loved him—because of the gifts of Spirit that he gave us. He "inclined unto us, and heard our cry, and put a new song in our mouth" (Psalm 40:1)—a song celebrating the recovery, redemption, and transformation of the fallen human being into spirit. He led us prodigal children back to our true selves, and I know he lives.

TABLE OF CONTENTS

Preface

Overview

To Change Your Life

Learning to Fulfill the Needs of Your Self:
It's an Inside Job

Chapter I	Zeke's Story	1
Chapter II	The Freedom Healing Process	11
Chapter III	The Security Need	29
Chapter IV	The Belonging Need	69
Chapter V	The Self-Esteem Need	89
Chapter VI	The Autonomy Need	109
Chapter VII	The Freedom Healing Process as a Means to Transcendence	131

Discoveries & Conclusions:
The Freedom Healing Process & Five Correlative Systems

Appendix I	Codependency	185
	Codependency & the Chart	
Appendix II	Brain Structure & Functioning	203
Appendix III	Mental Health Diagnoses	228
Appendix IV	The Hierarchy of Needs & the Chakras	250
Appendix V	From Chaos to Harmony	254

To the Reader: From My Heart to Yours

Notes

Notes for Appendices

Bibliography

The Hierarchy of Needs

"Dependency" needs
(Empty, incomplete, unintegrated, needing to take in, be filled, nurtured)

"Being" needs
(Filled, integrated, whole, needing to express)

- PHYSICAL - EMOTIONAL -
- SPIRITUAL -

HIERARCHY of HUMAN NEEDS (Maslow)

Level	FEELINGS Experienced when the NEED not met	WHAT THE DEFENSES SAY	TYPE	MENTAL HEALTH DIAG.
UNITY				
SPIRITUAL SELF REALIZATION	Absolute isolation. Despairing, alienated, fragmented, incomplete, separated, bitter. Lonely, alone, empty, afraid, unfulfilled, fragile.	PRIDE HUBRIS EGOMANIA MACHISMO — Self-sufficiency, sense of superiority. "I am the only one that matters... I am a law unto myself... other people and the rest of creation don't matter." "No one really cares... I can do it myself. I don't need any help... I can take care of my family... myself." "I am all I need... I have no interest in or connection with anything outside me."	EVIL ONE OPPRESSOR DOMINATOR DICTATOR	THE LOST SOUL
SELF-ACTUALIZATION (Expression of self)	Bored, futile, meaningless, empty, apathetic, useless.	Cynicism, denial of feelings, hyperactivity, sophistication, compulsive socializing and spending, overconsumption, taking up hobbies, self-improvement. "I'm OK... the world is wrong."... "I have everything I need."... "Why am I still unhappy?"... "Something's missing..." "Why bother to try? Life's a bitch and then you die... Who really cares? Everything's pointless... Let's go on a trip!"	THE CYNIC	
AUTONOMY Self-defining Self-governing	Self-doubting, ashamed, guilty, helpless, powerless, feeling incompetent, trapped, rejected, hurt, enraged, defiant.	Blame, arrogance, rationalizing, defensiveness, self-righteousness, dependency, narcissism, grandiosity, anti-social acting out, rebelling, lying, analyzing, making trouble, projecting, illicit drug use/addiction. "I'll by... if I do that! That lousy...", "You know what he did to me?" "No-body's going to tell me what to do!" "Why can't you understand?" "It's your fault... if you hadn't..." "It's not fair!"	ANTI-SOC NARCISSISTIC PASSIVE AGGRES. PERS. DIS.	THE TROUBLE TYPE
SELF ESTEEM	Inadequate, worthless, inferior. Self hating. Not good enough, less than.	Self justification, bragging, envy, jealousy, projection, denial, sarcasm, suspiciousness, volunteering, over-achieving, compulsive talking, caretaking, theorizing, criticizing, bragging, alcohol abuse/addiction. "I can drink more than any man in the house!" "I have to get this done today!" "Work isn't my problem, you are!" "I just know she hates me!"	COMPULSIVE PERS. DIS.	THE PERFECT TYPE
BELONGING ACCEPTANCE	Abandoned, lonely. Grief-ful, unacceptable, neglected, rejected, sad.	Depression, rage, silence, isolation, self-pity, fantasy, solitary activities, compulsive overeating, TV-watching, romance novel reading, has pets, Pornography, masturbation, sexual anorexia. Often sexual abuse survivor. Paranoia, loose associations, incongruency. "I've gotten used to it." "Never mind what they said to you; you wouldn't remember it anyway." "I never fit in any-how." "I can't get out." "You're no good!" "Dumb!" "Stupid!" "Fat girl!" "Lazy!"	AVOIDANT PERS. DIS. AGORAPHOBIA PANIC DISORDER SCHIZOPHRENIA	THE FORGOTTEN TYPE
SURVIVAL - SECURITY	Anxious, insecure, fearful, worry, angry.	FIGHT — Life of the party, funny, sarcastic, obnoxious, on the go, worry, verbal abuse, agitation, tackling, accusation, provoking, planning, physical abuse, hyperactivity, competitiveness, violence, grandiosity, hostility, homicide, obsessive focusing. Controlling behavior: Prescription drug abuse, alcohol abuse/addiction. FLIGHT — Checking out, tension, depression, scattered thinking, denial, dissociation, shyness, lying, spaced, sleeping difficulty, fantasy.	ADD, OCD, ODD, MD, MPD DISSOCIATIVE DISORDERS	THE CLOWN TYPE

← when met
← when unmet

MENTAL & BEHAVIORAL DEFENSES which block pain of unmet needs

FAITH H. CHARLES, CAC
Freedom Counseling
2325 North 52nd Street
Philadelphia, PA 19131
(215) 879-9887
Copyright Pending

PREFACE

The system of healing presented in this book is based on the concept that for us to be happy, fulfilled, and productive, and attain our highest possible degree of evolution, our basic emotional needs must be sufficiently met. Accomplishing this is necessarily a spiritual process. As set forth here, that process involves two things: first, releasing—one might even say *exorcizing*—the patterns encoded in us when children, from unmet needs, the ghosts which haunt and dominate our adult lives; and second, replacing them with healthful new patterns based on a realization of the truth and power of our nature—that is, that we are essentially spiritual beings dwelling in physical form.

This shift in consciousness, in how we see ourselves, is *an inside job*: it can be done only *by* you, not *to* you, although external support and guidance are typically necessary and nearly always desired. As this shift is accomplished, we experience an ever-increasing sense of freedom, joy, love, peace, and all other gifts and qualities of spirit, most especially the realization that *there is only good*, because now having eyes to see, we perceive that the bad events are stepping stones that bring us to our good—"the past is perfect."

The Freedom Healing Process© presented here is thus transformative: confronting and releasing old harmful patterns dissolves them as current influences, freeing us to choose our thoughts and actions in accord with our needs. Accomplishing that Process© leads us to develop values and govern ourselves according to them. By continuing to use the same Process© in the present, we eventually realize our deepest truth: that we not only *have* an Inner Power, we *are* that Inner Power: "I am *that* I am" (Exodus 3:14). So, if we want freedom, health, love, and joy, and anything else, we can create them daily within us:

"Be ye transformed in the renewing of your mind."

(Romans 12:2)

"You are waves; I am the ocean. Know this and be free, be divine.

"Man must give up the desire for objective pleasure, based on the illusion that the world is many, manifold, multi-colored, *etc.* and not on the truth that the world, nature, all creation is One. When one is conscious only of the One, who desires what? What can be acquired and enjoyed by the second person? The Atmic vision destroys the desire for objective joys, for there is no object distinct from the subject."[1]

Satya Sai Baba, in Samuel H. Sandweiss, M.D.
The Holy Man and the Psychiatrist
Birth Day Publishing Co.
San Diego, California, U.S.A. p. 207

The following quotation, written by a client, gives a precise summation of the system presented in this book. Its clarity, simplicity, and grace so perfectly reflect the nature of the Freedom Process© that it makes an appropriate introduction. The writer, Mitchell Karp, kindly gave his permission for me to use it.

An Overview of the Freedom Healing Process

We were all born with a certain set of needs. To a lesser or greater extent these needs were met or not met by our parents and significant others in our early childhood. As we grew up, we found ways to compensate for our unmet needs. We formed certain behaviors and thinking patterns, a set of defenses if you will, to cover up the painful feelings caused by our unmet needs.

What served us then is now a disability for us. Our job in recovery is to learn to discharge these painful feelings so that the defenses will fall away. So long as we hold on to these feelings, the destructive behaviors and thinking patterns will continue. After discharging the feelings and thereby altering our behaviors and thinking, we can learn how to meet the needs that were so neglected as we grew up in our families. We do this with positive affirmation, prayer, meditation, deep breathing, and relaxing. Time and patience are the keynotes here. We need to be gentle with ourselves and vigilant in our path to recovery.

If You Want to Change Your Life

If you want to change your life,
    you have to change your behavior.

To change your behavior,
    you have to change your thinking.

To change your thinking,
    you have to change your feelings.

To change your feelings,
    you have to meet your needs.

To meet your needs,
    you have to meditate.

The butterfly was flapping its wings—a good five-inch spread—against the window as I walked into the garage. It was the largest and definitely the most anxious butterfly I'd ever seen. Afraid it would be hurt, I ran back into the house and got a large strainer and a pot lid, hoping the wood frames of the windows wouldn't block my rescue attempt. As I approached I saw the butterfly's gorgeous markings, velvet black on top of dusky black, blurring into each other from his fluttering. Miraculously, as I put the strainer over him, the pot lid slid past the frames of the window, enclosing him safely. Trembling with anxious success, I made for the door. Once outside, *my* intent was to liberate him onto the honeysuckle bushes lining the driveway fence.

But the butterfly had his own plan. The minute we were outside the garage, to my utter astonishment, he burst the bounds of his benign cage—which I *still* think I was holding tightly shut—and, wings whirring into a blur, he turned on the afterburners, and rocketed himself *straight upward* to the heavens—and *freedom*!

I

Zeke's Story

Zeke was a fifty-six-year-old man in recovery from addiction and codependency.[1] In the group therapy session I was leading, he had revealed his troubled childhood and adolescence, and how he had been struggling for several months to free himself from some very painful and persistent feelings stemming from that time. When he was three and a half, his father was severely injured in a fire, and was laid up for over a year. Consequently, in addition to suddenly becoming sole caregiver for him, his mother had to take on the entire job of running the house, paying the bills, and finding a job. Shaken by her husband's incapacity and overwhelmed with a load of new responsibilities, she paid hardly any attention to Zeke beyond survival necessities.

This drastic and sudden loss, shocking and incomprehensible to Zeke, made him feel abandoned, rejected, unwanted, not good enough—and baffled. If he had been old enough to put his feelings into words, it would have gone something like this: "Why doesn't mommy play with me anymore? Why doesn't mommy love me anymore? I must be bad...unlovable...no good...undesirable...I must be a different person from what I thought I was..." Zeke was already losing the positive self he had developed during the first three and half years, and was installing a new one, exactly opposite: negative, pessimistic, and isolated.

By the time Zeke's father could walk again, about a year and a half later, his mother's life was filled with so many different obligations that she had even less time for Zeke. The effect on him was drastic and life changing: he had by now developed a mind-set that would stay with him for the rest of his life (until he entered group). Instead of that feeling of belonging and connectedness with his mother that had made him a confident and loving little boy, he now felt empty, withdrawn, and lonesome, the beginning stages of the pervasive sense of disappointment, depression, rage, and rejection that were to shape his life.

As he grew into manhood, his later relationship troubles with women reflected this early disconnect. With his need for bonding perpetually unfulfilled, he unconsciously related to other people—women in particular—as though they were there to meet his needs. It hadn't entered his mind that, as an adult, he could meet those needs *himself*. Physically he was grown up, but emotionally he was still a child.

Little did he know that this night God would give him a gift. It was clear by the way he walked into the room that he was upset.

"I need some time," he announced to the group, and continued without pausing, "That woman is at me again about money!"

"More trouble with the girl friend?" asked a sympathetic group member. The group was familiar with Zeke's relationship and its troubles, so the identity of the woman was no mystery to them.

"Yeah," said Zeke. "She wants a new dining room set! I'm already working overtime three nights...I just can't do it any more! I got really pissed off and told her what I'd do if she didn't stop!"

Learning to Fulfill the Needs of Your Self

"You were really furious," said one of the women.

"I still am!" he replied, his face now red and his veins standing out. "I better work on the pillows." He went to the stack of cushions in the corner and pounded with intensity for several minutes.[2]

When Zeke stopped, his face had cleared somewhat, and after a few minutes of deep breathing he said, "What came up while I was pounding is—surprise!—*my mother!* She was always after me to do something—fix the doorknob, go to the store, cut the neighbor's grass—to make more money! It was never enough. *It still isn't!*"

This anguished outburst made it clear that Zeke's feelings toward his mother, the source of his irritation with his girl friend, needed more work. Customarily I would at this point have suggested a role-play or psychodrama to help him release them and look at what he brought to the relationship. But this time I didn't, because a new energy/idea entered my mind, and after a moment's consideration, I decided to go with it.

"Zeke," I said, "I'd like you to close your eyes and do some deep breathing, and please everybody else give support by breathing with him."

To my surprise, Zeke willingly complied, as did all the other group members. After several minutes, when I saw that his breathing rhythm was well established, I again followed the energy/idea that came into my mind.

"Now, as you inhale, expanding your abdomen, let yourself experience the healthful energy filling you, and as you exhale, contract your abdomen and experience yourself releasing the unhealthful energy." Evidently he was listening, because his inbreaths became deeper and longer and his outbreaths more vigorous and complete. He continued for about ten minutes. Fascinated to be witnessing something new and apparently effective, and aware by now that it had a direction of its own, I gave all my attention to tracking its flow, listening for each suggestion.

The signs of agitation and anger in Zeke's face brought up by the pounding—reddened nose and cheeks, visible veins, scowling expression—diminished, giving way to a drizzle, then a torrent, of tears. Several other group members showed similar signs. As I continued to watch, all the while breathing in sync with him and the group, I saw his tears gradually subside and his face become relaxed. So I continued:

"As your breathing returns to normal, keep your eyes closed, and say silently to yourself on the inbreath: *peace*, and on the outbreath: *be still*...and keep repeating it." (Subsequent use of the process taught me to vary the message to suit the need). Zeke stayed with this for a significant length of time—maybe eight or nine minutes. When he opened his eyes, his countenance showed that he had experienced a deep change: his skin was a beautiful healthy pink, his eyes were sparkling, and his lips were wide open in a beatific smile.

"I feel so peaceful," he said, "like *cleansed*...I've never felt anything like this before..." The blue of his eyes had deepened; they looked like a baby's when he awakens—as though he had gone back to his world of origin and was reluctant to return to this one. The group appeared transfixed, their faces still and shining, apparently awed by what had taken place, new to them as it was to me. Several expressed feelings similar to Zeke's.

"What was *that?*" he asked. "It was incredible...I feel so relaxed...more than relaxed...a feeling I don't have a word for..."

"Blissful?" I suggested.

"Yes!" he exclaimed. "If only I could do that myself!" The results of the process—bliss—defined it to me as a variant form of meditation.

"You discovered something you really like," I said. "You'll remember the steps."

"I shouldn't have yelled at her and threatened her," Zeke said, all of a sudden spontaneously able to look at his behavior and correct it (Step Ten, to those in a Twelve Step program). "I see now I have to acknowledge that to her" (Step Nine). The group uttered expressions of support and affection, happy to hear him complete his process with an action they understood. Their faces suggested that they had experienced a mood change similar to Zeke's, if not as intense.

"It's not really about her, anyway," he continued. "When I was breathing, something came up that I haven't thought about for years—maybe even since it happened. It's what I was crying about. When I was three and a half, my father burned his leg, third degree, ankle to hip. He'd been cleaning paintbrushes in the kitchen sink, standing right next to the hot water heater, and he knocked over the can of paint thinner. Some of it splashed onto the open flame of the water heater, which leapt out and set his left pant leg—and the whole damn kitchen—on fire.

"He ran down the cellar stairs—'flaming like a torch' he later described it—to find a blanket to smother the fire consuming his leg, while my mother, outside hanging up the wash, seeing the smoke pouring out the kitchen window, ran up the stairs to put out the fire consuming the kitchen (she did, too, by God, even before the fire engine got there!). Afterwards, neither remembered having passed the other"— here he stopped and swallowed a bit and a few more tears rolled down his face—"they figured it out after. Also, neither of them could remember where I was—kind of an omen—and I don't remember either...although I do remember my mother's yell when she saw the smoke, so I guess I was outside with her.

"Well, Dad was laid up for a year, Mom had to go to work, and my world was gone...She got a job teaching. It was a long time ago—in the mid fifties—in the country, in a one-room schoolhouse, all eight grades together! She couldn't afford baby sitting for me, especially on top of Dad's medical bills (no health insurance then!), so she took me to school with her. I sat in the schoolroom all day long with nothing to do but watch the older kids do stuff I couldn't even understand, and felt like a dunce, invisible and useless, pretty much how I still feel around other people. She had no attention to spare, and there were no kids my own age to play with—they were all two years older or more, on up to thirteen—and not particularly interested in me. When we got home in the late afternoon, she had to take care of *him*!...so I wasn't five before she started leaning on me to do stuff—stuff that would have been *his* job! I felt that old rage just now toward them both—how dare they just use me and forget me like that!—then I felt again that lost, alone, empty, forlorn, desolate feeling...God, what an awful feeling!" Here Zeke paused, and spontaneously took three or four deep breaths.

"Before the fire," he went on, "she was very attentive and gentle and understanding—which is probably why I didn't end up totally insane. I remember once when I broke a dish she comforted me, instead of scolding me; and she read to me a lot, and sang me 'Lullaby and Goodnight' at bedtime. But all that went up in the kitchen flames.

"Now that I look back on it I don't think they ever really recovered from it, and *what it did to them shaped me*. I felt so unwanted. Just thinking of being around other people frightened me, because they might reject me. The only way to make sure that couldn't happen was to stay alone. That's why I'm fifty-six and have a girl friend rather than a wife. Sometimes I'm amazed I have a girl friend." He paused again and sank into a brief trance, absorbing this flood of memories and feelings. Then his face brightened and he said: "But if I can get that feeling—that *bliss*—again, I can see that some changes might happen!"

His transformation was apparent, and for the first time he allowed himself to have a group hug. The breathing process had taken him into the core of his trauma, released it, and brought him out on the healing path. From this new vantage point, the seemingly irrelevant tiff with his girl friend took on new meaning: it was there, he now saw, on purpose to uproot and release the life-defining trauma that was blocking his progress, and to give him a process by which to heal and find his bliss.

As I continued to use this Process© over the years, I learned many things about it and from it. During the time immediately following its appearance via Zeke, as I practiced it myself and with clients, what impressed me the most was its short and simple three-part structure: the first part pounding, leading into accessing and experiencing feelings; the second part experiencing and releasing feelings; the third part fulfilling the needs of Your self, thus becoming self nurturing and free of dependency.[3] I named it the "Freedom Healing Process©" because, as Zeke's story shows, it brings new healthful energy that liberates old pain, and transforms the energy of old negative patterns into positive. And you don't need a group to do it—just this Process©!

P.S. For those who want to know what happened with the girl friend, he stayed with her and with the help of his new process and the release of resentment about his mother, they were able to negotiate their differences and live happily ever after!

A few words about what to expect in the coming chapters:

Chapter II describes the Freedom Healing Process© in detail so it will be familiar to you when you read the chapters on the four basic needs.

Chapters III through VI introduce in turn the four basic needs, and describe the characteristics of each and the kind of thinking and behavior typical of each. Each chapter then takes you step-by-step through the method of healing specific to that need. The re-presentation of the Freedom Healing Process© in each of these five chapters is deliberate and therapeutic. The repetition insures the fulfillment of your needs: it hastens the shift in consciousness from depending on others, to relying on the eternal source within you to meet them. Furthermore, because the Process© is experiential, the repetitions will be imprinted in your feeling brain so that eventually you will come to use it automatically whenever you feel troubled.

One other consideration, a practical one, supported this format: it struck me as more reader-friendly to have the Freedom Healing Process© exactly where you need it in the moment you need it, rather than in a separate chapter where you would have to turn to it.

The sequence of chapters is also significant: it follows the structure of the main Chart© (see page facing Chapter III) from the primary need, security, to the final need, unification, following the order of growth from infancy through adulthood to our ultimate state of spiritual union. Your maturation/spiritual growth process will advance no matter at what level you start, since each chapter takes you up one level. My intention and hope are that in addition to presenting and describing the Freedom© Healing Process©, the presentation will also give you the *experience* of it, since it is through *experiencing* that our feelings learn and our growth develops.

Chapter VII presents the three spiritual needs that make up the top third of the main Chart©, first discussing feelings and the defenses they generate when not met, then taking the reader through the Healing Process© for each one. In contrast to the *dependency* needs of the previous four, these are *being* needs—that is, the needs of the evolved person, someone who has successfully completed the initial four dependency needs.

"DISCOVERIES AND CONCLUSIONS" consists of five additional conceptual systems, each one of which correlates to the Freedom Healing Process©. In order of discovery, they are:

Codependency

The Structure and Functioning of the Brain

The Mental Health Diagnostic System

The Hierarchy of Needs and the Eastern System of the Chakras

From Chaos to Harmony

A final note. While this book may be interesting because of its theory (I certainly hope so) and you therefore may want to read it through without doing the exercises *en route*, you will get a much greater benefit if you practice the Process© for each need until it can be reliably met from within. The Process© doesn't just put you in a better mood; if worked sufficiently, it reconstructs your view of Your self.

II

The Freedom Healing Process

When you undertake the Freedom Healing Process©, you will find that it consists of a combination of physical and psychological processes that together gradually transform you from a need-driven person to a need-fulfilled person, one who experiences freedom. The core of the Healing Process© is the breathing procedure demonstrated in Zeke's marvelous experience: it channels energy from our spiritual self (consciousness) to our human self (thought, emotion, and body). Participating in both realms, breath unifies our human-self with our Spirit-Self.

The Process© consists of three distinct phases:

Phase 1: accesses feelings, bringing them from the unconscious mind (where we cannot experience them but which determines our behavior) to our conscious mind;

Phase 2: gives us the opportunity to experience our feelings and, using our conscious mind, explore their messages, retaining the beneficial ones and releasing the harmful ones, which

Phase 3: enables us to choose our behavior and fulfill the needs of our human self *from within*, no longer dependent on outside sources.

Once you've learned to practice the Process©, you will find that you can do it anywhere. For example, a friend of mine, who loves opera above all (well, *almost* all) else, intercepted a family disagreement that threatened her attendance at a performance of *The Magic Flute* by a timely release of feelings—quietly—in the Ladies' Room at the Metropolitan Opera!

The experiential segment which follows, the Freedom Healing Process©, is the core of this book. It presents the concept and the procedure that the book was written to give you: that is, the Process© by which you can liberate Your self *in the moment* from the pain of unmet needs and from dependency on others to meet your needs. After all, *You* know, better than anyone else, what Your self needs—safety, understanding, approval, love, respect, *etc.*

As you release more and more of the distress that damaged you in childhood, your inner self undergoes a transformation, like David, who recorded and celebrated the joyous revelations of his inner self, as in Psalm 40:2: "He (the inner spirit) hath established my goings . . and put a new song in my mouth." Experiencing is not just the best teacher—it's the *only* teacher. That's what "practice" means: *experience*. The following section guides you through the Process© step by step. It consists of three parts:

**1
Accessing Feelings**

**2
Experiencing and Releasing Feelings**

**3
Meeting the Need: Infilling
& Self Nurturing**

The Freedom Healing Process

I. Accessing Feelings

This exercise activates your feelings, brings them to the surface, and starts the process of releasing. Kneel on a pillow in front of a sofa or a pile of cushions (sturdy ones). Close your eyes, clench your fists, and pound the sofa or cushions like Zeke did. Pound only from your elbows; raising your arms over your head can result in a pulled muscle and isn't any more effective. Continue the pounding, with pauses to get your breath, until your anger is gone or reduced so greatly that it's negligible.

Some people, especially those who have deeply repressed anger, feel uncomfortable doing the pounding. While they are the ones who need it the most, they are, ironically, also the ones who often reject it, on grounds that it will make them more angry, instead of less:

"I'm not ready for this." (fear)
"It won't work." (frustration and discouragement)
"It will just make me upset." (frustration and anger)
"It will make me more angry." (anxiety)

But what actually happens is that the Process© removes their defenses so that they can release the painful feelings they have been repressing or acting out. Better to access the anger, bring it out into the light of consciousness where it can be dealt with, than to store it up. Contrary to popular opinion, it is the *repression,* not the *expression,* of painful feelings that harms us: the more we repress them, the less we can control them and therefore the more underground pain they generate. In that state, when someone or something gets our goat, we "go off" and react with a defensive statement or behavior.

This action has two negative results: it represses our painful feelings further and hurts the other person as well, setting us up for a karmic response. When we can break through the defenses by doing the Healing Process© and allow ourselves to experience and consciously release the painful feelings—privately, not at the other person—we will be able consciously to dissolve the pain, cease acting it out, and stop making somebody else responsible for our actions.

For those who were exposed to violence as children or adolescents, the pounding may awaken frightening memories. The Process© can go one of two ways: the memories may bring about a therapeutic discharge, or they may be too intense to handle. If the latter is the case with you, here is an alternative process: bend your head and torso (from the pelvic area rather than the waist) and let your head and arms dangle down loosely. Now start shaking your hands, arms, and head gently and knock your knees together, *sideways, not front to back!* Stay loose and relaxed as you do all this: remember it's a tension *releasing,* not a tension *creating* activity. After not more than a couple of minutes *slowly,* pull up your torso and head and, eyes closed, shake your head back and forth, drop your jaw and let it hang loose, keep knocking your knees together, and shake your *derriere.*

All of this is to be done loosely, and if it has no other effect than making you feel giggly and silly, it will have served its purpose. (Those of you who want to put your recovery into the fast lane can do *both* the pounding and the shaking, in that order). Finally, sit down slowly and gently, and notice the tingling sensation in your lower legs, hands, and arms: that's new energy giving your body/mind a spring-cleaning. You will feel refreshed and clear-headed and free of old pain.

Always do the pounding twice even if you have to shorten the length of time of both poundings. The first process awakens feelings and brings them to the surface; the second begins the process of releasing them. Both phases are necessary to get the full result; if you do only the first pounding, you'll be left with a bellyful of anger and no way to relieve it. Doing it a second time dislodges the anger and relieves the pain. As you gradually allow yourself to experience the anger, you will become able to release it consciously and deliberately, so it doesn't disrupt your inner state or cause you to take it out on somebody else.

Continue this exercise as many times as needed, with brief rests, until your painful feelings have diminished or disappeared. You will experience relief from your negative feelings and a sense of comfort, wholeness, and self-confidence. When your feelings have been released to the degree that you want, you are ready for the next stage of the Process©.

II. Experiencing and Releasing Feelings: Breathing

This breathing process will not be new to you if you have done hatha yoga or meditation. But as you will soon see, it is designed here to do a specific job: clearing your mind and body of the toxins produced by painful feelings. To start the Process© either:

1. Sit with your back straight, both feet on the floor,
or
2. Lie down on the floor, lower legs resting horizontally on chair or bed, upper legs vertical, knees at right angles, small pillow under the back of your neck. This position is the easier from which to learn; after you've practised it several times, you'll be able to do the Process© sitting up or adapt it to any condition you want to change. In either position, lay your hands flat across your abdomen, below your navel.

3. Now you are ready to begin. Always start by exhaling: blow the breath out forcibly, as if blowing out the candles on a birthday cake. As you exhale, *deflate* your abdomen (below your navel) by contracting your abdominal muscles, pulling them back toward your spine. (Pushing your abdomen inward with your hands helps.) This forces the breath out, as you know if you've ever had the misfortune to be punched or hit below the belt. Don't, however, exhale fast. Make your exhalation deliberate, steady, and thorough; you must govern it, not let it govern you.

4. When every last bit of breath has been squeezed out, inhale through your nose, deliberately and fully, inflating your abdomen by directing the breath into it; its expansion should push your hands out. Exhale as before, and repeat the exercise for about ten minutes.

5. When you notice your mind wandering—which it will—just direct it back to the breathing. Picture and feel the column of breath as it moves in and out, in and out, like being rocked in a boat. This is the crucial part of the Process© since it is *through exhaling that the pain and toxins are released.* The exhalation must therefore be thorough and completed. Since it is hard to remember a sequence of instructions, you might want to tape them (read them into your recorder *very slowly*), or ask a friend to read them to you (*slowly*):

Here is the brief version:
1. Sit or lie down, as described above.

2. Exhale: *blow out* through your mouth as you *deflate* your abdomen (beneath your navel).
3. Inhale: *breathe in* through your nose as you *inflate* your abdomen.

If this way of breathing (exhale/deflate) feels awkward to you at first, it may be because you've been breathing the opposite way (exhale/inflate, inhale/deflate) and you may need to practise it a while to catch on. (The other way can cause you to hyperventilate). When you feel as if nothing is happening is exactly the time to stay with it. As your system gets accustomed to the Process© it will gradually speed up and you will feel wonderful. You don't have to get it all the first time you do it: *it's a learning thing.*

By the time you have breathed like this for three or four minutes, a steady rhythm will be established. The next step is to focus on your painful feelings and as you inhale, feel your inhalation drawing them in. Hold your breath for a moment at the top to experience them fully, then puff your cheeks up and exhale as described above—long, slow, and complete. Blow your pain out into the universe where it will be dissolved and recycled. Feel your breath releasing as the contraction of your torso squeezes it out, just like an accordion.

The purpose of the inbreath is to awaken the unconscious feelings held in your body (in the very cells!) by your defenses, and bring them into your awareness, so you can consciously release them. *To release feelings it is necessary to feel them.* Let them happen as they will; don't fight, force, or try to control them, and continue to do the Process©. They will intensify and then dissipate and you will be rid of that batch of painful feelings. This is the cleansing part of the Process©: releasing toxic chemicals generated in the body by painful feelings and thereby giving the immune system a boost.

This type of breathing is not aimed at making you feel relaxed and soothed; on the contrary, it is hard work, like labor. It is reassuring to know that you have a built-in healthy defense system that will govern this part of the Healing Process© so that it won't get more intense that you can handle. You won't fall apart or go crazy. Indeed, those outcomes are more likely to happen from *not* doing the Process©.

After each inhalation, you will experience a lessening of the feeling-charge, of the obsessive mental chatter, and of the urgency to act out. Your whole system will become relaxed and *clear:* you will have reversed the cycle which keeps you dependent on others to meet your needs, and you will be able to meet them from within, from You-as Spirit. "I just had to call and see if she's alright!" turns into: "I have a choice whether or not to call. Let me think which would be better."

If you don't get dramatic results at first it doesn't mean that you—or the Process©—has failed; it means you need to prime the pump a bit. Deeply buried feelings surface gradually. And for a good reason: if they all gushed up at once, you would feel overwhelmed. So keep at it—it works *if you work it.* Trust the Process© and trust *your* process: it knows how to regulate itself to what your feeling system can handle. You will be transformed a little bit each time you do it, so that eventually you will metamorphose from being a *troubled person* to a *person who sometimes feels troubled.*

III. Meeting the Need: Infilling and Self-nurturing

Once the feeling-charge has been released, you are ready to do the third part of the Process©, the infilling part. Turn your breathing back to your body to regulate, but still breathe into and from the abdomen.

By now your breathing will be very shallow and slow, with a significant interval—ten to fifteen seconds or more—

between the end of an out-breath and the beginning of the next in-breath. Continue to experience your breathing, and let Your self enjoy the intense peacefulness that happens in the interval between the exhalation and the inhalation. You may even feel weightless, as if you are floating, and your usual mental chatter will be almost non-existent.

Next, as you inhale, speak silently to Your self, conveying whatever message it needs to hear. This will be determined by whatever need is most deficient at that moment. Specific messages designed to meet each need are provided in each of the four needs chapters that follow. Here are four examples, one for each need, with a sixth that covers all contingencies.

> "You are safe, secure, and protected, surrounded by My presence."

> "My love enfolds you and you feel lovable, loved, and loving."

> "You are valuable and precious to Me."

> "You are free of the opinion of others: You define and govern Your self."

> "Wherever you are, I am, and where I am there are safety, love, protection, worthiness, and self-assurance."

> *"There is no place you can be that I am not."*

At first, you may balk at saying these things to Your self out of disbelief or modesty. That's your thinking brain playing saboteur. As you continue to say them, they will accumulate in your feeling brain, which accepts and stores—*forever*, without comments or questions and—whatever comes to it. Many repetitions are needed to implant these new beliefs into your feeling brain, where the change must take place, so don't be discouraged if it takes more time than you expected. In fact, *don't expect*: part of the job of the Process© is to teach you to observe and guide Your self and its pace.

Repeat your Declaration with every breath, varying or adding to the message as needed, continuing each session as long as you can: ten minutes is a good start, twenty is effective, thirty is transcendent, and thirty plus is ecstatic. *Make sure to use the word "You" when talking to Your self*, as though speaking to another person. This identifies You-as-speaker with Your inner or higher power, and you-as-listener with your human self. Since power is a property of our spiritual rather than our human self, we must speak from our spiritual nature to our human nature to make the affirmation fully effective. Throughout the book, therefore, the word "yourself" is written "Your self," to remind us of our true nature.

When used over a period of time, this Process© removes the accumulated patterns of toxic emotion and behavior stored in the feeling brain (limbic system) and throughout the body, and replaces them with affirmative messages that fulfill the deficient needs. Had you been given such messages consistently in childhood you wouldn't now be needy.

The effectiveness of this Process© is not lessened because it is You doing the talking: while Your thinking brain, which makes distinctions and requires proof, will say something like, "This won't work! I need somebody else to tell me I'm OK," your feeling (limbic) brain will absorb the new messages automatically. It doesn't distinguish between then and now, male and female, good and bad, self and other, past and present. Indeed, the limbic system lives in the eternal present: every emotional experience that ever happened to you is stored in it awaiting only the appropriate signal to surface and be released, rather like the juke box in a diner. It is incapable of doubt, and records and believes whatever you tell it. It won't be long before you begin actually to experience within you *the feelings you would like to have,* that heretofore you have thought you needed other people to give you.

The Freedom Healing Process© will be most effective if repeated daily on a regular basis, twice if possible, for about ten minutes to start with, then gradually building up to twenty five to thirty minutes as you become more experienced. Shortly after you get up in the morning is the best, since at that time you are nearest to your unconscious where the old feelings are stored. Second best is when you get home from work—it clears out the accumulated stress of the day and prepares you for a relaxed, happy evening.

Any time in between that you feel off track it's a good idea to do the Process© even if you have only a few minutes. It needs to be done several times for each hurt you experience: the older and more serious the hurt, the more repetitions needed. As the repetitions accumulate, you will experience a gradual, steady improvement in your entire system: your feelings will be more good than bad, your thinking will become clear and insightful, your behavior more governable.

The infilling part is as important as the releasing; the two should always be done in sequence. When you change the oil in your car, what happens if you put the new oil in before draining out the old? *Right*! The new oil will be contaminated and overflow, and therefore not be able to do its job properly. And if you drained out the old and didn't put in the new, what then? *Right*! The car wouldn't operate! Likewise, if you add the affirmations before draining out the sludge of your repressed feelings, they will be contaminated and rendered ineffective; but if you release the old feelings and don't fill the void with clean new feelings and beliefs, you will be running on empty—and the world will rush in to fill the vacuum with whatever is handy, without regard to its appropriateness, value, or truth. As your system gets used to the benefits of the Process©, it will respond by spontaneously setting the Process© in motion, thus gradually transforming your neediness into self-fulfillment.

The fact that this method is based on healing from within doesn't exclude outer ways of meeting needs as well. Physical exercise, making a successful presentation at work, painting a beautiful picture, joining a club involving your favorite pastime, doing volunteer work, founding your own business and making a bundle—without a doubt, all these do a lot for all your needs. It's not a question of having to choose between the inner and outer. You can and will have both, on one condition: the sequence in which you use them. The *inner process must come first.* Then the outer will happen naturally with little effort and will produce a positive effect.

A little reflection will make this point very clear. When you have a sense of inner security, you act naturally and spontaneously in ways that increase the security, and you draw more of the same from other people. Ditto for the other three needs. But not *vice versa.* If you do the outer ways first, the inner lack of security will still be there and will draw to you experiences in like kind, and the outer activities will become contaminated and ineffective. Then you will be driven to still more accomplishments, since whenever you're not accomplishing, the pain returns. Presto! You have reinforced your unmet need and created another addiction.

Moreover, your inner neediness, knowing where its true good lies, will constantly criticize and challenge the outer activity: "You could have done better!" "What about that remark you made to the boss? You saw he didn't like it!" "Joe's *wife* makes more money than you do—what's wrong with *you?*" *etc., etc.* If you get the inner right, the outer will follow. *As within, so without. What you think about you bring about.*

The biochemical aspect of the Process© underlines the importance—indeed, necessity—of feeling feelings and releasing them. Here's how it works: when a painful feeling occurs, say fear or anger, it registers in the feeling (limbic) system of the brain. The pain is encoded there in chemical messengers called neuropeptides, and transmitted by them to receptor cells in the appropriate endocrine glands. These then promptly release adrenaline, which re-routes the flow of blood from the adult thinking brain (neocortex) to the fight/flight control center (amygdala) located in the feeling brain. This gives you the energy to attack or run, whichever is appropriate, and thereby use up the adrenaline and with it the feeling. (It also reduces the functioning of the thinking brain—not needed in an emergency—which is why you can't think clearly when upset).

However, if you don't release the feelings (as described above) and thus also the adrenaline, they will come out and play again another day. Since mostly we *don't* do the releasing, we keep ourselves in an almost constant revved-up state—an adrenaline high, you could say. When a few moments of order occur, allowing us to feel a smidgen of peace, we feel flat, as if something is missing, and impulsively seek some way to turn up the intensity (the 11:00 news, sports violence both on and off the screen, spending sprees, verbal or physical abuse, video games, pornography, picking a fight, *etc., etc.*). We create a storehouse of energy to fuel the defensive thought and behavior patterns and keep neediness and anxiety alive, when we could be directing that energy instead to create more of whatever we value most for Our self.

The way out of this—the breathing—is so simple that your first reaction to it may be skeptical. But in addition to its time-tested effectiveness, it makes complete sense both physically and psychologically: when you do the Process© of releasing feelings and fulfilling the need, you cleanse your mind/body of toxins, both emotional and biochemical. This restores the flow of blood to the thinking brain, so you are back in your "right" (*i.e.* adult) mind, and your entire being is restored to its natural state of balance and harmony.

Having practiced the Process© somewhat, or even just read the description of it, you can see that expressing and discharging feelings does *not* mean: acting out, giving opinions, making a scene, making judgments, calling names, blowing up, screaming, yelling, "letting her have it," "giving him a piece of my mind," "telling it like it is," *etc., etc.* These clichés, when you can get the person to repeat what he *actually* said (instead of a *description* of what he said), almost invariably consist of accusations, attacks, criticism, judgment, advice, disapproval, threats, *etc.* All of these fall into the category of verbal abuse. They are defenses, and they hurt and scare the person on the receiving end, often provoking some form of retaliation. Here are some examples, translated into feeling statements:

Defensive Statement
   I feel like you're always putting me down.
Feeling Statement
   I always feel put down.

Defensive Statement
   What's the matter with you? You're never on time!
Feeling Statement
   I feel frustrated and annoyed and disrespected and angry when you are late.

Defensive Statement
   I can't take this anymore! All you do is criticize me.
Feeling Statement
   I feel fed up because I feel constantly criticized.

None of the defensive sentences says what the speaker is *feeling*; instead, each one accuses or blames the other person. They are precisely what *not* to do, since they are destructive both ways: they block the expression of the speaker's feelings and hurt the recipient's feelings. In contrast, the feeling statements are about the speaker: he names the emotion *he* is experiencing, thereby owning it and beginning his process of releasing it. He deals with it within himself, instead of tossing it into the opponent's territory. The differences between defensive statements and feelings statements are summarized in the following chart:

Defensive Statement	Feeling Statement
1 Is about the recipient	1. Is about the speaker
2. Is done compulsively	2. Is done by choice
3. Represses feelings of the speaker	3. States feelings of the speaker

Examples of the healthy release of feelings happen spontaneously in our lives, but are often met with criticism or denial ("Nonsense! You're not hurt!"). For example, a baby's crying, which is the signal of a need and as such is a healthful function, often evokes a repressive or angry reaction from the caregivers. Adults will tickle, bounce, overfeed, distract, shake, or worst of all, hit or isolate the baby in their efforts to stop his crying. When, however, his crying is not stifled but *stayed with*, then his security need is met and he can take a step toward feeling that his universe is safe.

If this way of handling frustration is followed, he will be happier and healthier not only in the moment, but will also outgrow the tantrums and will naturally, as he matures, find less dramatic (or at any rate less compulsive) ways of releasing his feelings. Among many other possible examples of good healthy discharge, one more example comes to mind. Did you ever see a wide receiver, having blown a catchable pass, flop down on the field and pound it with his fist three or four times? If you instinctively understood his actions as releasing frustration, you'd be right on target, and wouldn't be surprised that he caught the next pass perfectly and took it all the way!

These examples show that releasing feelings is a process built into us by nature. We come with the instinct and the equipment to do it—if we are allowed to, and not given a spanking, a lollipop, or a "time-out" *(i.e.* neglect and rejection) to get us to stop. Such manipulations, while they may produce immediate results, in the long run work counter to our four dependency needs and are therefore toxic.

In contrast, releasing feelings is a part of the system nature gave us and it works to meet our needs. It does this by dissolving defenses, stopping the repression and accumulation of painful feelings, thereby allowing the unmet need to be identified and met in a healthful way. It thus prevents repetition of the needs cycle. All we need do is *release rather than repress our emotions, in a place and in a way that doesn't make a scene or upset another person.* Then the defensive thinking will clear and the defensive behaviors can be changed. We either accumulate or release—there's no third alternative.

In conclusion, practising the Freedom Process© awakens the inner power that moves you out of the limitations and self-defeating patterns generated by neediness. Your true self then appears: a person unintimidated by life, who knows how to deal with painful feelings and unmet needs when they occur. You will develop the ability to choose your behavior according to your values. It is essentially an exercise in awareness: You-as-monitor of your human consciousness assess and guide your thinking, feeling, and behavior. Since we are at every moment subject to "the law of retributive justice" (*what we put out comes back to us; we draw to us what we are; what we think about we bring about*) it follows that only when this freedom has been attained can we achieve "the esteem of wise men and the means of doing good."[1] I have seen such transformations many times, each one amazing (like Zeke), a seeming miracle of healing. But you don't have to take my word for it—just try it yourself!

Unmet Needs cause...	Painful Feelings cause...	Mental & Behavioral Defenses : constitute... The defences of this role are all variations of the primitive biological defences of:		Type of Personality	Feelings When Needs Met
SECURITY SAFETY SURVIVAL	Anger anxiety fear insecurity being intimidated threatened hostility jealousy	FIGHT aggressiveness argumentativeness agitation invasiveness worrying hypermentation sarcasm mania hyperactivity/tantrums joking/teasing/needling practical joking taunting acting/creating a scene homicide competitiveness physical or sexual abuse violence	FLIGHT checking out dissociating shutting down compliance/placating passive aggression rituals fantasizing depression daydreaming silence non-responsiveness suicidal thinking or attempts wandering thinking distractedness geographical cure anorexia prescription drug use	THE "CLOWN" TYPE	protected safe secure relaxed calm reassured

III

The Security Need

Riddle #1

Your company is having its annual training conference next month. The supervisor asks you to coordinate the activities of all the divisions—an indication that you are in the running for promotion to assistant supervisor. Already anxious about blowing the opportunity, you set off vigorously to make the rounds, snapping out orders and wisecracks and motivational blurbs as you go: "GEE WHIZ, BETTY! What a slew of papers! Whatever you lost, I hope you find it! JACK! Where are you hiding the report I gave you this morning on T.B.I., Inc.? You running a treasure hunt? C'mon, c'mon, everybody, move it, move it, we got a lot to do! MORRIS! Call divisions 1–4; TOM! (who jumps), you take 5-8. MAKE IT SNAPPY! We're all happy campers here!"

What's driving your behavior?

The Security Need

From birth to death, we human beings are in continuous development. All our dimensions—physical, emotional, mental, spiritual—have characteristic needs that make us happy, successful, and loving if they are fulfilled, and miserable if they are not. The purpose of this book is to show you how you can fulfill these needs *from within—it's an inside job*!

Our primary needs, each of which marks a stage of growth from birth to adulthood, are four in number and begin with the need for *security*, followed by *belonging, self-esteem,* and *autonomy*.[1] Like the rings of a ladder, each of these needs gives support to the one above it and gets support from the one below it (except for the first, the security need). Each need is described in detail in its own chapter; together these four needs chapters constitute the core of the book. (See Master Chart© facing p.i and Security Chart© on the page facing p. 29).

The first step on this ladder, and the subject of this chapter, is the *Security Need*. It is the foundation of the four essential needs that define our emotional-mental-spiritual growth, beginning with our total dependence on others and culminating in our need for dependence on self, a process that necessarily takes considerable time, and is more often not completed than completed. The following three chapters present the remaining needs, describe the characteristics of each one, and then show how each shapes our personality and behavior, both when met and not met. In each of the four chapters, the discussion of the need is followed by directions for using the Freedom Healing Process© specific to that particular need.

Security is our earliest need: developing it is what our first three years are primarily about. If it is not met sufficiently during that period, emotional growth stalls, preventing the remaining three needs from being met also. The result of this non-development is a child in adult clothing: physically you appear to be adult and are legally perceived as such, but emotionally you are a three-year old. *Being* that of course prevents you from recognizing it, but your behavior makes apparent to other people that you are still in the security stage: you expect them, rather than yourself, to meet your need. (For further discussion of this topic see Appendices A on codependency and C on mental health, which explore and explain in detail how emotional immaturity affects adult life).

We need security every moment in every area of our lives: physical, emotional, psychological, relational, domestic, sexual, professional, financial, legal, medical, *etc*. Any area where it is deficient gets our attention and keeps it until a sufficient degree is restored. Then and only then can we continue our upward emotional growth into adulthood. But as the Chart© on page 28 shows, this is a rough journey: when any one of the four needs isn't met, we experience *painful feelings*, which generate *mental and behavioral defenses* that in turn determine the *type* of our personality. So if we're grown up in years but not in consciousness, we have to work our way up the needs ladder to become truly adult.

Due to the nature of the birth process, the period of our greatest urgency is during birth and infancy, and the incredibly formative first three years. Numerous regression experiences recounted in Jenny Wade's fascinating book, *Changes of Mind; A Holonomic Theory of the Evolution of Consciousness* dramatically testify to the pain, fear, and stress the infant must endure.[2] There is no way that being squeezed, ejected, and pulled out of the birth canal can be anything but an experience filled with a high degree of anxiety, a symptom of insecurity.

As adults, we remember our birth unconsciously in nightmares, panicky feelings in tunnels or crowded elevators, traffic jams—all of which make us often insecure and anxious without quite knowing why. Anyone who has undergone the panic of being trapped pulling off a tight-fitting garment over her/his head, arms stretched straight up and helpless, experiences a miniature version of what birth must be like: going backward is impossible and going forward to un-charted

The Security Need

territory scary, painful, and possibly suffocating. (Hence the extreme panic toddlers exhibit when pulling a tee-shirt on or off–their little psyches must be saying: "Oh, no! Not this again, and so soon!").

These vestiges of the pain and insecurity of our first experience on earth are deeply embedded in our unconscious (the feeling brain), from which they surface when events in the present awaken our primitive memory, even into old age unless dealt with therapeutically. The pain of the birth itself is aggravated by the anxiety of being separated from our nine-month home, and from our mother, by being taken to the neonatal unit for physical examination. Here we may be kept for the entire first day or two of life, deprived of the security of our mother's arms. Such events register in the infant's consciousness (the feeling brain or the limbic system) that as yet has no understanding of or defense against the pain and fear they create. (The fact that many hospitals are changing this procedure—leaving the baby with the mother and examining him there—is encouraging.)

The shock of separation compels the infant to seek security, which in the womb he experiences continuously, and a way to restore that oneness. If he doesn't get a sufficient amount now he will seek until he does. For some this means all their lives. If, however, his need for security is sufficiently met, he will be able gradually to venture out on his own. Until then, the mother (and father, too!) must provide *as much holding as he needs,* since *being continuously held in a safe place* was his original experience as a sentient creature. As a gentle, kind pediatrician once told me: "Don't ever miss a chance to give him a hug."

Responding to his anxiety isn't spoiling him; *it is meeting his need for security.* He doesn't yet have the necessary equipment to comfort himself, and he'll never develop it if his caregivers don't do it for him until he *can* do it himself— and only he can know when that is. It's amazing what body contact—holding, rocking, blowing on his tummy, stroking his feet—does for his mood and his security. It is certainly not too hard to do, and surprising to most adults, feels good to them to do it: "To comfort is to be comforted." He will copy these comforting behaviors, learning how to comfort himself, and will consequently develop compassion for others—playmates, animals, siblings, and even parents! As a parent, you haven't lived until your three and a half year old says, "Mommy, I bring band-aid for your cut."

The insecurity is intensified by the dramatic differences in the baby's new environment. Everything is exactly the opposite of what it was in his original dwelling. Light is bright rather than dim; sounds are loud rather than muffled; touch is rough rather than smooth and flowing; the pull of gravity is an entirely new feeling, in contrast to the "oceanic bliss" of floating in the amniotic fluid; smell and taste are unprecedented sensations and can, the baby soon discovers, be unpleasant; hunger, digestion, and excretion are not only new but often stressful and sometimes painful. The newborn is thus dumped out of Eden into a fallen world, filled with challenge, discomfort, and danger, in which he must eventually stand on his own.

So, transferred thus from a state of total security into one of total insecurity, we are now totally dependent on entities outside us to survive. This is the force underlying the security need: *survival.* Its paramount importance to human beings is demonstrated movingly in the story of Cain and Abel. After God evicts Cain from Eden for slaying Abel, he does a remarkable and compassionate thing: he "set a mark upon Cain." Why? "Lest any finding him should kill him" (Gen. 4:15), not, as we generally think, to punish him. (Apparently God did not—does not?—believe in capital punishment). The message is clear: survival comes above all other considerations. Hence the baby's feelings of insecurity and fear, since left to himself he could not survive.

If our environment and caregivers do not provide enough security in our first years, we become chronically fearful, and instead of absorbing security, we absorb fear into our feeling brain (limbic system). The shattering experience of our entry into the world can be repaired only if we find out in the years following what's wrong and how to fix it. (Considering the high levels of anxiety in this country, it is safe to say most people have not found how to meet this need adequately). Our ability to develop psychological health is thus derailed. This drastically affects the other three needs, since they can't be fully or properly met until the security need is. Our emotional maturation then stalls.

Given the child's inability to obtain security by himself, how then does he achieve it? The primary source is of course parents. But others abound—grandparents, older siblings, aunts and uncles and cousins, nannies, good day care workers, teachers, coaches, all varieties of cuddly stuffed animals, a favorite book or song, and thanks to Linus, the security blanket—second only to parents. All of these can be security-makers, if parents recognize that his cry is the expression of a need that he himself is not capable of meeting. The "let him cry or you'll spoil him" school of thought is counter to his need, and running counter to a need causes dysfunction and neurosis.

All too often in public I see children ignored, yelled at, hit, threatened, roughly pushed into a grocery cart, *etc. etc.* I wish I could give the parents a ticket. Examples: a baby, not more than a month old, lying in a shopping cart, lips purple and trembling, arms waving frantically, screaming in continuous panic, while his mother slowly packs her groceries, all the while seeming not even to hear him. A boy, about four, waiting in line at the post office, crying with panicky, gulping sobs, arms raised beseechingly to his mother to be held, she staring fiercely down at him, her arms crossed, saying: "I am *not going to pick you up*! I told you if you cried I'd make you wait outside by yourself!" The threats and panicky sobs went on, loudly, until the woman and the little boy left. And *nobody*, including me, did anything to stop it, all of us afraid to confront her, or to make a scene in public. But I was also afraid, and so others might have been, that interfering might make her even more vicious toward him. To this day that memory makes me sick. Imagine what that one scene did to his security and belonging need—and remember: the fear and sense of abandonment go away only from the thinking (neocortex) brain; they stay embedded *forever* in the feeling brain (the unconscious) from which they emerge instantly when anything even remotely similar occurs, to relive a pain of which they have no conscious knowledge.

The beginning of the solution is to *pick him up,* releasing the still-unfamiliar pull of gravity and providing the warmth of another's body, thus replicating his original earthly home (the womb) and satisfying his survival/security need. If the crying does not stop soon, we have to turn on our sensing device, and explore possibilities: is he (1) hungry, (2) lonely, (3) cold, (4) enduring a diaper in need of removal, (5) sleepy but won't give in to it, (6) colicky, *etc., etc.* All of these conditions make him anxious, because they threaten his security. It requires patience, understanding, true love, and time to sort it out, plus a full awareness that the *child* is not an *adult:* he doesn't yet have the thinking brain that adults have. He can't, therefore, function according to rationality (not that adults operate on their thinking brain twenty-four and seven, either). He is still operating on the *feeling* brain, which means he functions on emotions, not logic.

When this need *is* met consistently, he gradually develops an inner sense of security, and becomes able to relinquish outside help bit by bit, one of the signs of emotional growth. If his caregivers continue their support after he's three, diminishing it in proportion to his growing ability to reassure and support himself, his sense of security becomes even stronger. From such a foundation he will grow upward to the next need, belonging and acceptance.

But if he reaches adulthood chronologically without this need sufficiently met, his attention is held in bondage by the security need and he cannot attend effectively to any of the other needs—which will, necessarily, be deficient to some extent also. Nor can he continue his growth into the spiritual dimension.

He is then in a state of pain overload, a state which brings him to behaviors that look similar to the adult condition referred to as a "nervous breakdown." When that happens, the aware parent will not scold or criticize, but instead will gently guide the child to release his feelings—by crying, pounding, running, jumping—by any means necessary so long as he doesn't hurt himself or anybody or anything else, including animals, sofa cushions, toys, *etc.* This pattern will be repeated many times to guide him bit by bit until he learns how to overcome his fear instead of letting it threaten his sense of security.

Let us now look at the emotions that develop when the need for emotional and psychological security is deficient or threatened. (The Chart© at the beginning of this chapter shows the whole cycle.) Just as we do when our physical security is at risk, we become anxious and angry. These feelings instinctively set off the *fight* and *flight* defenses, so that we either attack or retreat or both in order to hide the feelings and suppress the pain. This defensive pattern becomes a cycle: the lack of *security* generates painful *feelings* that fuel the *defenses* that have *consequences* in the world. The diagram at right shows the pattern.

The *defenses* (as in the Chart©) are the thoughts and behaviors that we unconsciously use to protect us from feeling insecure. They occur in psychological and symbolic form as well, because we need to feel secure emotionally as well as physically. Some examples of *fight* defenses against insecurity include behaviors such as competitiveness, hyperactivity, agitated thinking, and verbal abuse—all of which direct the anger/anxiety energy outward toward other people.

Unmet Need for Security	Mental & Behavioral Defenses	Type of Personality
Unmet needs cause…	Painful feelings lead to…	Defenses lead to…
PAINFUL FEELINGS: fearful angry hostile jealous nervous insecure	MENTAL DEFENSES: worry denial checking-out loss of focus domination mania BEHAVIORAL DEFENSES: taunts argues lies jokes teases aggresses/attacks murders/suicides daydreams/isolates sleeps/fantasizes shuts down/checks out dissociates/placates	THE "CLOWN" TYPE

In contrast, the *flight* variety of defenses includes behaviors that turn the defensive energy inward. Examples are checking out, shutting down, and fantasizing *etc.* (see Chart©). This internalization represses the emotional pain and causes depression, a defense against anger. Since the cause of the depressive condition (insecurity) is rarely recognized, medication is generally provided. This is not only unnecessary—it can also be harmful, because the medication covers up the cause and thereby becomes another defense.

If your toddler or youngster exhibits behaviors of either fight or flight to a more than average degree, acknowledge his distress and allow him to say whatever he needs to say without comment, even if it's something preposterous or something you said or did; this is not the time to get your ego involved—it's not about you, it's about him. Don't pry him with questions, or attempt to make him explain: chronologically he's not yet capable of doing that.

Try your best not to get angry or defensive; instead, *listen* to him and paraphrase back to him what he said, *e.g.* "you were really scared." This will make him feel heard—and therefore understood—and therefore secure: he'll nod his head and say emphatically "yes" (or "yeth," depending on his age).

Don't tell him "not to worry," "don't be afraid," "there's nothing to be afraid of,"—to *you* that may be true, but right now, *he's scared,* and telling him he isn't confuses him. It makes him unable to trust his own perceptions and therefore can lead to a variety of neurotic defensive behaviors. This approach will *not* make him more scared, nor a "sissy"—on the contrary, it will in fact prevent such a development, because being heard and understood satisfies his need for security and thereby dissolves the fear.

Because both the fight and flight defenses do such a good job of repressing our feelings of insecurity (fear, anxiety, jealousy, *etc.),* we use them routinely in our discourse, not thinking of the damage they cause. For example, instead of saying our feelings directly—"I felt hurt when you said I was stupid"—we push the feeling out of our conscious awareness by verbally attacking the other person (just what he had done to us)—"You think you're so smart? It's a miracle you got through high school!" Or we defend ourselves behaviorally: in response to the insult, we shut down, walk away, and don't talk to the other person for a week. Both kinds of defensive reaction create the destructive cycle shown in the diagram above, in which each component sets off the next.

Whether our defenses are fight or flight, until we learn to recognize them and hear and understand their message, we cannot experience our feelings and therefore cannot identify *what need is unmet*. When that is the case, our emotional growth stalls, and we continue our childhood pattern of relying on others to meet our needs. To intercept the cycle, we must learn to notice our defenses when they occur, release the repressed feelings that generate them, and then meet the need from within as described at the end of this chapter (see also the end of Chapter II).

Insecurity occurs more often in the youngest child of the family than in any of the others. (Of course, in a healthy, functional family, it occurs only rarely). There are two reasons for that. First, by the time the last child is born, the family dysfunction has deteriorated to its most severe state so far, and is at its lowest condition to provide support and security. Second, whatever deficiencies have happened to older siblings are likely to be acted out in some way on the youngest, who unwittingly absorbs and copies them. This inheritance makes him the child most heavily laden with defenses, and therefore the one most at risk. Alternately, he is sometimes the most pampered and indulged by older family members, both parents and siblings, who coddle him to defend and repress their guilt.

Since the defenses of the insecure child can be either fight or flight, the question arises, what determines which set a child adopts? There are four factors involved. The first is *gender:* typically though not invariably, whether through sociological or biological factors, if you are a male, you adopt fight defenses; if female, flight. The second is *situational:* you instinctively choose whichever alternative feels appropriate to the particular situation. For example, if your parents are having an argument and you feel scared, but you are too little to try to stop it, you might run to your room and turn on your TV to distract you from your fear. The third factor is *availability:* if both types of defense are modeled in your environment, you may experiment (unconsciously, of course) to see which works best for you. Or you may use both alternately, depending on the situation and the personnel involved.

Last, there is an *emotional-physiological-chemical connection* between feelings and defenses. For example, most people instinctively, if not consciously, understand that someone who is very thin, moves and talks quickly, jumps from one topic to another, doesn't complete her sentences, and laughs frequently for no particular reason, is nervous and has feelings of anxiety or fear that cause her behaviors, thus outpicturing her feelings. Practise observing people's behavior and you will see how it works.

The internal chemical reactions, triggered by feelings that we think of as non-material, in fact reach over into materiality by generating chemicals such as *adrenaline* and *acetylcholine*. These particular chemicals work for our safety in a situation of danger by reducing the flow of blood to the thinking brain (neocortex)—less important to survival than the feeling-instinct brain—and sending it instead to the amygdala, the flight/fight "button" in the feeling brain. Our body responds with either the fight or flight defense, depending on the size of the threat.

These defensive processes were demonstrated in a television story on 20/20, about a treatment center in Boston for children exposed to spousal abuse.[3] As the narrator described the problem, the video showed a five-year-old boy tricycling toward a much bigger child and, without any provocation, whacking him with a stick. The narrator explained, "John is repeating what he saw at home." True, but this is only part of the reason for his behavior. Having many times witnessed Dad beat up Mom, John's inner state is jittering with fear: if Dad really damages Mom, or kills her, *what will become of me?* And, *will Dad do it to me?*

Of course John doesn't reason consciously like this, but his entire emotional/chemical/physical system registers fear at what it recognizes to be painful, destructive, and life-threatening—*insecurity of the highest degree.* So he makes a preemptive strike on someone older, symbolizing his father, but not enough older to be as strong a threat. Since he has lived in this condition of insecurity all his five years, his fear and anger are by now chronic, unconsciously absorbed into his psyche, and therefore so too are his defensive behaviors.

There are two major consequences of this experience. The first is that these feelings, encoded in John's feeling brain, are thereby woven into the development of his personality, which by five years old is already defined by insecurity, nervousness, and aggression. Perhaps it has occurred to you that these defenses are similar to ADD and ADHD (see Appendix II, for further discussion), a hunch validated by the fact that one of the products of insecurity is an inability to pay attention.

Insecurity makes a mind of any age jumpy, nervous, and easily distracted—all symptoms of "ADD," but more important, of *fear.* ADD and ADHD, while certainly identifiable, aren't really diseases, like polio or cancer or tuberculosis; they are *behavioral defenses,* and as such are *symptoms of unmet needs.* If treated only with medication, they are notoriously difficult to cure, even if therapy is added (see Appendix III). Although the medication may tame them, it can't actually heal them, unless they identify the cause—the lack of sufficient security.

But due to the tendency to define the "disease" as genetic in origin, getting to the cause is rarely undertaken. This puts recovery on a track that leads nowhere. The condition is actually environmental, as is shown further on in John's story: that is, it is brought about by the behaviors of others (generally the parents, sad to say) that damage the child's security and over which he is ultimately powerless. His "ADD" is the result.

Recovery depends first on determining what dynamic in the family is causing the dysfunction, then working together to eliminate it and learn how to establish security-for-all instead. This takes awareness, willingness, and some humility (plus good counseling) to achieve. There should be no feelings of shame or blame in such cases; very few families are totally free of dysfunction, and where it occurs, it always has its roots in the parents' family of origin, which grew out of the previous generation, *etc., etc.*—all the way back to Cain! For an adult, recovery is slower and more difficult, due to the longer duration of the insecurity, and must come from within himself (see the Freedom Healing Process© at the end of this chapter) though not without help, understanding, and directions from other people.

Recovery, always gradual, depends for a child primarily of course on his parents. But when the patterns are deeply embedded in the limbic system, it is hard even to try. In fact, most of us *practise* our defenses and cling to them as though they will save our life, when in fact they are taking our life away. If you had practised the piano as long and as intensively as you have your defenses, by now you'd be in Carnegie Hall!

The second consequence of John's experience is that because his body is constantly filled with the above-mentioned chemicals generated by his feelings, it is in constant motion, agitated and vibrating, like a dog at the vet's. These traits are guaranteed to irritate most of the adults in his life, especially teachers, and often other children as well, not to mention how much it unnerves and confuses him. To block the fear and anger, and to work off the adrenaline, he behaves aggressively (like the dog), copying the fight defense from his father's model. Despite his fear of Daddy's violence, he repeats what his father does, not only because kids copy their parents (sometimes; sometimes they do the opposite), but because attacking somebody bigger than himself gives him what he is otherwise lacking—a sense of power.

It works for him as a defense against fear. If it didn't, he wouldn't use it, despite Dad's modeling of it. He would find a defense that did—most likely a form of flight. John's aggressive behavior is a visible defense (symptom or diagnosis) of a predictable sequence that began from an invisible unmet need, and is an indicator of that unmet need, *security*.

We can use John to complete our profile of this need. In school, he will be restless, agitated, and hyper, his hand always in the air even if doesn't know the answer: it's the attention he wants. But he generally gets ignored, since the teacher and other students soon tire of his aggression and dominance. In any situation he will be easily distracted. He will by eight or nine already wisecrack his way through a tight spot. He may beat his dog and by eleven or twelve begin sexually molesting or abusing his sister (or his brother).

In high school, if he doesn't drop out and hit the streets and drugs and gangs, he will be the class clown, life of the party, and chief of the debating team, where his aggressiveness, mental quickness, and sarcastic wit become legendary, along with his capacity for alcohol.[4] He doesn't, typically, get into contact sports—too reminiscent of dear old Dad and therefore too threatening to his sense of security. Tennis, golf, swimming, or track appeal to him more, since they offer a high degree of control combined with no direct physical threat from another person.

His chief strategy in life, at which he excels, is *getting attention*: it distracts him from the ever-present, churning,

The Security Need

inner anxiety by giving him an illusory, if momentary, sense of control and security. But no amount of external attention can reach the deeply embedded insecurity, and so, ironically, all his various defenses actually *prevent* him from getting his needs met. He is therefore trapped in his attention-getting pattern and his self-defeating "Clown" personality type.

The television story had an interesting sequel. As the narrator completed her account of John's case, she added, in a puzzled and seemingly irrelevant footnote, "Most of our children are aggressive, like John, but some of them, surprisingly, are passive and withdrawn"—not surprising when you know that such children are using the flight defense, rather than the fight, against fear and anger.

It is not hard to imagine a history that will demonstrate and explain this, and serve as an example of the flight type of codependency. Let's say John has a younger sister—Sally—who, suffering daily the same traumatic conditions as John, instinctively adopts the flight defense. There are at least three reasons for her choice, all of them both logical and effective. First, she sees John get beaten when he acts aggressive, and she's not stupid, so why would she copy that? Second, she sees passivity and submission modeled by her mother, and also sees her get hit less than John, and third, because *flight works to repress her fear*, thus giving her a temporary sense of control and security.

Sally is shy, probably inarticulate, prone to daydreaming, fantasizing, and making up imaginary playmates; absent-minded in school, maybe dyslexic and diagnosed with a learning deficit; out to lunch when it comes to social and play activities with peers; has by seven or eight learned to smooth over a difficult situation by changing the subject, and to handle her parents' fighting and their probably arbitrary and harsh "discipline" (*i.e.* abuse) with silence or the word "whatever;" has taught herself to avoid feeling her natural fear and anger by so quickly and thoroughly *repressing* them that they turn into chronic *depression*, and nobody, including her, knows she has them in her.

By ten or twelve she's discovered pot, alcohol, and her mother's Xanax, or all three, and if not yet physically addicted, has become psychologically dependent on some or all of them, even though, ironically, all of them are depressants. The drugs of course aggravate her depression. Her whole motivation is to become detached from the reality around her—it's too overwhelming to endure. "Checking out" is her safety. But whether she's in it or out of it, the bottom line is that the feelings which signal her unmet need for security are, like her brother's, hidden by her defenses and thus never met.

For both of them, for the rest of their lives, any subsequent event which triggers their early experiences of insecurity and fear, even in one tiny particular, will set off these same defenses: each has developed a pattern and a persona that, unless they get adequate treatment (such as the Healing Process©) will shape their entire lives. The earlier in life it happens, the more severe and lasting the damage.

The pattern is: *unmet needs* create *painful feelings* that generate *mental* and *behavioral defenses* that determine *behavior and personality type*. Some security-deprived people use both kinds of defense. This indicates that the insecurity was so extreme or constant, from such an early age, that neither fight nor flight is in itself a sufficient defense. They then combine in a jumbled mixture, confusing alike to both the person and those who live with him; or they may alternate, each defense living in his body, so to speak, for indefinite intervals.

An example is a client of mine from many years ago whom I'll call Alan. He was the youngest, and the most fragile, of the eight children of a family in which both parents worked—had to—and even though they managed to work different shifts so one of them was always home (no money for day care) most of the children were deeply insecure. The parents, well intentioned though they may have been, were perpetually puzzled and irritated by the outrageous behavior their kids exhibited most of the time. They had no way of knowing that the generator of the behavior was the insecurity the children experienced due to the parents' work schedules. But the mayhem was too much for them, so one day they decided to decrease the caretaking and the pandemonium by one child: they sent Alan to live with his aunt across the street.

Being uprooted from his family and familiar surroundings at the age of three completely undid Alan. (*He* didn't know they were crazy). He cried nonstop for mommy and dada, and for his next older sibling, a little girl four and a half, who loved him and whom he loved. At this age he had few of the internal resources with which to reassure or comfort himself, so his anxiety level stayed high all the time. His distress soon became despair; he lost his voice and completely shut down. His aunt, never having had children, had even less understanding than his parents of what was wrong and what to do about it. "What makes him cry so-o-o much?" she wanted to know. His parents didn't know either and had no time or resources or, apparently, interest in exploring the answer.

After about three weeks, Auntie Rose had had enough, and sent Alan back home. Once there, his tears started in earnest, since the others, each wrapped up in their own troubles, gave him no real attention, so across the street he went. Two more weeks of steady crying, and Alan's voice shut down again. Nonetheless, the habit of sending him back and forth continued, sometimes for holidays or birthdays, though both he and his birthday were often forgotten.

By the time he was ready for high school, he had what his family called "moodiness," that is, severe chronic depression, the result of too many changes too often and too early. Since his world was always unstable, he couldn't establish a sense of security inside himself and desperately needed a competent adult to show him how. The chief symptom and outcome of this dysfunction was extreme fight/flight behavior. He smashed his beloved sister's dolls, stole his brother's wallet and lied about it, often "checked out"—that is, shut down, ignored questions, and was absent most of the time, both physically and mentally; showed signs of drug and alcohol use, and began at about nine to disappear in the late afternoon and not return till midnight or later, often to the house he *hadn't* just left. His symptoms got more severe, and the family was at their wit's end. It hadn't occurred to them to seek professional help; the world of psychology was unknown to them.

Eventually Alan landed in the hands of the police. He'd been caught, attempting a stick-up, and when questioned, his insecurity skyrocketed, sending him into a psychotic state. His answers to the policeman's questions were incoherent and preposterous: "The moon was in Mars, so my gun had to be with me...It jumped across the street..." "*What* did?" the cop wanted to know. "The *car*, the *car!*" Alan answered, frustrated by the cop's "stupidity." At this point the cop caught on and took Alan to a psychiatric hospital instead of jail.

It was probably the first break Alan had had in his life. The people at the hospital were—amazingly—kind to him, and his condition ("manic depression" or as it is called today "bipolar disorder") was effectively treated: medication for a specified period followed by intensive, long-term therapy. After a lengthy stay, he was moved to a group home, from which he came to therapy at the agency where I was then employed. By working the Freedom Healing Process© for a couple of years, Alan gradually learned how to fulfill his needs himself, not totally and not always, but enough to keep him sane, functional, and relatively non-aggressive most of the time.

His progress enabled him to join a recovering group home, and he even got a job that made him self-sustaining. In his sessions with me, he learned that his "symptoms" of "mental illness" were actually thought and behavior patterns developed in childhood to block out of his conscious mind the overwhelming fear and anxiety caused by his family's dysfunction. Just finding the cause of his pain and learning that it wasn't his fault was a big boost to his self-esteem, and did a lot to help him recover.

Alan's story exemplifies how most of us live: *defensively*, our behavior driven by our feelings and thoughts, and our feelings and thoughts driven by our unmet needs. Most of the time, we are unaware of what is happening inside us and are therefore unable to direct our behavior consciously and in accord with our values. If you doubt this, try the following experiment: as you drive to work (or school or the mall *etc., etc.*) in the morning, direct yourself to remain calm *no matter what the other drivers are doing* and *to respond with courtesy rather than react with anger.* See how long you can do it!

The advice often given at this juncture is to replace such "negative thinking" (defenses) with positive thinking. If you can do this, fine. But it is harder than it sounds because the pain of the unmet need is lodged in your feeling brain (the unconscious), where it is inaccessible to your thinking brain (the conscious brain). Instead of yielding to the logic of your thinking brain, your feeling brain sets in motion another cycle of its stored-up pain and does so much more quickly than the thinking brain can replace it with "positive thinking."

In addition, trying to switch your thinking from negative to positive is not only hard to do, but is also actually damaging, since it *represses* the painful feelings which cause the negative thinking, but does not remove or change them. The pain of the unmet need remains and will inevitably set off a new cycle. *Unmet needs create painful feelings; painful feelings generate mental and behavioral defenses; mental and behavioral defenses dictate our behavior.*

How to break this logjam? The solution is in the problem, as the Chart© at the beginning of this chapter shows: start with Column 3, which lists the defenses, the thoughts and behaviors that your feelings set in motion to cover up the pain of your unmet need. To find out what your particular feelings are, read Column 2, and to identify your unmet need read Column 1. This is the key to recovery: once you know this formula you will recognize your defensive thoughts and actions and use them as both a signal of and guide to the hidden feelings that in turn will identify the unmet need. In other words, in blocking your feelings, the defensive thoughts and behaviors act as *signals of them*—as the cat's hissing, while intended to scare me away from her kittens in the woodpile, actually signals me of their presence.

You can say that painful feelings and defenses have a *symbiotic* relationship: *painful feelings generate mental and behavioral defenses, and defenses block and signal—conceal and reveal—feelings.* Painful feelings and defenses can't survive without each other. Consequently, once you have become aware you are in a defense—that your thinking or your behavior is out of control—you can use it, instead of letting it use you, as a signal that you are out of touch with your feelings, and therefore with your needs. Becoming self-aware enables you to discover what painful feelings are inhabiting your unconscious, and bring them to the surface to be released. This is the foundation of the Freedom Healing Process©: it shows you how to recognize and release your defenses so that you can identify your feelings which in turn will tell you what your unmet need is and how to meet it. Then you are a *whole,* and *free.*

Confronting our own defensive statements is hard for us to do, because they are there specifically *to cover up* our feelings. Instead of "I feel unheard, but I'm afraid to say so," which is honest and non-aggressive, I say: "You never listen to me," which is untrue and aggressive. Not only does such dialogue make the other person feel accused, it promotes your negative process by hiding your feelings from your conscious mind, thus allowing those feelings to dictate your behavior. *You are then out of control of Your self.*

The Security Need

In contrast, learning to identify and break through your defenses to explore your feelings, which bring you both false and real messages, is essential if you want to enjoy your life and be a constructive person. To do this, you must first deal with your defenses: recognized and read correctly, they *open the door to your unconscious—which is exactly what the Freedom Healing Process© does for you.*

It takes practise in being aware of Your *self*—its words, actions, feelings, and needs—to recognize your defenses, and still more practice in self-awareness to catch and acknowledge them *in the moment*. On a scale of awareness of our defenses, the Process© looks like this:

+5
+4
+3
.........beginnings of awareness
+2
+1
0
___
-1
-2
-3
.........unawareness
-4
-5

Before you can enter the awareness zone, you have to climb up through the unawareness zone, from minus to zero. Not until you get to plus two or three can you *begin* to notice that you are using a defensive word or doing a defensive action. It comes about gradually, first by an after-the-fact realization that yesterday, for example, in that little incident with your friend, you justified a behavior of yours that hurt her feelings by the following mental defense: "Well, it was just a joke!—How come you took it so seriously?" Excusing yourself and criticizing her is mean, unfair, and bad karma: it sets you up for a return in kind.

The alternative, if you've been paying attention to your feelings, is simply to acknowledge your guilt, making your friend feel better and, amazingly, you too! As you continue to practice self-observation, the length of time it takes you to notice your defensive action will shorten and eventually you will recognize *while you are doing it* that you are being defensive. This is a liberating and exciting event, because it provides the key to self-mastery.

What follows is a version of the Freedom Healing Process© tailored specifically to the security need. It will teach you step-by-step how to determine whether your security need is unmet and if so how to fulfill it yourself. The effectiveness of the Process© increases the more often you do it; it's not a once and for all exercise. Daily is essential, even twice daily, since we have feelings all the time. The following directions repeat the general ones given in Chapter II, and add directions specific to the security need.

If you read the directions over a few times, you will soon be able to do the Process© through without having to refer to the instructions as you go so as to avoid interrupting the flow and impairing its effectiveness. It helps to have a friend, mate, sponsor, or counselor with you to talk about what's troubling you before you start, and to read the instructions aloud as you do the Process©. This allows you to stay in the feeling mode and not have to keep switching to the cognitive. Your reader may also provide support as you work through your feelings, which are likely to be intense.

Make sure to warn him or her that you may cry or yell or otherwise exhibit painful feelings, and if so, he or she should not intervene in any way, but allow the release to happen. So long as you are *discharging*, the Process© can't in any way harm you (unless you are psychotic, and even then it's unlikely)—the harm lies in *repressing* your feelings. So as your feelings begin to release, let go and let them out. If you prefer to be alone, you can read the instructions into a tape recorder. Read slowly with adequate pauses at appropriate places so that when you play it back, you'll have enough time to do the feeling work.

The Security Need

The Process© will come to an end when the feeling is fully out. You have a built-in regulator that will stop at the point where you've done enough, just as with a physical workout. After your first two or three experiences, you'll be able to go through the whole thing without referring to the directions.

Favorable times to do the Process© are either in the morning, after you are thoroughly awake, or in the early evening. To get quicker results, do it both times each day. If you do it too soon after awakening or too close to bedtime, you're likely to fall asleep. Indeed, regardless of when you do it, you may fall asleep the first few times, because it's so relaxing. If you hit a rough spot in your day, doing even a short version of it is helpful.

To determine whether security is your primary unmet need, study Column 3 of the Healing Chart© ("mental and behavioral defenses") thoroughly. If three or more of the defenses match how you typically think and act, it is indeed your main unmet need. The Healing Process© presented at the end of this chapter is therefore where you should start. However, if the mental and behavioral defenses of the security need *don't* match your typical thinking and behavior, look at column 3 in each of the other three Charts© (pp. 68, 88, 112) to find which matches your defenses most closely and follow the directions in the corresponding chapter for healing that need.

But before you undertake that journey, do the Healing Process© this chapter presents, even if it isn't your primary need, because it introduces the pattern for the remaining three. The book is structured so that you do the Healing Process© four times, one for each of the four needs chapters. The repetitions gradually teach you to listen to your thinking and observe your behavior, so that instead of your feelings controlling you, *You experience and take care of Your feelings.* This increases your sense of security and improves your self-esteem, making interaction with other people smoother, more enjoyable, less oppositional, and less tense. Ready, set, GO!

The Freedom Healing Process

I. Accessing Feelings: Pounding

Begin by doing the pounding as described in Chapter II, and do it long enough to activate and release any anger or frustration you are harboring. Stop, get your breath, then do it again—and again and again. It often happens that the pounding will bring up tears, a very desirable event. Tears are not the *hurt*; tears are the *healing* of the hurt (an important concept to practice with your kids) so let them flow freely; they are washing away years of distress. This is, indeed, the purpose of the pounding: to arouse unconscious memories from childhood of rejection, criticism, violence, *etc., either witnessed or experienced.* While most people find great release from this exercise, for some it may be too restimulating to be therapeutic. If that is the case with you, use the alternative process in Chapter II, page 11.

Next, do the deep breathing process in two stages:

Start by exhaling slowly and completely, making sure to *contract fully* your abdominal muscles as you blow out your breath.

Next, inhale, slowly and completely, remembering to direct the incoming breath into your abdomen so that it expands (laying your hands across your abdomen lets you know this is happening) and feel the breath as it next fills your chest and then your thorax (the hollow at the bottom of your throat). Do this breathing for at least five to ten minutes, long enough to activate and release any painful feelings indicative of insecurity, such as anger, frustration, fear, anxiety, *etc.* Stop, get your breath, then do it again—and again and again. If the pounding scares you it is probably an indicator of unconscious memories from childhood that are too intense to handle at this stage. If so, let it go and move on.

II. Experiencing and Releasing Feelings: Breathing

You may either sit or lie down to do this part. If you sit, make sure your back is straight and relaxed; if you lie down, rest your lower legs on a sofa, at right angles to your upper legs. In either position, close your eyes and lay your hands on your abdomen just below your navel. Continue breathing as described above. This is the complete yogic breath, and when you do it fully, it is extremely satisfying and fulfilling, both relaxing and energizing at the same time. During the Process©, your shoulders should not move, whether you are sitting or lying down.

Next, while exhaling in the manner just described, focus on the painful feelings as you release them, and then picture them going out into the universe to be recycled. Let yourself *feel them fully*: this disperses them, while burying them, paradoxically, keeps them alive. Continue exhaling thoroughly until you have squeezed out every last bit of breath and the painful feelings with it; then inhale slowly and deeply into your abdomen, inflating it fully, and enjoy the pleasurable expansion of your lungs as you inhale the new oxygen. Feel it pulling up the painful feelings and let Your self focus on them, *experience* them, and they will dissipate and dwindle into non-existence. This is the cleansing part of the Process©. The basic recipe is, in the following order, first *exhale*: blow out forcibly through your mouth, *deflating* the abdomen; then *inhale*: breathe the air in through your nose, *inflating* the abdomen.

Sometimes, especially if you are in an anxious state already, the breathing process can be confusing. There are two main reasons. First, you may find it difficult to get your breath. This is caused by inhaling when you should be exhaling. To correct it, *blow out fully through your mouth*, pulling your abdomen back toward your spine, and you will automatically inhale. Second, if you get confused about which breathing action goes with which abdomen action here are two ways to remedy it: (a) memorize the following: *exhale and deflate; inhale and inflate*; (b) think of your abdomen as a balloon: when you pull the air in, the balloon inflates; when the air is squeezed out, it deflates, and your abdomen retreats back toward your spine.

Some people find it easier to begin the breathing process by starting with the abdomen: for example, quickly expand your abdomen and the inhalation will follow; or, pull your abdomen sharply inward and you will be forced to blow out. Since most of us have a tendency to breathe backwards when agitated, doing this Process© effectively takes practice and repetition. Persist, and it will suddenly click—and you will wonder why you didn't get it sooner.

Not being used to this intensity, you may feel anxious. Be assured—this is how the Process© starts; it will not harm you, or make you "break down" or "fall apart" *etc*. Releasing done consciously and deliberately like this is not *losing* control, it's *taking* control, and is the key to healing your unmet need. The pounding and the breathing bring up the buried feelings, releasing the defenses, whereupon you are out of pain and can think clearly and choose behavior wisely. So trust the Process©: continue to breathe and release the painful feelings; they will dissipate and you will feel lighter and more clear—*free*. As you repeat the cleansing breathing, with each inhalation search back in your life for earlier times when you felt the same feeling, so you can release old insecurities as well.

This Healing Process© used daily will gradually relieve your unconscious of its accumulation of painful feelings, and prepare the way for your entire system to be rebalanced. Doing it twice daily is good; three times is better; four times and you'll be floating! It does this by discharging the toxic chemicals created by those feelings, and generating the production of healing chemicals (which also gives a boost to your immune system). The longer and more often you do it, the better and more free you will feel. You are now ready to move to the next part of the Process©.

III. Meeting the Need: Infilling and Self-nurturing

The third part of the Healing Process© is fulfilling the need. As your feelings diminish, keep your eyes closed, and let your breathing also diminish, so that the body regulates it according to its need. Focus on your breathing, now quiet and shallow with long spaces in between, because you are so fully oxygenated from the preceding exercises that you need only small and infrequent breaths. Continue to breathe into and from the abdomen. Now on the inbreath, speaking from Your Spiritual Self, say silently to Your human self (Your mind, feelings, and body): "Peace, be still;" then on the outbreath silently repeat whichever of the following Declarations meets the needs of Your self at the moment.

Talk to Your self just as you talked to your babies or grandchildren, with love and gentleness and without criticizing; comfort and guide Your self when it is afraid or disappointed; refrain from being cross or critical or in any way negative; allow Your self to express its feelings and ideas, and validate them. Start with the Declarations below, and let Your mind wrap around them; let it explore whatever it wants to about each one. Repeat that Declaration in rhythm with your breathing until Your self feels safe, secure, and protected. You, and only You, can make that happen, by repeating it over and over until You *experience* the self that You are. This is how the healing takes place: *it's an inside job!*

"Be comforted; You are safe, secure, and protected."

"I hold You in the security of My love."

"Wherever You are, I AM, and where I AM there are safety, protection, security, stability."

"I AM protecting You; only good can happen."

Repeat Your chosen Declaration in rhythm with your breathing until Your self feels safe, secure, and protected. and *you fully believe that you are what it says you are:* this is how the transformation is accomplished. You will be in a state of deep peace, and may find additional Declarations coming into Your mind spontaneously. This is Your inner voice, You as spirit, indicated in the Declarations by capitals. Become even more still, and focus intently on what your *inner voice is saying.*

Consider what is happening. It is so amazing we shy away from even *thinking* it: *You* are making something happen in Your being that hasn't happened before, *ever*! And you probably didn't even notice that You were doing it without any help from other people. Just by choosing one of the Declarations below and repeating it over and over, You have created a new and permanent (unless *You* decide to change it) component of your feeling brain.

Before you started this Process©, you most likely would have thought of the brain as a fixed organ and never even had the idea that *You* could do something to *it*. Now watch yourself use it to take care of your needs or just daydream and weave an interesting story. The limbic system is our playground, as centuries of poets, playwrights, composers, novelists, teachers, singers, musicians—all creators—have amply shown us. We are then, to ourselves and also to others, what God is to us, *creators*. We create "in His image"— proving that we are his offspring, just *smaller—considerably* smaller!

So, here You go, talking to Your self, just the way you probably talked to your babies or grandchildren: with love and gentleness and no criticizing; comforting them when they needed comforting; guiding them through their fears and disappointments; refraining from being cross or in any way harmful to them; not foisting your feelings, views, or ideas on them, but allowing them to express their feelings and ideas, and validating them. Do this also for Your self, starting with the Declarations below, and let Your mind wrap around them; give it free reign to explore whatever it wants to about the particular Declaration.

You will be in a state of deep peace, and may find additional Declarations coming into Your mind spontaneously. This is Your inner voice, You-as-Spirit (indicated in the Declarations by capitals). Become even more still, and focus intently on what your Inner Voice is saying. During this exercise you may want to picture Your human self sitting on Your lap, so You can talk to it directly. Talk to Your self as you would talk to a baby—lovingly, gently, understandingly—for five to ten minutes, using the Declarations given above or whatever variations suit you. The longer you do it, the stronger your feeling of security will become. Each time you say the nurturing phrase, focus on your heart area and the gentle, soothing, expanding and contracting of your rib cage.

Let Your self experience the comforting sense of peace and safety filling it a little fuller with each breath. (Remember to use the word "you" when speaking to Your self, because in so doing you align your identity with Your Spiritual Self, the source of power). Each repetition contributes to encoding this message into your feeling brain, so that after enough repetitions you will have incorporated a sense of security into Your self in place of the old insecurity. *Your self is being transformed because you are learning to meet its needs instead of relying on other people to do so.* Remember, you don't have to believe the Declaration to say it; *you have to say it to believe it.* If you already believed it, the Declaration wouldn't be necessary.

At this point in each practice, if you've been thorough, your mind will be able to focus more intently, almost without a break, because your defenses—that obsessive chatter which passes for thinking most of our waking time—will have been cleared out by the release of negative feelings. If your mind does wander, draw it back to the breathing and repeat the phrase. Be gentle with your mind; don't scold it—it's suffered enough! Just guide it; it will serve you well if you direct it. If you don't, it will revert to its habitual automatic patterns. Trust the Process©; it knows what it's doing. *It will happen for you the way you need it to*, so you can be sure that whatever way it directs you is *right*.

Be gentle as well with Your feelings and Your body as you practice the Process©. Your self has been conditioned in one way all your life up till now, and here you are asking it to do a number of things entirely differently! So if it takes several repetitions of the Process© until you get the hang of it, be reassured, everything new takes practise. As with physical exercise, the effect is cumulative and depends on repetition. The idea is to set aside time in your daily schedule, say two fifteen minute periods to start with, gradually building up to thirty minutes each time, so that the process becomes part of your routine, a psycho-spiritual work-out.

Just as important as the scheduled times are the impromptu, probably briefer, sessions at times when something gets to you. You will learn to do a mini-version (two or three minutes) of the Process© in your office between phone calls, while taking a short walk on your lunch hour, in the restroom on your coffee break, in your car at a stoplight (or even while driving—as long as you don't close your eyes!). The difficult moments that each day brings are thus bonuses—upsets in the present that often connect to pain from long ago. When we bring the old pain to light through this Process©, we give ourselves an opportunity to release the painful, destructive patterns of childhood that caused our insecurity and all the damaging behavior it spawned. The principle is: *accumulate or release*—there is no alternative.

For most people, this Process© of releasing and healing takes a significant period of time to become fully effective. One cannot dislodge huge and long-standing emotional patterns and attitudes, accumulated and repressed over many years, all at once. Because your feelings are so deeply embedded, it takes many repetitions of the Process© to bring about transformation, and regular use of it thereafter to ensure continued serenity and spiritual growth. This is because you are working with your feeling brain, which needs more repetitions than your thinking brain to get it right.

The feeling brain is the repository of all the feelings and experiences you've accumulated since you breathed your first breath, many of which are negative, and it operates at the unconscious level. This means that most of us, most of the time, haven't a clue what we're feeling. Consequently, we rely mainly on our behavior—itself not a very dependable source of accurate information—to tell us how, or what, we're feeling. You can test this anytime by observing the reactions of Your self in situations of insecurity and anxiety such as the supermarket; driving in heavy traffic or a severe thunderstorm; missing an important and long-awaited phone call; discovering a sudden and major illness in yourself or someone you love.

In any of these situations, does Your self revert to a terrified/angry state that persists for several days? Or can you, when afraid and anxious, remember to initiate the Process©, that is, start the deep breathing and releasing of painful feelings, then, like a good mother would do, give Your self reassuring messages until it feels safe? And then, can You discipline Your self to practise the Process© daily for several weeks or months—whatever it takes—to build a sense of security in yourself? When you can say "yes" to these questions, you are ready to move to the next level,

Chapter IV, and from there progressively up the hierarchy of needs, from wherever you began, to autonomy and beyond.

It is important for a full understanding of the security need to remember that the fight/flight defense is grounded in our biochemistry. (This is true for the other three needs also, since each of them uses variations of the same fight/flight defenses). When this defense occurs in response to a physical threat, the adrenaline surge provides the energy to attack or run, thus using up the adrenaline. However, if the threat and fear are psychological rather than physical, running and attacking are both useless, so the chemical isn't used up and you are left with a "chemical imbalance:" too much adrenaline.

The same thing happens if the fear is repressed, meaning that our feeling brain has automatically shut down our fear by pushing it into the unconscious, like packing a suitcase and then locking it in a closet. So we have to rely on what our body chemistry is telling us: the neuropeptides carrying the fear message can't find the receptor cells in the immune system, can't therefore be reabsorbed or neutralized, and so remain in the system continuing the damage and the cycle. If the fear you experience is chronic, that is, either it has been in you, repressed, for many years, or it comes from an ongoing condition in your life, you will have a virtually chronic "adrenaline high," meaning you will be agitated and nervous a lot of the time. This in turn results in continual fight/flight defenses that, as we have seen, form the basis of several mental illnesses (see Ch. VIII, section B).

If another situation of insecurity occurs at the same time, the adrenaline will shoot up even higher, causing anxiety or panic attacks. Your system eventually gets used to this state and feels down and depressed without it, like being in withdrawal—in fact, it *is* withdrawal, and you will, consequently, seek a "high" to feel "normal" again. You need the Process©!

The Security Need

A good example of this pattern was a shocking case in South Carolina in which a policeman, angered by the length of time it took a driver to pull over, roughly dragged her, unarmed and nonresistant, from her car, pushed her to the ground and held her down (even though she wasn't struggling) by planting a knee in her back. A chemical chain reaction in the policeman explains (but does not, of course, excuse) his atrocious behavior, and provides a chemical substrate to his out-of-control actions: his anger triggers the release of adrenaline and acetylcholine, decreasing the flow of blood to the neocortex and increasing it to the amygdala, the fight/flight "button" in the limbic system. It has momentarily overpowered the neocortex, rendering the cop unable to think rationally or to behave properly or to "follow correct procedure." *The fight defense took over.*

A similar chain reaction must have taken place in the frightened driver, who without doubt also suffered an adrenaline rush. But *her* rush, being set off by fear, would have led to the flight defense (here meaning submission rather than trying to escape). Given the brutality of the cop's action, we might speculate that pretty soon *her* adrenaline assumed the "fight" reaction, enough to propel her into some safe kind of response, preferably legal and aggressive.

Many people in our culture—indeed, the majority, if my case load is indicative—are in such a state daily, fraught with insecurity of every kind: physical, financial, professional, social—in families, schools, jobs, cities, streets, environment, etc. People aren't just *mad as hell*; they are *scared to death*. That the security need occupies the largest, as well as the initial, slot on the Chart©, says a lot about our culture: it puts money and position first, with little regard for those who are born into poverty, most of whom live in it the rest of their lives.

This situation, plus the fact that the security need, the first of the needs, is more unmet than met, thereby creating a breeding ground for increasing violence, crime, and accidents, is a frightening comment on the emotional health and values of our nation. They are far from what the founding fathers had in mind when they wrote about "life, liberty, and the pursuit of happiness."

Writing and *doing* are two different things: the diabolical institution of slavery had already corrupted those values *and* the founding fathers that had established them. Without those corrupted values that allowed them to engage in the shameful slave trade, the "fathers" could not live the grand and pleasant life they had grown accustomed to. So they turned their eyes and hearts from what they were actually *doing,* to the grand and noble documents they were *thinking* and *writing.*

These "gentlemanly" activities, revered enough to camouflage a variety of crimes, started with the systematic eradication or evacuation of all the indigenous nations of the continent. They moved on to *stealing people from their homeland* and shipping them to the "New World" in the atrocious conditions of the infamous slave ships. Then, once on the *land they had stolen*, they introduced the Africans to auctions, beatings, lynchings followed by the inhuman, diabolical—*but beneficial to them*—separating of families.

Since this kind of treatment naturally brought a deservedly antagonistic response from the indigenous people and the African slaves whenever they could risk it, the white land owners and settlers also shuddered—but, because they had guns, they won. *Thus the very beginning of this country was born in insecurity: all three groups lived in varying degrees of fear or terror.* The indigenous population and the forced immigrants must have lived in constant anxiety, with the first having only their homemade weapons for protection, and the second with nothing to protect them from the white man's power, will, and guns. The degree of their terror is painful to imagine, considering the "weapons of mass destruction" that the invader/settlers had in their hands, ready for action.

Security is a national, not just an individual issue: when a country allocates it to those who have ninety-nine percent of almost all the wealth (the modern equivalent of the settlers' firearms) and deny it to those who have little-to-none of the wealth, there will come a time when the tables will be turned and the insecure will wise up and rise up and demand that *their* rights to security—financial, academic, legal, professional—be met, and met equally and permanently.

What I am saying here is certainly not new news: those of our countrymen who are aware of the huge gap in the security need between the "lower" class and the "upper" class have evidently become so accustomed to it that *it feels like normal, especially to the latter.* Indeed, they actually defend it, as witness the recent statement of Trent Lott to the effect that this country wouldn't have the troubles it's having if the ancient Strom Thurmond had been elected president in 1948 instead of good old Harry Truman.

Instead of stirring up possible war in foreign countries, our leaders should be taking care of business here at home. Think of the crumbling schools with not enough teachers, partly because the classrooms are too full and the pay isn't full enough; hospitals with overworked nurses and doctors; inner cities and country areas both in poverty (many of which still use outhouses!); houses falling apart; old roads in bad shape and new ones not plentiful enough; the poor and the aged often unable to get the medical treatment and medications they need, *etc.* How awful to be living daily in a state of insecurity in your old age as well as your youth!

As all this almost willful devastation worsens day after day, rogue stock-exchange traders make billions of dollars illegally and take it to Bermuda; a rogue president, illegally elected to office by a corrupt Supreme Court (which broke its own jurisdiction by moving into and making a decision in a state issue in which it has no standing) beholden to the

Learning to Fulfill the Needs of Your Self

new president's father, pays—so far—no attention to the problems of the "homeland" other than trying to create two new bureaucracies and needlessly use up our—the taxpayers—money.

If memory serves, it is the Republicans who like to complain, when the Democrats are in power, about their supposed propensity for "big government" and its reputed evils. It's a replay of the "founding fathers/slave workers" scenario: the government and the stock market play with their toys and send the bill to its citizens. Even more alarming are the two neo-Hitlerian ideas of (1) allowing CIA agents to arrest and/or shoot anybody whom they think is a threat, without due process, and (2) allowing the "Homeland Security" operatives to enter any house they think is suspicious without a search warrant.

Eradicating these internal threats on our national security should be every citizen's primary concern, and one way to start that would be for every citizen to send President Bush (he who professes such devotion to the Bible!) a copy of the *Sermon on the Mount*, the *Ten Commandments*, and the *Constitution of the United States*. What is needed is an all-out, nationwide campaign to eradicate the dangerous ideas that run counter to those three documents. Creating a nationwide sense of insecurity borders on the idiotic and the diabolical: it's not only *children* who need security. But when, for a sufficient amount of time, a sufficient amount of security is denied nationwide, the nation will rise up like Marie Antoinette's France, or the famous "Boston tea party," and call to account those who have brought it to this state. Such a step can create only harm and internal dissent in our country: an all-out forward press against it is urgently needed.

I have no solution for this nationwide dysfunction; my work is with individual people and small groups. But the same Process© my clients use would certainly help those who live, work, go to school, and play in conditions in which no human being could possibly feel safe and comfortable, especially since the method works no matter how severely depressed or angry the person is. Repeated use of the Process© on any issue or need or problem will bring resolution. Removing stress as soon as possible after it happens, and doing a Process© as many times as needed, depending on the severity of the problem, will avoid "toxic build-up," and enable you to think clearly and choose your behavior in accord with your values and goals.

The Riddle Rewritten

After the boss gave you the project, you thanked him, went to your office excited and scared, and sat down and did some deep breathing for about five minutes. Towards the end, feeling less scattered and no longer scared, you repeated to yourself for about five or six minutes: "Peace, be secure. The boss likes you. Take your time, make a plan. You can do it." An idea for organizing the project came to you, and you spent about half an hour working it out on your computer. Then you called the staff members into your office and told them, "As you know, we're coming up on the yearly training conference. Betty, I'd like you to handle the travel and accommodation arrangements; Jack, the meals, snacks and drinks; Morris, you take the technical set-ups—the PC, overhead projectors, displays, etc., and Tom, you get the agendas and presentations and programs together. Do you each feel suited to your job?" You listened to their responses, making adjustments where indicated, and provided them with a printout of instructions for their project. They left smiling and you felt relaxed and self-approving.

What brought about the change?

Unmet Needs cause...	Painful Feelings cause...	Mental & Behavioral Defenses: constitute...	Type of Personality	Feelings When Needs Met
BELONGING	uncomfortable around people	isolation/fantasy	THE "FORGOTTEN CHILD" TYPE	happy
CONNECTEDNESS	lonely	repressed rage & outrage		loved
LOVE	outcast	panic/depression/silence		treasured
NURTURANCE	neglected	solitary activities		heard
COMFORT	resentful	compulsive overeating		accepted
	deserted	anorexia		taken care of
	rejected	drinking or taking pills		joyous
	self-pity	TV watching		acknowledged
	abandoned	romance novel reading or writing		included
	self-loathing	pornography		nurtured
	unloved	masturbation		wanted
	grief-full	sexual anorexia or addiction		desirable
	lonely	passivity		
	sad/forlorn/lost	lack of assertiveness		
	sense of justice	minimal social skills		
	betrayed	has teddy bear, small pet		
	panic	(cat, dog, hamster)		

IV

The Belonging Need

Riddle #2

Your wife leaves for work earlier than you and takes the kids with her. Sometimes you're still in bed when she leaves. Yesterday, such was the case: when you got up and realized she hadn't said goodbye, you felt outraged and depressed. That evening you were mean to the kids, and yelled at your wife, "How come you're always late? What's wrong with you?" You refused to eat dinner with the family, and stalked off to your bedroom.

What's driving your behavior?

We now move on to the *Belonging Need*, the second level of the hierarchy. This consists of the "childhood" years, in which the baby gradually relinquishes the delights of infancy, and the child inches toward the perplexities of adolescence. If the security need has been adequately met in the first three years, the baby will move seamlessly into the stage of childhood, which correlates to the need for belonging and acceptance, that is, for love.

Love is, indeed, the core ingredient of all four needs: in the first two, the love comes from outer sources; in the second two, increasingly from inner sources (if the first two needs have been adequately met). This need is where we most encounter the feeling of love—the need to get it and the need to give it. While in his first three years the baby receives love and gives it freely, he and his caregivers must still concern themselves first with security in all areas, for two reasons: the security need is the foundation of all the other needs and for the baby, security *is* love. When, and only when, the security need is met sufficiently, can the child safely receive and give love.

The way the belonging need is met, and the love conveyed is, of course, through the acceptance, approval, encouragement, support, and especially the empathy of the parents. The result is a deep bond and connection between parent and child. When this need is well met during the childhood stage, the foundation of a successful, non-rebellious adolescence is established (which helps prevent the parents of adolescents from inheriting insanity from their children).

The need is met also by all those who inhabit the child's expanding world: siblings, cousins, aunts and uncles, grandparents, pets, schoolmates, teachers, ministers and priests, even doctors and dentists. I know a young child who *loves* his doctor *and* his dentist, because both are gentle and affectionate: "I go doctor, doctor make me better;" and I know a crossing guard whose warmth and attention to her charges gives them feelings of safety, protection, and affection, which make a significant difference in the beginning and ending of their school days.

During this period, the child's development and attention increasingly look to the acceptance, approval, and companionship of other children as a source of this need, second only to parents. As puppies and kittens gather together for warmth and play and companionship, so kids are drawn to kids. If they have a good foundation of security from their parents, they will make friends easily, and they will make good friends. Acceptance and popularity are important all through our lives, but they are crucial at the second stage of development. Being accepted by the most popular of one's peers is the most gratifying of all, and rightly so, for it is the foundation for the next stage, self-esteem.

In contrast to the three years of the security need, fulfillment of the belonging need requires significantly more time, generally about eight years. This is due to the expansion of the child's activities and relationships: a whole slew of new playmates to be sorted out and allied with or not; teachers (some likable and some not); principals (ditto); homework (yuk!); technology (telephones, computers, *etc.*); and very likely, if not already, a new sibling or two to contend with.

With all this going on, we can see how important it is that the parents continue to be supportive, mindful that whatever their child's age or problem, he can be certain that his parents are there to supply security and strengthen his growing sense of belonging. Consequently, he will be able to face the notoriously difficult stage of adolescence with security and confidence, and without interest in using or even experimenting with drugs, roaming the streets, engaging in random sex, or playing car games.

However, when the belonging need is not met sufficiently we, adults as well as children, stay stuck at that emotional level, still expecting other people to take care of us and nurture us. How do we feel and what happens to our inner life when the need for belonging is deficient? The Chart© facing page 69 gives a clear answer in column 2: we experience feelings of neglect, rejection, sadness, self-loathing; we are filled with grief and a deep sense of injustice; we feel resented, resentful, and alone, even—or rather, *especially*—in a crowd.

But worst of all, we feel abandoned, not wanted: as it says on passports, *persona non grata*: "person not welcome." These feelings are an appropriate reaction to such rejection from those who should nurture us: acceptance by our family is our birthright, a law of nature. As Robert Frost says: "Home is where, when you go there, they have to take you in."[1] When that birthright to be loved, nurtured, and treasured, *to belong*, is violated, we are outraged, enraged, and terrified, because absence of nurturance is against nature and is therefore life threatening.

In such a state our painful feelings become super-highly charged, and set off the defensive pattern: sequences of thoughts and actions over which we have very little conscious control, and which generate consequences in two ways. First, they cycle back within us and create more pain, and second, they have effects on the world around us that inevitably return to us. We will be eventually submerged and lost— *truly* lost—unless we can figure out what's wrong, and get help if we need it. But mostly we don't get help, because we, or our parents, don't know that a crucial element in us is deficient. Moreover, we compare ourselves to others who exhibit confidence and get along well, it seems, with *everybody*, wondering morosely why we can't do the same. Even as young children we can become "loners," resorting to isolation as our only safety.

This condition is similar to getting a shot of Novocain to deal with a toothache: the pain is suppressed but re-emerges when the drug wears off, a *short term gain* but *a long term pain*, since the *cause* of the pain hasn't been dealt with and is therefore increasing. *There is no lasting or permanent cure without removing the cause; conversely, the effect can't happen if the cause is removed.* Many medical as well as street drugs do the same thing: they camouflage the pain and ignore the cause, giving us an illusory belief that we're now okay. Although the pain may be temporarily alleviated, the cause is still there, and will remain until identified and released.

The loss of self happens most typically either to the last or next-to-last child. In either case, your share of attention, already less than that given to the kids before you—who needs another girl?—was further diminished when your baby brother was born only eighteen months later, and most of the attention you were getting was diverted to him. The shorter the time between the two of you the more severe your loss and therefore your damage: you haven't yet had enough time with Mom to develop a sufficient sense of security, let alone belonging. You are at least seven or eight years away from being able to comfort yourself or ask for reassurance.

The result is that you suffer painful feelings of desertion, desolation, and abandonment that you are too young to verbalize, and that, unless recognized and remedied by mom or dad or someone trained in healing this kind of distress, will remain with you for life and can lead to serious mental illness. (See the Main Chart© on page facing p.i for the correlations between the defenses and mental health diagnoses). Buried deep in your unconscious brain, these old feelings will surface even when you are chronologically an adult, in any situation where other people are getting more attention than you are. If you let the feelings show, the world will see you as selfish, temperamental, and insensitive to others.

When this need is unmet in an only child, the outcome is even more severe, since without a sibling there isn't even a possibility of alliance or support. Zeke in Chapter I is a good example. Another is Jane, whom I met early in my practice. Her mother came from a preacher's family, and was the third child *and* the third *girl*, so she didn't get much attention or many of the basic necessities. Jane laughingly told me that her mother used to say that the first two kids in her family who got to the laundry basket in the morning got socks. The not surprising consequence of this childhood was a deficit in Jane's mother's need for security, in every area: money, social standing, job, house, marriage, *etc.* This need was so intense that in order to keep herself together she always had to be the controller, the center of attention.

In contrast, Jane's father was extremely deficient in the belonging need. His parents, using the discipline of the day—scolding, humiliation, and constant criticizing and correcting everything he said and did to prevent him from becoming "conceited"—produced an introverted, self-absorbed, and timid child. (Thank God we have a better psychological understanding today!). It is not surprising that he grew into a scared, anxious, nervous, needy, absent-minded, preoccupied, dreamy, insufficiently loved and nurtured man, rarely present except to his wife, to whom he was excessively attentive because she was his only source of belonging.

This of course put him at her mercy. His unconscious revenge took the form of passive aggression (hiding a bill, forgetting to pay it, not locking the car door, hiding his dirty socks ostensibly so she wouldn't have to wash them, *etc.*). This defensive behavior ensured him a monopoly on her attention until the day he died. The more he played the child, the more she played the mother; the more she played the mother, the more he became the child. Each sought in the other what each lacked in childhood. The controlled became the controller and the controller became the controlled.

It's not hard to imagine the effect all this had on Jane. Enmeshed in her parents' dysfunctional dance, Jane got little attention. Only when at eight years old she contracted pneumonia was the focus on her, and even then her parents' attention was minimal. As a teenager, Jane was connected to her parents even less. For example, although they lived within a half an hour from the airport, they were not willing to make the trip to welcome her home after a year in Europe. Instead, they sent her ex-boyfriend (and they knew he was ex) to meet her and drive her home. And they neglected to inform her of the arrangement! The shock, disappointment, and sense of being deceived by their evasion were still apparent in her recounting of the event, fifteen years after it happened.

Amazingly, her parents added a second dose of neglect by packing her off alone to her first year in college, with a year's worth of luggage to handle, and all the unfamiliar routines to deal with by herself. Being the forgotten child, she was unable to find her voice to protest the mistreatment, but plowed through the unfamiliar activities in constant anxiety. After a diligent four years, she graduated *cum laude;* but her parents once again abandoned her—they couldn't face the perils of a train ride from Long Island to New Jersey to see their daughter graduate.

There are, of course, innumerable scenarios that produce the same result of insufficient bonding with one's parents and lack of a sense of belonging, of being accepted and loved by them. Not only were you not wanted, you weren't even remembered: you were the child who got left at the beach and whose absence wasn't noticed until bedtime; lost in the crowd at the carnival and not missed until your parents were paged; left at home alone when too young with only the television for company—and for safety. If a thunderstorm came up or a door creaked, the feeling of aloneness and terror was almost fatal.

You were the silent little kid whom the teacher couldn't remember even while you were still in her class; whose birthday, coming so near Christmas, was not celebrated; who got one letter per semester in boarding school (while most of the other kids got at least one a week); whose mother camouflaged her failure to bond by giving her style of child-rearing a legitimate-sounding name: "benign neglect." Your desperate need for attention and affection may lead you to anorexia or bulimia. You are so attuned to rejection that you feel it in actions or words not intended to convey it. You are caught in a terrible dilemma: to live as a loner—the illusion of safety—or to reach out to other people to get the need met, and run the risk of rejection—your greatest fear.

Such feelings are unbearable and, paradoxically, tend to be intensified by being around other people, especially in large numbers ("I feel lonely in a crowd"). Seeing groups of people talking and joking, socializing with apparent ease and lack of self-consciousness, or looking into brightly lit houses at night while you are walking your dog alone and seeing a *family relating*—eating dinner, washing up, playing cards, *etc., etc.*, amplifies the loneliness beyond enduring. The "left-out, shut-out, I-am-forgotten" feeling is overwhelming.

The typical defenses against this unmet need, such as withdrawnness, silence, solo activities, and lack of communication, at first appear puzzling: why would somebody so neglected make herself *more* alone? Given that emotional disconnection is the generator of this system of defenses, the answer is ironic: only by being alone can we be certain of not being more forgotten ("I have to be alone so I won't be rejected," a client said once). We thereby gain a sense of control over the perpetual threat to our psychic intactness—at the terrible expense of making our need even more pronounced. The same cycle we saw with the security need occurs here: an *unmet need* causes *painful feelings* that generate *mental and behavioral defenses* which create consequences and reactions from other people. The diagram on the next page shows a clear picture of this cycle.

As you can see, each component generates the next: the cycle cannot stop itself, and as it continues the pain in the child deepens. A child naturally depends on his parents, especially Mom, for nurturance and belonging, but when he experiences abandonment instead, he feels his acceptance into the family, and his very existence, threatened. Since these conditions are against nature—even *animals* protect and nurture their young—he feels *outraged*, because those

Unmet Need for Security	Mental & Behavioral Defenses	Type of Personality
Unmet needs cause…	Painful feelings lead to…	Defenses lead to…
PAINFUL FEELINGS: abandoned deserted neglected rejected unwanted lost forgotten	MENTAL DEFENSES: imagining fantasizing shutting down retreating repressing self-deprecating BEHAVIORAL DEFENSES: isolation reading solitude activity anorexia pornography sex addiction television headset pets loner	THE **"FORGOTTEN CHILD"** TYPE

whose job it is to love and nurture him instead abandon him, either emotionally or physically.

He becomes another *forgotten child*, and falls into a state of despair alternating with rage that he struggles to keep suppressed, but it occasionally erupts and spreads ashes all over his life. Hence the concept of *desertion* (different from and more devastating than *loss*), which we use in reference only to people who are our caregivers. We don't, for example, speak of a sales person or a gas station attendant or bank teller *deserting* us (though sometimes it feels that way) but only of a mother, father, older sibling *etc.*, doing so.

The rage, even though it is a feeling, functions as a defense against the pain and, in comparison to the desertion and despair, feels like relief. But while it effectively defends the forgotten child against his feelings of neglect, rejection, and abandonment, the rage prevents the painful feelings from being released, in turn blocking the need from being met. A secondary form of this defense is *outrage*, of which this country has lately seen an alarming amount. Whether the forgotten child defends himself through rage or outrage, the result is the same: he is caught in an endless, downward-spiraling process that prevents healing and blocks emotional growth.

One of the consequences of this treatment is fear of a negative reaction from those whom you expect to protect you (somehow you never are able to stop *expecting*). The rage you experience when they let you down is immediately repressed—way too dangerous to confront. The result looks like depression, but is more precisely called *compression*, since your rage accumulates and is packed down year by year, like trash in a compactor. While depression drags you down into apathy and disaffection, able at its worst to make you *not care about anything*, in contrast, the compressed rage of the *forgotten child* is explosive, a disruptive component in his intrapsychic make-up.

The effort to keep the rage repressed often fails, and the resulting negative energy disturbs normal elements of living like eating and sleeping (who can eat or sleep on a full unconscious?), diminishes or increases libido, thereby distorting normal sexual activities, and makes you uncommunicative, prone to long or continuous silence, self-absorbed, irascible, and hostile (which you call "self-conscious" or "shy")—and as we discussed above, *dangerous*—a bomb waiting to be set off.

If this condition is treated by traditional medical methods, you will most likely be diagnosed as clinically depressed and given medication. As you become habituated to it, the effectiveness of the medication will diminish, whereupon you or your doctor will increase the dosage to get the same effect you got at first—that is, you will become addicted, first psychologically and, if you keep taking the stuff, eventually physically. In any case, the medication cannot cure, because it does not reach, the cause: the unmet need for belonging. Until that happens, you will continue to be symptomatic and your behavior will continue to be driven by your unmet needs.

This rage is also *explosive*, in proportion to the degree of abandonment and rejection you suffered as a child. When it erupts, it is similar, sometimes indistinguishable from, a panic attack, and is uncontrollable and dangerous, often being the cause of irrational or mass violence. Our country has suffered a number of such catastrophes in the past decade or two: the Unabomber (see Appendix III: Mental Health Diagnoses for analysis); several school shootings, most notably Columbine; several murders by teenage boys of family members or peers; the Government Office Building in Oklahoma; the Atlanta bombing; and 9/11.

In each of the cases for which such information was released, somebody (generally a neighbor) who thought he knew the perpetrator well, said something like, "It's a mystery why he did it…he was always a quiet kid, kind of a loner" or, in the case of 9/11, "why do they hate us?" To which they might reply: because they have so little and we have so much, a statement applicable to the forgotten child as well, but in respect to emotional, rather than material, issues.

From Ted Kaczynski to the Oklahoma bomber to the Columbine duo, a neighbor or schoolmate unwittingly let us know the cause of the disaster in just one word: "loner." In each case, the belonging need was so drastically unmet that the rage and desolation it generated exploded, tragically bringing others down with it.

In cases where the lack of connection to another human is absolute, the loner feels invisible, as though he is dead, and becomes so terrified that he must make his presence indisputably known. He must destroy those he feels are destroying him. In all cases, whether public or domestic, the reaction from those affected is, understandably, terror, outrage, and rejection, exactly what the perpetrator suffered from. In some domestic cases, the parent uses silence, refusing to speak to the child at all for an extended period of time. The worst case of this I've heard of is a *year.*

To a child, the psychological damage of such treatment is catastrophic: shut out from what he needs most, he can only turn inward, conditioned to see his "self" as worthless and unacceptable, and therefore afraid to join with other kids. By now, his consciousness is so filled with a sense of being unwanted it will continue to create more rejection. He sees and treats himself with neglect and lack of attention, the way the family does, and, enacting their subliminal message, may even take his own life. To be a perpetual reject is a fate worst than death.

When your belonging need is chronically unmet, you eventually conclude that you are *persona non grata,* even hated. Your ability to develop self-love and self-esteem is virtually destroyed. There is no way out that doesn't incur more pain: if you erupt, or even try to say your feelings, you get attacked or yelled at; if you remain silent, you get ignored. Of the two, the latter is safer, since it at least gives you immunity from attack and overt rejection. Your defenses function like medication—a short term gain but a long-term pain: by blocking your feelings they keep the needs cycle in perpetual motion.[2]

Sooner or later you give up any attempt to break out of this pattern, and you grow into adulthood without having developed the emotional and social skills of an adult. You are as a result uncomfortable–even terrified—around other people. At first glance, your reluctance to socialize and your apparent self-sufficiency appear to disqualify you as a loner, but they actually put you in that category, since it is precisely your sensitivity to other people's reactions that makes you isolate and against which your isolation defends you. Your needs control you, and though you still have the expectation that they are supposed to be met by other people, you cannot bring yourself to reach out for help and connection. *Checkmate!*

If your need for belonging wasn't met in your childhood, it probably hasn't been met in adulthood either. To remedy this deficit, you can learn to give to Your self the nurturance it lacks. Using the Freedom Healing Process© repeatedly will gradually release your childhood trauma, diminish present hurts, and bit by bit build a sense of inner acceptance and self-connectedness. This opens the door to start moving, gradually, toward connecting with others, which for a while feels like learning to ice skate: very, very slippery and for a long time not very rewarding.

Healing for this deficiency lies not in continuing to live alone, nor in becoming even more dependent on others for your belonging need, but on changing the belief that the need can be met *only by others* and that your whole emotional life is at the mercy of other people. As you practice the Healing Process©, and learn that You-as-spiritual being can create and generate feelings of love within and for Your human self, your desperate loneliness will gradually fade away. You will eventually find Your lost self and how to nurture it (described below).

In addition to the freedom and joy of living this brings you, it gives you choice when to be alone and when to seek companionship. Other people will notice the change, even though they may not say so, and will respond differently

The Belonging Need

and positively, now that *You* have *remembered Your self*. So let us now turn to the Healing Process©.

The Freedom Healing Process© for the second need follows the same procedure as that for the first. Having assessed Your self and identified the components that constitute Your personality type (see Chart on p.68), you are now ready to undertake the Healing Process© to fulfill your need for acceptance. You will quickly see it's an *inside job: nobody can do it for you.*

As you come to recognize and clear away your defenses, you gradually learn to experience and release your lifetime of painful feelings and give Your self the belonging and acceptance it has yearned for all its life. You will enjoy a gradually increasing sense of self-affection and a slowly developing ability to connect with other people. Learning to acknowledge your painful feelings and blow them away frees you to begin living a more enjoyable life. Reviewing the defenses for this need (Chart, Col. 2) will increase your awareness of defensive thoughts and behaviors *as you are doing them*, and this awareness will become a signal to engage the Healing Process©: "Oh dear! There I go again, imagining that Jim will scold me. Maybe I better go do some breathing..."

The Freedom Healing Process

I. Accessing Feelings: Pounding

The first part of the Process© consists of learning to access your feelings. Begin by pounding a pillow or sofa cushion as described in Chapter II. Clench your fists and pound as hard as you can, just working with your forearms. No need to raise your arms above your shoulders—it's not any more effective and it can pull a muscle.

Continue to pound for about five minutes, pausing to catch your breath when needed. Then do it again for two or three minutes. Don't fret about the amount of time; a better measure is how you're feeling. If the anger and hurt are still painful, pound some more. Different hurts require different amounts of work: a severe childhood experience may require doing the Process© daily for several months, while an offhand snide remark by a co-worker may need only one session. Since the effectiveness of this procedure is increased by yelling (a good type of discharge) as well as by the pounding, it's a good idea to do it when nobody else is around—not difficult if you're a loner!

II. Experiencing and Releasing Feelings: Breathing

Next, when your frustration and rage are sufficiently reduced, start the deep breathing. Sit with your back straight and both feet on the floor, or lie down on the floor with lower legs resting horizontally on a chair or sofa. Start by *exhaling*: as you pull your abdominal muscles back toward your spine, blow your breath out through your mouth, squeezing out every last bit, expelling all the toxins you can, then *inhale* the fresh air *all the way in* until your abdomen inflates like a balloon. Let Your self experience the buried feelings of loneliness, abandonment, betrayal, and unwantedness, as you inhale them from the unconscious mind into the conscious mind and then release them to the universe. Feel the clean new air pulling the toxins out of your blood, and as you exhale picture your breath blowing them all the way across the universe. Repeat until you feel calmer and more whole.

As you release the accumulated pain that caused your defenses, they gradually fall away and you find Your true self—a moving experience that generally involves tears. Let them flow: the crying carries out the pain. Not only will it make you feel better, but, as you have already experienced in Chapter III, the emotion will run its course and stop of its own accord if you don't try to manage it. As you experience this Process© and the relief it brings, your reluctance to do the intense feeling work will diminish, and you will gain freedom from your pain and increasing governance of your behavior.

Each time you do the Process©, repeat the pounding and breathing until the feelings have subsided, noticing how soothing it is to experience them draining out of you. If you get light-headed or dizzy, check to see if you are *inflating* on the *inhale,* so that your abdomen *expands.* Sometimes we get forgetful and reverse it, and find we are *pulling the abdomen in* while *inhaling,* the reverse of what you want. If this happens, be reassured, it won't hurt you. A few minutes of reversing your breathing will make the lightheadedness pass. Then move on to the release breathing on the exhale and cleansing breathing on the inhale.

Don't rush the Process©. You don't have to get out all the old stuff in one session: in fact, you can't. It's something you do repeatedly, daily, a spiritual and emotional workout. Allow the Process© to take the time it needs, without expecting or setting a specific time span.

III. Meeting the Need: Infilling and Self-nurturing

When the feelings have subsided significantly, you are ready to start doing the nurturing part. Because your blood is now highly oxygenated by the deep breathing, your breaths will become brief, shallow, fulfilling, and very peaceful, and you will notice a sizable interval between them. Start saying silently to Your self on the in-breath, "peace," and experience that feeling expanding in your chest and abdomen. Then, on the outbreath, search for the specific Declarations that will meet your need to feel that you belong, you are connected, wanted, welcome, loved. Then say them silently to Your self. Do one per session, saying it over and over to give the limbic system time to incorporate and store it.

This is the core of the Process©: first, through the breathing, you remove the old patterns embedded in your feeling brain by your childhood experiences; then, by many repetitions of the Declaration, you gradually implant the new messages, bit by bit moving your mindset from negative to positive, and Your view of Your self from unlovable to lovable. Here are some examples; add your own as you wish. Keep the pronouns as they are, remembering that You-as-Spirit are speaking to you-as-human:

"You are always acceptable to ME."

"You are lovable, loved, and loving."

"I AM always with you; My love fills you with feelings of acceptance and belonging."

"My love supports, sustains, and envelops you."

"Wherever you are, I AM, and where I AM there is unlimited love, acceptance, and belonging."

Pick one of the messages and repeat it for several minutes, addressing Your self as "you," not "I." The "you" is the human being, the locus of neediness; the "I" is the spiritual being, the locus of fulfilledness. The needs of your human self cannot be met by your human self, but only by the "I," the spiritual self. As You-as-spirit continue to say the Declaration Your self will begin to experience warmth, love, and fulfillment expanding in you.

The longer You-as-spirit talk to Your human self, repeating the specific message it needs most to hear, the more quickly and completely it will progress. You will transform it from a childlike state of neediness and emptiness and longing, to an adult state of fulfillment, serenity, and joy. Herein lies the spirituality of the Process©: You-as-Spiritual Being have the power to heal you-as-human being.

If you do this exercise thoroughly (all three parts) twice a day for fifteen minutes each, gradually expanding to thirty minutes, in a relatively short time your sadness and sense of unwantedness will begin to lift, and within three to four months (no longer than it takes to get physically fit!), you will be feeling wonderful feelings, very different from what you have been used to, inklings—maybe more—of the state described in the Upanishads:

> From joy all things are born;
> By joy all things are sustained;
> To joy all things return.

Doing the Healing Process© for the belonging need builds the foundation for working on the next need, self esteem. Signs that you are ready to undertake it are: being able to handle everyday situations such as work, shopping, children's activities, *etc.* with less stress; developing a new unforced calmness in social situations; and remembering to do the Healing Process© promptly to restore your sense of belonging when something happens that makes you feel rejected. You will no longer be terrified of going out of your den, or of trying to make a friendship or even—imagine!—develop a relationship. Even if it falls apart, *you* won't—because *You are able to give Your self the love and nurturance it needs.*

The Riddle Rewritten

When you opened your eyes it was 7:45, and the house was still; Marge and the kids must already have left. Disappointed at not seeing them off and kissing Marge goodbye, you spent some time deep breathing, then spoke reassuringly and lovingly to Your self: "Peace, be comforted. You feel like they forgot you. But you know they love you. Peace, be comforted. You are accepted and loved." When you got home after a good day at work, you gave them all a kiss, and said to Marge: "When I woke up this morning and realized you'd left, I felt real disappointed at missing my morning kiss—so let's have one now!"

What brought about the change?

Unmet Needs cause...	Painful Feelings cause...	Mental & Behavioral Defenses constitute...	Type of Personality	Feelings When Needs Met
SELF-ESTEEM SELF-WORTH	inadequate inferior worthless not good enough less than invaluable stupid clumsy inept incompetent guilty unappreciated unapproved easily embarrassed tense stressed self-doubting	over-achieving/over-working self-justifying/rationalizing ("Somebody has to do it.") care taking/volunteering directing/organizing ("If I don't do it, it won't get done.") criticizing/judging bragging ("If I do it, I know it will be done right.") perfecting competing ("I'd rather do it myself.") constantly proving ones elf people pleasing/social climbing false altruism/martyr-izing back biting/envying/complaining declining help ("I can do it myself") gossiping/chameleon compulsive drinking use of antidepressants/sedatives/painkillers	THE "PERFECT CHILD" TYPE	self-confident adequate capable as good as intelligent competent self-approving valuable willing to accept help nonjudgmental non-competitive valuable

V

The Self-Esteem Need

Riddle #3

Your parents are due in about an hour for Thanksgiving dinner. You've prepared the regulation meal; cleaned the house; set a beautiful table which you suddenly realize is missing something. Flowers! And the water goblets have spots on them! What will Mom think—and say? "Honey," you ask your husband, "could you run over to the farmer's market—they have the freshest flowers—and pick up a nice bunch of roses and carnations with some greens and baby's breath? Make sure they're all fresh!" Your husband replies, "Look, honey, it's just your folks—not the *Pope!* They probably won't even notice!" You're now literally up to your elbows in hot water dealing with the goblets and feeling very pressured—only one half hour till they get here—and this is too much. *"Just do it,"* you holler. "You know Mom will have a comment!"

What's driving your behavior?

This chapter describes the *Self-Esteem Need*. It is the third of the four dependency needs, and is the one that we meet and must fulfill in adolescence if we are to continue our emotional growth. If we don't learn how to give value and esteem to ourselves, our growth will stall at this level even though chronologically and physically we reach adulthood. The Chart© facing page 89 shows the feelings and defenses that develop when the need isn't met. Achieving self-esteem will be a smooth process if your caregivers have provided you with a good foundation in the first two needs, security and belonging. Likewise, to the degree that you fulfill your need for self-esteem, you lay the necessary foundation for the next need, thus insuring yourself a healthy sense of autonomy.

The relation of self-esteem to adolescence—that period of growth through which we transition from our childhood dependence to our adult independence—is like the sighting of land to a storm-torn ship: it's the exact thing you need *if you can just reach it*. It is by definition an *inside job*, though not exclusively. External support is helpful, so long as it is secondary: parents are needed still, not only to support and affirm the sometimes overwhelming physical, social, and intellectual challenges and development, but to supply guidance and discipline; siblings, both older and younger, can provide, respectively, support and admiration; teachers and coaches can be inspirational, and also good watchdogs for unwanted behavior; and, finally, *friends*! Well, anybody who thinks friends aren't everything to a teenager has been living under a rock: not only is their approval essential, but their mutual interactions (activities, achievements, dreams, goals) are all deeply important to the development of this need in each one.

Accomplishing the fulfillment of this need teaches us that "learning to love Your self" is indeed the "greatest love of all." Without it, no amount of affirmation from others, pleasing though it may be, can fulfill your need for esteeming yourself. Support from others at this stage isn't *bad*; it's just *not enough.* No more seeking people who will do for you what you don't or won't do for Your self. Since You are the one who knows best what Your self is feeling from one moment to the next, You are the one best equipped to give that self, by inward talking, whatever it needs: love, approval, support, encouragement, validation.

As you move more fully into adult consciousness, in which self-definition and self-governance are the main characteristics, it will matter less and less whether other people validate you, because You can give Your self what You know it needs *in the moment.* You thus become the monitor of Your self, the necessary qualification for adulthood. How to do this is explained fully in the second part of this chapter, pp. 102–107.

The emotional and mental transformations that occur during this period are no less dramatic and life-changing than the physical, and all three metamorphoses are necessary to entering adulthood and continuing to grow in it and beyond, to the spiritual dimension. Awareness of self is the necessary gate to the development of spirituality, as the various Eastern metaphysical paths show us. (For further discussion of this see Ch. VII).

You can tell when Your self-esteem is adequate if You can stand up for Your self and maintain Your beliefs or position in the face of disagreement, criticism, antagonism, or mistreatment; if You can refrain from doing or saying something in order to get approval from others, and can instead validate Your self; if you can resist the urge to step into other people's lives and direct, correct, or try to fix them; if You can conduct Your self in a way that elicits respect; if You can manage (most of the time) not to get defensive or feel guilty if someone blames you; and if You can be honest with Your self and others.

All of these goals are actually not *met* so much as *worked on*—constantly—and it's all too easy for a fledgling adult to revert to an issue in his belonging or self-esteem stage. Just because one becomes adequately autonomous (next chapter) doesn't allow us to disregard the earlier needs. If they get shaken, the whole tree trembles. Following are two examples, one that demonstrates high self-esteem and one that demonstrates low self-esteem.

The first example came to me from a delightful teenager who had been seeing me for guidance in strengthening this need. It happened that right before Mother's Day she and her mother had an argument. Not having been able to resolve it before the special day arrived, she wrote the following message on her card: "Dear Mom, when I'm mad at you it doesn't mean I hate you. It just means I'm mad." Her mother was, as you might expect, delighted, and with pleasure saw in her daughter's comment a sense of her developing self-awareness and self-validation.

The second example, equally telling, involves a young man, eighteen years old, from an inner city Afro-American family, who had achieved brilliant success in his academic work. His high school record in every area was outstanding; but in physics and math it was off the charts, and his SAT scores were in the top one percent. When he opened the letter from MIT, and found he'd been given a full four-year scholarship including books and room and board, he said (after he stopped crying:) "If I'm so damn smart, how come I feel like _____?"

When we don't develop a sufficient sense of self-esteem, our growth stalls at this stage even though we reach adulthood in years. We are then in for a rocky ride, one which will lead us into adulthood only in name. We remain emotionally immature, still seeking other people to support us and meet our preceding three needs. The result will be chronic feelings of inferiority, inadequacy, guilt, incompetence, embarrassment, self-doubt, self-disapproval, and self-rejection (see the Chart© at the beginning of this chapter) no matter what age we are chronologically.

The origin of these painful feelings is most likely to be a support system that is either too demanding and critical, or too permissive and lax, in providing healthy boundaries and standards. In their zeal to *make* you succeed (generally a mark of their own sense of inferiority), your parents may become overly ambitious and establish goals that are beyond your abilities at this point. Having been conditioned to think you are inferior, and already feeling inadequate from so many expectations, you strive for perfection and when you don't achieve it (who does?) you blame Your self and vow to try harder. Then when what you have done is critiqued—it's not good enough, or it could have been more thorough, or more quickly done—your self-esteem is further damaged.

The self-image thus created is unbearable, and must be camouflaged by defenses proving to other people that one is OK, competent, valuable, intelligent, capable, *etc.*, which in fact you are—you just have difficulty believing it. Hence the defenses listed in the Chart©, many of which advertise the self to be better than other people, or other people to be worse than the self. Since the feelings are chronic, the defenses are also. Consequently, the patterns of obsessive thinking and compulsive behavior gradually accumulate, covering up the underlying causative feelings and taking over the original self, like ivy making its slow, destructive way up a sycamore tree. When you are in such a state, your conscious mind cannot access and release them, and consequently the need cannot be met, so the painful feelings keep being generated, and the defenses likewise. *The defenses are the disease.*

The defenses generated by low self-esteem are variations of the fight variety, that is, defenses that are based on outer-directed energy, and as such are forms of aggression. Although you do them (unconsciously, of course) to hide your sense of inadequacy, they are felt by other people as invasive, controlling, competitive, condescending, derogatory, taking charge, taking-care-of (when it is not wanted or needed); taking a valium (aggression against one's mind/body system) "because I get so stressed out;" telling stories about

The Self-Esteem Need

the achievements or virtues of yourself or your children or about the socially eminent people you had dinner with last night, at which you had "a few too many" drinks to "handle the stress"—after all, alcohol is legal and socially acceptable!

All of these defenses are typical of the person whose self-esteem is low to nonexistent, and who is almost entirely defined by others rather than self: martyr, workaholic, overachiever, caretaker, enabler, maybe alcoholic. Lest this array of defenses overwhelm you, remember, *You* are not *Your type*. *You* are *Consciousness*: that which can at this level begin to observe Your self, made up of thoughts, feelings, and behavior, and govern and change it, unlike the child level, which rarely exhibits self awareness and self examination (at least not consciously). (This concept is examined more fully in Chapter VII.)

The problem lies in the solution: you are trying to use outer sources to meet an inner need. Since outer sources are themselves subject to circumstance and change, and are therefore ultimately undependable, the need is never met, thus perpetuating the cycle. The following diagram at right shows how this happens.

Follow the arrows and the numbering and you can see how each component generates the next: (l) the *unmet need*, self-esteem, sets off painful (2) *feelings* of inadequacy, worthlessness, *etc.*, which cause (3) *mental and behavioral defenses* such as criticizing, envy, complaining, correcting, *etc*. Although these defenses repress the pain, giving you some temporary relief, they leave it to the feelings to determine (4) *behaviors* that are also *defensive*: *when You are not aware of Your feelings You can't choose your behavior*. Instead, your *feelings* will choose your behavior—and not always for the better. The resulting compulsive ("not chosen") behavior is unlikely to be in line with your values, damaging your self-esteem further, resulting in more painful feelings and causing consequences in the world that always come back on you, generating another round of the cycle.

Unmet Need for Security	Mental & Behavioral Defenses	Type of Personality
Unmet needs cause…	Painful feelings lead to…	Defenses lead to…
PAINFUL FEELINGS: inadequacy inferiority worthlessness lack of motivation	MENTAL DEFENSES: gossips corrects gives directions always has the right answer plans brags worries BEHAVIORAL DEFENSES: overworks excels plans overachieves dictates fixes tells other people what to do and how to do it always has the answer	THE **"PERFECT CHILD"** TYPE

How did you get to be this way? Well, you are likely to be either the oldest child or the only or the first child of your sex, any of which makes you the first in line to be a parent lieutenant or surrogate. You grew up in a non-supportive and over-demanding environment, in which you were expected to do everything that a parent would do but did not have time—or energy or knowledge—to do. Your training as a parent substitute was entirely on-the-job: instructions were either non-existent or delivered in such a general way that they were impossible to follow without error (maybe they were a set-up? You sometimes wondered).

In fulfilling your appointed role, you were expected to be unfailingly and perfectly responsible, effective, and efficient. You learned all this, not by patient, loving training, but by being scolded, yelled at, criticized, or ridiculed—or beaten—anytime you fell the tiniest bit short of the mark.

Once in a while you suspected it was *because* you did so well that you got so thoroughly shamed. It sometimes happens that parents who themselves have low self-esteem feel unconsciously threatened by their child's abilities and achievements, and by such criticism or physical abuse unconsciously compete with or even try to defeat them. Your training as a parent substitute was entirely on-the-job; instructions were either non-existent, or delivered in such a general way that they were impossible to follow without error, which made you feel slightly paranoid: "Maybe they're trying to trap me?" The result is commands like the following:

"Take care of baby while I'm out."

"Get the house in order."

"Make dinner."

Not exactly a blueprint! Especially to an eight or ten or even a twelve year old. Nevertheless, you learned to do it, and to do it to near perfection, from fear of the inevitable criticism. You drew the conclusion that *not getting it perfect* or *making a mistake meant that you were unacceptable and worthless—a failure*—and you *still* believe that. This idea impedes growth, since making mistakes is one way we learn: a mistake is just a *growth opportunity we don't like*, and one that we can therefore change and learn from.

If, however, you *did* do it well, you didn't get appreciation or praise, just the absence of criticism. From this conditioning, you developed a permanent "knot in the pit of your stomach"—a built-in sense of dread that at any moment in any situation you'll get it wrong and make a fool of yourself, when actually you perform very well.

Your perception of Your self is skewed and inaccurate: anything you do that is less than perfect in your eyes is worthless, because Your unconscious remembers and expects the criticism, scolding, and physical abuse which followed not only a less than perfect job but even a job well done. You learned and now perpetuate the system your elders taught you, and you are your own toughest critic: if *you* don't think it's OK, no amount of praise from another will convince you, though you resent it bitterly if you don't get at least a little acknowledgment (praise is not even worth mentioning).

Moreover, you've *generalized*: even other people's imperfection scares you, since the unconscious doesn't recognize boundaries: if it's happening to somebody else, it's happening to you. As a result you, once the victim, now become the perpetrator, and inflict this system on others. You're a dreaded parent or boss or teacher, spotting the one spelling error in an otherwise exemplary book report, the one undusted windowsill in the house, the one call not made in a negotiation that accomplished a brilliant deal, the one fumble in the midst of four brilliant touchdowns, *etc., etc.*

Such a method of operating makes your children, your mate, and your workers feel demotivated and defeated, instead of approving and grateful. Nor do you, who as a child got little or no praise or approval and today give your self none, have any instinct for giving it to others. On the

The Self-Esteem Need

contrary, you begrudge it, since *perfect* is merely how it should be, not a cause for celebration by you or respect from others.

Your children, your mate, and your workers or co-workers are, naturally, intimidated and angered by this attitude, and not surprisingly they in turn reject and disapprove of you, generally in a covert but nonetheless painful way. You end up wondering why you, who do so much for others, are so unpopular, and you become resentful, an echo of the sense of injustice you felt growing up. Thus do the defensive patterns, designed to protect you, in the long run harm you, by keeping the need unmet and the dependent cycle alive.

Being the first child, whom "The Perfect Child" often is, contributes further to the compulsive need to excel and take care of others. I call it the *lost lap syndrome*. It works like this: the first child has sole occupancy of mother's lap until the next child arrives, whereupon she is displaced and scolded if she objects. If she is still a toddler she has no logical way of understanding why she has been bumped and some outsider has taken her territory. Moreover, her dethroning is repeated again and again, as many times as she has siblings, pushing her further away from her "rightful" original place, relegating her to the outermost position and losing more of her mother's attention and nurturance each time.

Successive children experience the same displacement at lesser degrees of rejection, since they see it happening to their siblings as well. But each time it happens is another trauma to the first child, because each new child, literally and figuratively, displaces the first child further away from the center, the lap on which one sits to be held, comforted, reassured, accepted, loved—*the place of valuation.*

The damage is in proportion to the amount of time between the first child and the next: under two years is the most severe. Moreover, the further removed she is from the lap, the closer she is to responsibility—that is, she is positioned to be designated "mother's little helper," and at first is flattered, since it is a unique title, and carries with it an assumed degree of attention and approval. But it ultimately turns out to be a scam, since the approbation isn't for her own selfhood—it's for what she does for Mommy. She thus loses Her self, like the Clown Type and the Forgotten Child, and becomes a role.

Here is Wendy, ten years old, with four siblings, eight and a half, six, four, and one and a half, who every week:

Makes the shopping list

Babysits (way too young)

Does her homework; getting straight A's is a given

Vacuums and dusts

Plans activities for "the kids" (she never refers to them as "the *other* kids")

Does the laundry

Where is the child in this?

At his inmost core, the person who suffers from low self-esteem craves praise and approval. If you are a boss, spouse, or parent, you will seek it (probably indirectly) from your workers, mate, or children, muddying boundaries and subverting the proper structure of the relationship. If, on the other hand, you are a worker, mate, or child, you will climb the highest mountain to get even a smidgen of praise from your superiors, but ironically, you will reject or discount it.

This need for approval from one's superiors or subordinates can play havoc with your priorities, as exemplified by the following dialogue. The speakers are a wife and her husband, an energetic stockbroker whose low self-esteem made him over-eager to impress the big-wigs at his strategy meeting:

The Self-Esteem Need

Wife: (calling husband on his car phone): Jack! Listen! Jimmy broke his leg—the ambulance is here—meet us at the hospital—the emergency room!

Husband: He'll be all right, honey! He's got you there...no need for us both to go. I'm on my way to the meeting—you know how important it is! I know you've got everything under control—say "hi" to Jimmy for me.

If your efforts meet with no praise or approval, you feel naturally hurt and resentful, but work all the harder and longer since the fear of disapproval has long since been engraved in your feeling brain and is therefore "always at your back, hurrying near."[1] Hence the overwhelming drive to prove yourself not a failure. If a situation includes people clearly more competent or accomplished than you, you may, instead of striving harder, resort to pointing out the other person's faults, inadequacy, venality, or whatever, to make yourself feel superior.

As a result of this conditioning, there is in you now, as an adult, a terrible inner tension caused by a chronic, impending fear of failure, and a chronic, urgent drive to be perfect, both of which are clearly unrealistic. The pressure thus created can have drastic consequences for body as well as mind, such as the "type A" problems—heart trouble, strokes, ulcers,[2] high blood pressure—and probably many more not yet recognized as consequences of the psychological stress of chronic low self esteem.

It is often these physical problems that bring such a person into treatment, because his high level of functioning blinds him to his psychological dysfunction. But it will not blind a physician familiar with the significance of these somatic signals of psychological issues.

For example, one such astute practitioner, a cardiologist, delivered the following diagnosis to a client of mine who had been suffering occasional chest pains for several months and had consulted several other doctors to no avail: "There is nothing organic wrong with your heart. It has become the *target organ* for your stress. I suggest you work on stress in your psychotherapy."[3] Naturally, being a perfectionist, you don't think you need therapy, because you are not conscious of your low self-esteem. But when convinced, you become an excellent client, your characteristic compulsivity making you strive to excel in recovery as in any other area. Recovery from perfectionism must be done to perfection!

It is important to acknowledge that some of the behavioral defenses of low self-esteem have positive results. For example, there's nothing wrong with a clean house, an excellent performance at work, a well-played game, a well-cooked meal, *etc*. But even these accomplishments, while gratifying to the doer, still have some negative effects.

First, such accomplishments are essentially *defenses*: they block feelings just as much as toxic defenses. Second, they are *compulsive*: they are done automatically, without consideration of their appropriateness, the doer's energy level, or the recipient's wishes. Meritorious though they may be, they keep the person with low self-esteem dependent on something outside himself to get his need met. As with the preceding two needs, the goal is to remove the compulsion and replace it with conscious choice. Remember, the Process© is an *inside job*: only You know what Your self needs.

In this respect, the person with low self-esteem has it backwards: he is convinced that if he can just get it perfect *this time*, he'll finally get sufficient approval from others to feel OK, or even good, about himself. This is the addictive pattern of doing the same thing again and again expecting a different result: no matter how many times he does well and gets approval, he is driven to do it *still better*. He doesn't understand that low self-esteem is part of his limbic makeup, an inner component that dictates his behavior, and is inaccessible to correction or fulfillment by outer means *now that he is nearing adulthood.*

The Self-Esteem Need

The reverse is the truth: it is from learning to validate and appreciate yourself (as described below) that you will find satisfaction in your work, product, activity, *etc.* Even if you still perceive it not to be perfect (which of course it can't be) you will be observing it from the attitude of self-esteem rather than self-loathing, a distinctly desirable result. Through the Healing Process© you will develop the ability to choose the level of excellence to achieve in any given endeavor: you will not "hafta" do everything you do perfectly.[4] Satisfied with your own approval, you will not "hafta" gain the acclaim of others. You will have broken the compulsive defensive cycle and be transformed. How to accomplish that is discussed next.

The Freedom Healing Process© for this need consists of the same procedure as that for the security and belonging needs. By now, if you have been working your way through the need levels, you will know what to do to release the painful feelings when this need isn't met and how to meet it from within. Move right on to the following sections, which present a condensed version of the Process©. If this is your point of entry to the Freedom Healing Process©, study the behavioral and mental defenses on the Chart© facing the first page of this chapter to see if they correspond to your thinking and behavior. If they do, then this is your main unmet need. Follow the Process© outlined below.

The Freedom Healing Process

I. Accessing Feelings: Pounding

Start by pounding out anger and frustration, always doing two rounds with a rest in between. Follow this with five to ten minutes of deep breathing, tracking your breathing as it flows in and out, establishing a good rhythm. Guide your thinking, and when it wanders—which it will—direct it back to the breathing. The kind of breathing here described helps focus and direct your thinking, so that with sufficient practice, it will obey your directions instead of you obeying it.

As you gradually gain control of your thinking, you will be amazed at how smooth and efficient Your life is becoming, compared to how bumpy and frustrating it used to be. The reason this apparently simple Process© produces such remarkable results is that using it activates two of the most important elements of our being—thinking and breathing—and correctly puts *the breathing in charge of the thinking*. Most of us do it unconsciously and in reverse, that is, we think randomly and ignore our breathing. However, while the breathing process is subtle, and requires time and concentration, it is well worth working for, as you by now have probably experienced from the preceding chapters. The results will make your life beautiful and happy.

II. Experiencing and Releasing Feelings: Breathing

Once you have established a good rhythm in your breathing and have become relaxed, focus on the residual feelings that have accumulated from years of being unappreciated, seen as incompetent, beaten for eating your food in the wrong order, told you were stupid, made to take care of everybody but Your self *etc., etc.* The resulting painful feelings create toxins that get stored in your body. As you continue the deep breathing, let yourself experience the inbreath pulling up these toxins, and picture your outbreath blowing them, and your painful feelings with them, as far away as you can imagine, to the outermost reaches of the universe.

Be as *"perfect"* in your breathing as you are in other areas of your life, extending each breath as long as you can. It is especially important to blow out fully, so that the breath is completely used up, and the toxins therefore completely released. Reassure Your self that the present pain is dissolving, and know that soon you will be rid of some old baggage. Releasing the old traumas and the toxic chemicals they produce empties your mind of its defenses, preparing it to receive the message you are going to give it in the second part of the Process©. When the painful feelings have significantly diminished, let your breathing return to normal and be regulated by your body, but still direct it into and release it from the abdomen.

III. Meeting the Need: Infilling and Self-nurturing

The third part of the Healing Process© is *fulfilling the need*. Focus on your breathing, now quiet and shallow (because you are so filled with oxygen from the preceding exercise), and as you inhale say silently to your feelings "peace." Then choose one of the Declarations below which meets your need. Repeat it to Your self (in rhythm with your breathing) until Your self feels valued. You have taken charge of Your self and given it what it needs to develop gradually a real sense of self-esteem.

"You are valuable and valued, just as you are."

"I appreciate you as you are; you don't have to get it right all the time."

"There is nothing wrong with you."

"You do not have to be perfect to be approved and appreciated."

"I approve of you no matter how you look, or how you perform."

"You cannot be without My approval."

"Wherever you are, I AM, and where I AM, there are praise, approval, appreciation."

Take several minutes, maybe eight to ten, to repeat whichever of these Declarations is the most helpful and appropriate for your needs, so that it has time to encode the message in your feeling brain. With enough repetition it will be established as true. Remember to address Your self with the word "you" as though it—the self—is another person. (See Chapter VII for in-depth explanation)

By undertaking this Process© you are starting to reverse the untruths about Your self incorporated in you all your life so far, by parents, siblings, schoolmates, teachers, *etc.* Be gentle with Your mind if it wanders and occasionally loses the Process©, though by now that will be much less likely. Just direct it to focus on experiencing the expanding and contracting of your torso. If you do that slowly and gently, it creates a comforting motion, like the gentle rocking of a cradle or boat.

These Declarations, as you may have noticed in the preceding two chapters, are indicators of a new, affirmative, and kindly way to look at and relate to Your self. You could see it as a kind of "emotional makeover" (rather than "emotional *hangover*"): a new you is emerging—actually, someone you always knew was there but couldn't quite allow to appear, lest it be ridiculed by less enlightened family members or friends.

You now, with clearer vision and help from the Process©, can begin to allow the *real* you—as opposed to the *pattern* of you that was incorporated into you in your formative years—to present Your self *as it is* (not perfect, because by now you recognize that *perfect* doesn't exist on this plane) but as a conscientous, helpful, and supportive person, making you feel comforted and good about Your self.

You will soon notice a gradually intensifying feeling of peace, approval, worth, and love for Your self happening

The Self-Esteem Need

within you, *independent of any external source*. This is an amazing and empowering feeling: to be able to create within Your self whatever mood and self image you want, whenever you want, without any external help, feels like a miracle!

For best results, the entire Process© should be done regularly at least twice a day for a minimum of ten minutes, increasing to twenty and eventually to thirty minutes per session, split equally between releasing and infilling. The three parts of the Process© should always be done together. If you release without infilling, you make Your self a vacuum for the world to rush into; if you try to infill without first releasing, you'll find your mind so full of jumble that your efforts are fruitless, and you will further repress your feelings.

In addition to your regular breathing sessions, the Freedom Healing Process© can also be done when you notice that your mental chatter has gotten louder and more insistent, or when you have just acted in a way that you don't like, both of which are defenses. To return Your self to full functioning, *the underlying need must be met*, and the earlier the better. Since by now you have practiced the Process© a great deal and experienced its benefits, your resistance will have greatly diminished. Therefore, you will undertake it effortlessly and eagerly, knowing from experience how it transforms Your self from a state of chaos, confusion, and misery to one of harmony, well-being, and joy. And you will be able to pull Your self out of a fit of compulsive caretaking or cleaning or overworking by recognizing your compulsivity and doing a process to release it.

The downward cycle of low self-esteem has been reversed by the upward cycle of healing. Evolving into a person who instead of scolding and rejecting Your self validates and loves it unconditionally, you will no longer have to prove your worth or display your abilities to establish it. If you have studiously practiced the three processes discussed in the preceding three chapters, by now you will be feeling secure, loved, and *valued by Your self* most of the time, and you will be able to restore those needs when a lapse occurs. You are ready to engage the next need.

The Riddle Rewritten

Your parents are due in an hour for Thanksgiving dinner. You got the turkey, *etc.* together, your husband did the vacuuming, and the kids set the table—reversing the knives and forks (Oh, God, are they dyslexic?) and putting the napkins on the right of the plates instead of the left (they must be!)—but you were nonetheless grateful to them for helping, and left the table as it was. But then you suddenly realized—NO FLOWERS! and WATER SPOTS ON THE GOBLETS! You stood still and breathed deeply 5 times. "It's OK," you said to yourself, "Peace, you did a good job." After repeating this for several minutes, your mind was emptied of its usual chatter and able to hear clearly the words of You-as-knower: "You need a little rest more than the table needs flowers. And I bet you nobody even notices the goblets! If Mom does say something, so what?" Then off to your bedroom you went and lay down for 20 minutes, breathing deeply the whole time. By the time your folks arrived you were rested, relaxed, and in a receptive frame of mind—and all Mom said was, "What a pretty table!" Your reward was seeing how much that delighted your kids.

What brought about the change?

Unmet Needs cause…	Painful Feelings cause…	Mental & Behavioral Defenses constitue:	Type of Personality	Feelings When Needs Met
AUTONOMY (SELF-DEFINING) (SELF-GOVERNING)	ashamed guilty self-doubting helpless powerless trapped hurt enraged outraged vulnerable needy incompetent victimized defiant resentful bitter sense of injustice feeling like a screw-up	blaming arrogance lying rationalizing projecting dependency narcissism grandiosity rebelling analyzing crossing boundaries making trouble anti-social acting out defensiveness self-righteousness passive aggression maverick dissenter scapegoat misfit	THE "TROUBLE CHILD" TYPE	self-defining self-governing self-vigilant self-directing responsible independent sensitive to others perceptive truthful acknowledged understood peaceable accepting/ accepted mannerly self-content part of

VI

The Autonomy Need

Riddle #4

You're having a cup of coffee at the AA Clubhouse, waiting for your sponsor, Lou. Returning from the snack bar you see a new guy, large and aggressive looking, sitting in your chair talking to your sponsor! As anger sends adrenaline throughout your body, it begins to vibrate with agitation and your legs feel weak and wobbly.

"GET OFF MY SEAT!" you holler at the intruder; then—too late! you notice he's about twenty years older than you and significantly bigger.

"Yo, kid!" he says back, "Didn't your mama teach you any manners? Guess it's up to me: step outside, son!"

Not everybody would react by decking the guy but you do.

What's driving your behavior?

The Autonomy Need

The *Autonomy Need* constitutes the fourth level of the hierarchy of needs, and correlates, in the stages of growth, to adulthood. To fulfill it, we must develop the ability to define and govern ourselves, thus becoming autonomous, which literally means "naming (defining) myself" and, by extension, "governing myself." As with the self-esteem need, only even more so, this need by its very nature can be met only from within. Depending on outside sources contradicts the meaning of the need: if *I* ask *you* to reassure *me* that *I am* self-defining and self-governing, I'm being *not* self-defining and self-governing—I'm being *dependent*, exactly the opposite of autonomous! No more crying, "It's *your* fault!" "The Devil made me do it!" "I don't know what happened—I just lost it—and down he went!"

We can therefore say that the entry fee for joining the adulthood club is self-vigilance and self- direction. To qualify, we must be able (at least a majority of the time) to govern what we think, feel, say, and do, unlike the hothead in the riddle above. Ducking responsibility for one's actions or shifting them to somebody else, while it may bring relief in the moment, will damage, even destroy your sense of self, not to mention what it does to the relationship with the other person.

In contrast, owning our faults, taking steps to repair them, and being able to maintain self- definition in the face of criticism, are necessary stepping-stones to this goal. Therefore, if the parents do their job of fulfilling the early needs, the child will have the "right stuff" to achieve autonomy and move on to lay the foundation for advancing to the three spiritual needs: *Self-Actualization*, *Self-Realization*, and *Unification*.

If you study the Chart© on the page facing Chapter VI you can get a good idea of how it feels when you are adult but are *not* self-defining and self-governing. Column 2 shows the painful emotions that result. First are shame and humiliation, the dominant duo of the autonomy need, and among the most painful of all feelings. Second are hurt, anger, and resentment, stemming from the denial of your autonomy by other people and a permanent sense of injustice due to being blamed for everything that goes wrong. An environment that perpetuates such abuse stirs up your defiance and makes you feel like an outcast, socially incompetent and trouble-prone—a maverick and a scapegoat. If you are currently struggling with such feelings this chapter is for you.

The development of autonomy in a healthy family normally begins in the middle to late teen-age years. However, when there is a deficiency in that development, it's not, as in the need for belonging, simply a matter of neglect by others, but rather of being *defined* by others, most likely your family. Unless you are the normal "good kid," and exhibit behavior they and your neighbors and your classmates are comfortable with, all three of these groups will be quick to define you, in a variety of ways: accusing you of breaking their basement window; calling the cops to break up the "party" you threw when your folks were away; reporting you to the school when you decided to play hooky for a few days, *etc.*

Your definition precedes you, and it can range from the merely derogatory—"he's a nut,"—to the alarming—"*he's the devil!*" As the scapegoating accumulates, it interferes with your emotional development and actually *diminishes* your autonomy, so that you live in constant emotional pain, while putting a good face on it and pretending everything is okay.

The pain shapes your sense of self: if you are being constantly defined by others, mainly your family, how can *you* know who you are or that you are not what they say? And if You can't define Your self, how can you respect and govern it? As a frantic 17-year-old screamed at his mother in a session: "DON'T TELL ME I'M IRRESPONSIBLE! IF YOU SAY I'M IRRESPONSIBLE, THEN I'M IRRESPONSIBLE!"

During this period of growth, the process of finding and defining his identity can feel to the fledgling adult and

The Autonomy Need

those nearest him like trying to tell a tornado which way to go. Often, whether out of frustration or anger, he resorts simply to running headlong right into it, naturally arousing strong comment, advice, and criticism in concerned others—parents, grandparents, siblings, neighbors, teachers, *etc.* "What to do with him" becomes the constant theme of the adults in his life, damaging his self-esteem and adding to his difficulties in learning to govern himself.

For an adolescent struggling to find his name and place in the world and transition into adulthood, the criticism of other people, especially those he reveres (probably not very many!) can be devastating. Just because it is his mission to achieve doesn't mean that he has no interest in how the world responds to his process—indeed, how it responds has a strong effect on him, both positive and negative, until he is firmly established in autonomy.

What, then, are some of the consequences of being defined by other people as wrong or at fault or to blame? If the message from the adult world is predominantly negative and critical, constantly hearing it eventually makes you unable to see Your self apart from that identity. Your thoughts, actions, and self-image are determined by it, rather than by you, and operate only according to that propaganda.

You come to believe what the family says you are, consequently losing touch with your real self, and driven by your unmet needs you develop defenses to block the pain. This is the same pattern we have seen in the three previous needs: (1) the *unmet need* (autonomy) creates (2) *painful feelings* (shame, hurt, resentment) which generate and are repressed by (3) *mental* and (4) *behavioral defenses*—such as blaming, rationalizing, being passive aggressive, not showing up for holidays, all of which in turn create more discord with other people and more painful feelings. The diagram at right shows the cyclic pattern.

As you can see, each component, rooted in pathology, generates the next—an endless cycle of confusion and suffering.

Unmet Need for Security	Mental & Behavioral Defenses	Type of Personality
Unmet needs cause…	Painful feelings lead to…	Defenses lead to…
PAINFUL FEELINGS: hurt rejected ashamed helpless dependent trapped guilty delusional	MENTAL DEFENSES: worry self-righteous analyzes blames projects rationalizes excuses BEHAVIORAL DEFENSES: hiding rebelling making trouble fighting anti-social behavior acting out stealing lying drug-use	THE **"TROUBLE CHILD"** TYPE

How, you might wonder, does the family decide whom to scapegoat? The answer lies, ironically, in one of his most valuable traits, one that makes his selection inevitable. He is *perceptive:* he has, innately, the ability to see the truth (he certainly didn't get it from his crazy family) and not be fooled by their denial of the family's dysfunction. From the family's perspective this makes him highly dangerous:

Billy: Hey Mom! Dad's drunk again and he just yelled at me and punched me in the stomach! (actual fact)

Mother: You have an *evil mind* to talk like that about your father! (defining, accusing). He's just stressed from work. (excusing) He didn't really hurt you—(denial)—you're just trying to get attention! (put-down)

Billy: Mom says she has a headache, but she's lying again: she's *drunk*! I can smell it six feet away and she's slurring her words! (actual fact)

Sister: Mom *is not* drunk! (denial) How can you say that about your own mother? (shaming) You're crazy *and* ignorant! (defining)

Billy: Hey Dad! Joe's father's got manic depression and Bobby sounds just like him! (actual fact)

Dad: How *dare* you even *think* your brother's manic-depressive! (shaming) How would a dumb-ass like you know anyhow? (defining, insulting)

It is the family members, not Billy, who are deluded: they all, except the scapegoat, have developed a system of denial and defenses to excuse and cover up the family dysfunction. This makes the scapegoat feel even crazier, since nobody but him sees the dysfunction for what it is.

The family defines the truth he speaks as insanity, in order to keep their system intact, when in fact he is earnestly and accurately reporting the truth.

His frustration about their denial makes him sound crazy: "But *Mom, listen!* Dad got drunk and *beat the guy up!* I saw it with my own eyes!" Mom replies: "Nonsense! *You* got drunk and *made it up!*" Blaming the messenger is one indication of a dysfunctional system, whether family, corporation, institution, or country, and a sure sign of defensiveness on the part of the organization.

So we see that the scapegoat has the great gift of insight, the ability to see the true state of things. It is a talent guaranteed to make him unpopular. His trust in this perception, and his willingness to announce it ("But Mommy, the Emperor *doesn't* have any clothes on") interferes with the family no talk rule, and thus threatens to expose the dysfunction of the system. Enough repetitions of this, and the messenger will, as we have seen above, become identified with the message: instead of being seen as the *identifier* of trouble, he is seen *as* trouble:

"Did you get into trouble *again*, boy?"

"What's the trouble *now*??"

"How come you're such a troublemaker?"

"Trouble sure does follow you!"

"You're just trouble!"

"Can't you leave trouble alone?"

It's only a step from this to a nickname:

"Hey, everybody, Trouble's at the door!"

"Mom, Trouble's on the phone—he wants to talk to you."

"Trouble just fell down the porch steps, Mom."

One is reminded of the ancient Trojan priestess Cassandra, who was given the gift of foresight on condition that no one would believe her. She foretold a number of catastrophes, most notably the fall of her city to the Greeks, which brought an end to the Trojan War and the Trojan civilization. Instead of heeding her warning, the Trojans, including members of her own royal family, ridiculed her as crazy, then blamed and ostracized her when her prediction proved accurate. People from Homer's time to the present don't want to hear the truth!

A more recent example is a young man who at nineteen was a full-fledged drug addict. James was the second child of an emotionally withdrawn father, a loner, and a controlling mother whose competence camouflaged her low self-esteem. His older brother was a carbon copy of Mom, while James, nicknamed "Trouble,"[1] closely resembled Dad. His characterization of the family dynamics showed his perceptiveness:

"Mom runs the show, Dad—when he's home—stays in his room pretending to take a nap...(sneering) Mr. Perfect (older brother) does whatever Mom says—it's like he's got a Mom IV tube...Dad and I hate him because he gets all of Mom's attention...Dad thinks Mom doesn't love him, and he's right...he never said this to me, but I can tell."

The family members were all in denial of their own needs deficits and were united in seeing "Trouble" as the problem, blaming him for anything that went wrong. After almost a year of recovery from drug and alcohol addiction, he had a relapse, and in the subsequent family session his father, pointing his finger at James, yelled, "We got five happy people in this family, and *you* got to go and screw it up!" Who's delusional here?

Denial is thus the vehicle for their scapegoating. By defining James as the troublemaker in the family, they can blame him for everything that's wrong. This unconscious strategy distracts them from noticing and having to deal with their own real problems, making them feel *they're OK—*

it's *James* who is "the problem." They thus defensively invert the truth and unconsciously reveal their own dysfunction, when in fact it is the dysfunctional system that causes James to be the way he is—and of course them too. Living that way they will never recover.

But scapegoating James doesn't remove their painful feelings; it buries them along with their unmet needs. Until they can allow those needs to surface and learn how to meet them, their dysfunctional system will continue, and so, therefore, will their pain. It's a never-ending loop, filled with suffering for all at every turn, because the truth, the only thing that can relieve their pain, never comes to light. This scenario leaves James little choice but to get away from them, either geographically or narcotically or both. Being scapegoated, that is, defined by others as the cause of the systemic problem, is the opposite of being autonomous, and is inevitable in a dysfunctional system.

Birth order also plays a part in the selection of the scapegoat, as it does in the other needs. More often than not he is, like James, the second child. Coming into the family with unimpaired vision, the scapegoat is perfectly positioned to see the already established dynamics of the parents and first child, who by now is displaying some characteristics of low self-esteem.

The Trouble Child learns early in life the futility of trying to get attention by doing well—his older brother has that angle all sewn up. Competing with him is likely to backfire painfully. But it doesn't take him much research to discover that getting into a scrape—spilling the milk, tying Susie's braids together, breaking a leg (his own or somebody else's), *etc., etc.,* beats straight A's for getting attention. "*So what*" (a favorite phrase of his) if it's negative—if you can't get a warm fuzzy, a cold prickly will do. In other words, acting out becomes a primary defense.

Unfortunately—or, come to think of it, maybe fortunately —*acting out* carries a price: it confirms and fulfills their

The Autonomy Need

definition of him. So he never gets understood, just blamed, and the resulting hurt, humiliation, shame, and rejection keep his pattern alive. His ability to see what's really going on when they can not intensifies his pain and his sense of being an outcast. To his clear eyes, their inability to *get it* is not credible, and he concludes, logically enough, that they are lying, which makes him feel slightly paranoid—"Why do they all want to lie to me?" he says, not unreasonably. When sufficiently provoked, he will accuse them angrily of just that: "You're lying, all of you! How can you stand there and tell me I'm the problem when Dad just got drunk *again* and beat you up *again?*"

The scapegoat thus faces a troubling dilemma: the family will accept him only if he agrees with their perception. They can't tolerate even the slightest bit of the actual reality of their situation. He must choose between his need for belonging and his need for autonomy.

In a dysfunctional system you cannot have both. If you want to achieve autonomy and maintain your identity, you have to forfeit belonging and acceptance by the family; conversely, if you choose belonging, you forfeit identity and your right to define yourself. In other words, *conform or get out*. It's a painful choice either way: to deny your own perceptions and abandon your real self is painful and damaging and likely to result in a lifetime of withdrawal and introversion.

On the other hand, asserting your personhood and standing firm on self-definition and self-governance, while courageous, often leaves you alone in the family doghouse, *outside*. James Baldwin's summation of the racial dilemma for the Afro-American, whom our national dysfunctional family has designated the scapegoat, who is blamed for problems not remotely of his making, and upon whom is projected the guilt of both those in power and those non-Blacks who have *no* power, expresses the scapegoat's situation perfectly: "This country will accept Blacks only to the extent to which they become white."[2]

Even when the scapegoat opts for belonging, he is often either unable to conform enough, or is so thoroughly defined as the different and difficult one that acceptance still is not granted. *Any family or culture which makes surrender of identity the price of belonging is a toxic system.* Sad to say but true, the belonging need wins more often than the autonomy need because of its priority in the hierarchy of needs. If you don't feel accepted, you can't develop a sufficient sense of self-esteem, and without self-esteem, you can't become truly self-defining and self-governing.

Moreover, for most people, it is less painful to surrender one's autonomy than to be an outcast (the only other alternative) since that can mean death. This is especially true if the scapegoat is female, due to both biological and sociological imperatives that have made women value—or at any rate, *choose*—belonging more often than autonomy. And because of those imperatives, women are much less likely to let themselves become the scapegoat, outcast, or iconoclast.

In contrast, a male scapegoat is more likely than a woman to give up belonging in favor of autonomy, placing greater value on self-definition and self-governance, no doubt also for biological and sociological reasons. But autonomy built on an insufficient sense of belonging and self-esteem is autonomy built on sand—shaky and unreliable, washed away by the slightest storm—bravado rather than true self-definition. A family or a society that sets these two needs at odds has violated its primary function to provide to all its members the unconditional acceptance and nurturance from which each one can develop her/his own true identity and still be accepted.

Not surprisingly, the defenses of the scapegoat are like those of the security need: psychological variations of the fight-flight defenses (see the Chart© p.). For example, aggressive behavior—blaming, arguing, fighting, stealing and other forms of antisocial acting out give a clear signal of the *explosive* feelings—such as resentment, outrage, and injustice—built into the scapegoat by the family's or society's treatment of him. Such defenses also block his consciousness from experiencing and expressing those feelings, generally apparent to others, especially his family members.

Likewise, passive and antisocial behavior such as lying, denial, alibiing, and over-depending are symptoms of *implosive* feelings such as hurt, rejection, shame, and humiliation. If carried to the extreme, these defenses can lead the scapegoat outside regular society into prison, a parallel world, *e.g.* camping out in the Florida Keys, going into the Armed Services, joining a religious cult, or becoming part of a counter-culture organization, such as the Nation of Islam, the Aryan Nation, a local militia group, a street gang, or the underworld.[3]

So the scapegoat becomes a maverick, a domestic and sometimes a social outlaw, in turn blaming and shaming the system that blamed and shamed him. The more he is blamed and shamed, the more he acts out, and the more he acts out, the more he is blamed and shamed. This assures him an important role in the family, which has both negative and positive aspects.

The negative aspect is that by being the scapegoat and taking the heat, he gets them off the hook, denying their dysfunction and enabling their denial of his perceptiveness. The "badder" he is, the more the family—plus relatives, neighbors, teachers, whoever—can say, "Goodness! What's wrong with 'Trouble'? The rest of the family is so nice. His older sister is first in her class every year and she teaches Sunday school every week. His little brother is always the life of the party, and the youngest one is as quiet and well-behaved as you can imagine!" What the uninformed speaker is missing, of course, is that he just described the three other dysfunctional types that stem from unmet needs!

While these three types are as pathological and damaging to themselves and to the family as the scapegoat is to himself, they are not as visible to others. The Trouble Child is the lighting rod of the family, attracting all the storms, absorbing all the shocks, and drawing all the attention so that the dysfunction of the other family members is not apparent. Without him as a buffer, the others would get hit instead. Therefore, while he sees himself as outside the family system (a position from which he can look in or stay out, depending) and they do, too, he is nonetheless indelibly part of it and plays an essential function in it. By taking the hits—even ones not meant for him—he, ironically, keeps the system operating (not something he enjoys hearing).

The positive aspect of this type is that the scapegoat, more than any of the others, discerns the truth. He knows the whole picture: the source of the problem, who plays what role, and how the dynamics of the dysfunctional system operate. (The compulsive do-gooder, whose problem is low self-esteem, is also sometimes aware of the dysfunction—but won't admit it).

In treatment it is the Trouble Child who is most likely to blow the whistle on the family. While his manner of doing this will be in character—blunt, antagonistic, and insensitive—it is nonetheless very helpful to the family treatment: it opens doors and mouths, if the therapist identifies it correctly and is not intimidated by his manner into allying with the family view of him as the problem. He is actually the bearer of the solution—if you can get him to work, with you, with the family.

But getting him into treatment is as difficult as getting the family to see his merit. Next to the compulsive do-gooder (covers her low self-esteem) whose competence and achievements in most areas of life cause her to develop a case of therapeutic immunity—"When I have the world by the tail, why would I need therapy?"—the scapegoat is the least likely to be willing to enter therapy. He figures, incorrectly but not unreasonably, that since he *perceives accurately* what's going on, *he is okay*—uncontaminated by it, merely an inevitable casualty and observer of it for whom nothing can be done. Much skill must be exercised in bringing him into the process of recovery, and in keeping him there. As a wise dog trainer put it: "He must come to you as he loves you not as he fears you."[4]

Success is most likely if he is approached through his hurt: *e.g.* "It must be very painful to see all this so clearly and not be heard by your family." Having his pain and perception acknowledged and validated opens his heart and mouth—and the door of recovery to him and to the family. "To be trusted is to be saved." When, through such therapeutic intervention, he is brought to see how crucial his persona is to the family's dysfunction, and therefore to its recovery (he really *does* belong, after all!) he is astounded and delighted, and consequently becomes eager to use his resulting sense of empowerment to start the family's healing process.

The first step in that process is to dismantle his conviction that it is the family (and society) that must change in order for him to be himself. For all his outspokenness about the family's (or society's) dysfunction, he is unskilled and naive about asserting his rights or setting his boundaries, and defensive about learning how to: "How come it's up to *me*? *They're* the crazy ones! Why should *I* change?"

It takes patient, persistent work, carefully adjusted to his RPM, and many repetitions of the Healing Process©, for the necessary paradigm shift to occur. He gradually comes to see that his insistence that *they* change to meet *his* needs is precisely what *keeps him powerless*—no matter how loud he talks—and that only *he* can change His self from victim to victor and only by ceasing to blame *them* for his troubles. If he can stay the course, bumpy though it certainly will be, he will reap the reward: that is, reclaim his true self, gain the power of choice, and achieve autonomy (eventually).

The process takes time: the results are effective but gradual. This could not happen without his realization (rarely achieved without therapeutic intervention) that he *does* have a place in the family system, as we saw earlier, and so in a sense he does belong, even though he doesn't feel accepted. Thus the goal of the scapegoat's healing is not to turn him into his opposite, something akin to the compulsive do-gooder. Rather, his healing path lies in learning how to motivate and teach himself to present his perceptions in a diplomatic rather than an accusatory manner (whether to the family or the nation), that is, to empower his ability to define himself, set appropriate boundaries, and communicate impartially.

His behavior must no longer be compulsive and impulsive acting out, but must honor and express his true position in the family: that he is crucial to its health and to the health of society, both of which need the dissenter, the critic, the passionate observer—Diogenes—willing to put His self on the line in the cause of health, both moral and mental.

The reader will think of several such notable dissenters in our century, men and women who thought "outside the box," such as Elizabeth Cady Stanton, Susan B. Anthony, Gandhi, MLK Jr., Malcolm X, Nelson Mandela, Bishop Tutu, and Mother Theresa, all of whom were willing to risk reputation, liberty, and life to identify and try to right what was wrong, sick, dysfunctional, unjust, or immoral. We run-of-the-mill scapegoats can, in our own humble way, profit by their model, as we marvel at their valor. You are now ready to do the Process© for this personality type.

The Freedom Healing Process

1. Accessing Feelings

The Healing Process© for the dissenter/scapegoat is set in motion by learning to recognize your defenses, the *signal of feelings you're not in touch with*. Studying the Chart© on page 113 will familiarize you with your particular defenses so that you can engage the Healing Process©. If you haven't done it yet, please read (or review) Chapter II, pp. 23-30.

The first step in the Healing Process© is accessing feelings. This is done by kneeling on a pillow and pounding a sofa cushion until you get out of breath. Then pause, get your breath, and pound a second time. Pound from the elbows only. Don't raise your arms over the head—it could pull a muscle. You can yell, holler, make caveman sounds—that helps too. (Best to do it when alone—unless your family takes to it also).

It takes time and energy to do this, but the results are well worth it, because the pounding releases anger and frustration like nothing else. If you are extremely upset, you will want to pound even more, and you will learn to follow your inner signals for how long to repeat it. The Process© will eventually complete itself each time, and you will become aware of a deep mood change—from outraged and furious to relaxed and peaceful.

II. Experiencing and Releasing Feelings: Breathing

When you have pounded a lot, and experience a significant reduction in painful feelings such as resentment, guilt, shame, *etc.*, begin the deep breathing: as you *exhale*, blow your pain out steadily and thoroughly, *deflating* your abdomen; as you *inhale*, breathe in slowly and completely, *inflating* your abdomen. Whether lying down or sitting up, laying your hands across your abdomen helps the Process© move correctly and comfortably.

Once you have established a good rhythm, after about five or six minutes, focus on the emerging feelings, and as you inhale and your abdomen expands, Your self will guide you in experiencing the feelings fully, then releasing them with long slow breaths, again and again, until the pain subsides. Let the Process© happen and follow it—it knows what it's doing. Remember, it's by *experiencing* feelings that you release them, and releasing them makes your defenses fall away, so that Your real self gradually emerges.

Being now very self-aware and honest, you will draw to you people who will "get it." You will feel validated and happy with Your self, even if your family still doesn't. This is the essential Process© in healing your scapegoat role.

After ten to fifteen minutes of this breathing process, you will notice a significant diminishing of the painful feelings on the outbreath, and a small, slowly expanding sense of peace and well-being on the inbreath. Do the deep breathing until you feel the beginnings of that state. Then let your breathing dictate the pace, which will be very short breaths with long spaces in between, because you are so fully oxygenated.

Stay with the Process© until you begin to feel a sense of peace gradually increasing in intensity. Be patient and give whatever amount of time you need to go deeply into the peace and then stay there. (Remember Zeke: "If I could just get that peace again.") *More is better*: the peace will be deeper the longer you do the deep breathing. Likewise, the more frequently you practice the entire Process©, the more quickly you will get the results, because your mind/body system will become familiar and comfortable with it and will produce results more readily.

III. Meeting the Need: Infilling and Self-nurturing

In the peaceful state induced by the release breathing, still keeping your eyes closed, start focusing on the need to feel more independent, less trapped, more respected, less invaded, less controlled or defined or blamed by something outside yourself. You are gradually moving toward *self- empowerment*.

Then with your next in-breath, say silently to Your self, "Peace," and on the out- breath, create messages to say to Your self that release the scapegoat/dissenter persona. Here are some examples you can tailor to suit Your self. Remember, *You-as-Spirit* are saying these declarations to Your *self*:

"You are free, respected, honest. It's safe to be you."

"I AM here, protecting you."

"Only I can define you. You do not have to be something you're not."

"Your perceptions are accurate; you see the situation clearly."

"Their opinions no longer bother you."

"You are what *I* say you are; not what *others* say you are."

"I believe you and trust you. Your hurt no longer makes you act out."

"Wherever you are, I AM, and where I AM, there are truth, honesty, and recovery."

Doing this Process© will embed the messages in your limbic system, and eventually a form a belief in them. Don't be deterred by the fact that you don't yet believe the messages. Of course you don't! If you already did, you wouldn't need to do the Process©. *The repetition will create the belief,* and when you believe the message your struggle and grief will be over. "What you think about, you bring about." You are creating a new mind set, re-storing the brain with what you want to hear rather than with what you don't.

At some point new messages will start coming into your mind without your consciously devising them. This is You-as-Higher Self speaking to you. The nicest thing about that Being is that It is incapable of saying anything but the truth. It will happen more and more as you do the Process©. Your inner feeling state and your behavior will spontaneously change and your body's systems will all become healthier.

Every time you do the Process©, You define and govern Your self a bit more, and little by little it accumulates confidence and self-respect. When these feelings reach a critical mass, the transformation will be complete: you will no longer be a scapegoat, but whatever *you* say you are. You will be *free*: safe, secure, accepted, competent, valued, and defining and liking who and what You are and how You govern Your self. *You will be loved and loving; you will be made new.*

The Riddle Rewritten

You're having a cup of coffee at the AA Clubhouse, waiting for your sponsor, Lou. Returning from the snack bar, you see a new guy, large and aggressive looking, sitting your chair talking to your sponsor! As anger sends adrenaline throughout your body, it begins to vibrate with agitation and your legs feel weak and wobbly. You turn around and head for the men's room, where you close your eyes and do deep breathing for a few minutes. As the anger and adrenaline are released, You tell Your self silently, "Peace, be cool. Peace. Your place with Lou is safe." You return to the clubroom, approach the intruder and say:

"My name's Mike—how ya doin'? First time here?"

"I'm Billy," he responds. "Yeah...I just got out of rehab."

"Well, good luck and welcome," you say. "Keep comin' back. Lou, can we have our talk?"

What brought about the change?

Postscript

These four needs chapters, focusing on the Freedom Healing Process©, were designed to carry you from the need level at which you started through autonomy. If you have done your Process© regularly, you will by now be living much more happily in four specific ways: (1) Each of your four dependency needs will be continuously filled *from within* whenever a deficit occurs, gradually accustoming you to an ever-increasing sense of fulfillment; (2) doing the Process© daily will ensure continuing development in governing your feelings and increasing the depth of your spiritual practice; (3) your thinking will be clearer, less obsessive and defensive, and when it reverts, you will recognize it more quickly and know what to do to restore its clarity; (4) and finally, your behavior will be *chosen* by *you* rather than *compelled* by your *feelings*, and therefore more in accord with your values and also more pleasing to other people. You will be free of the need to use defenses.

Since we reap what we sow—*what you think about, you bring about*—you will also enjoy a much-improved return from other people, in accordance with the "law of retributive justice." And best of all, when lapses occur and the old distressed you suddenly rears its anguished head, You will have exactly the right medicine to comfort and heal it!

You have completed the process of growing up Your self: by working your way up the ladder through to autonomy from whatever need was your point of entry, you have accomplished what you didn't have the support and guidance to do when you were growing up physically: *you have developed from a child to an adult.*

You are now ready to continue your growth beyond adulthood into Chapter VII, the realm of Spirit, which describes the three spiritual needs and guides you into a

Process© by which to fulfill them. Last but not least, the Appendix, "Discoveries and Conclusions," discusses five topics that correlate in interesting ways to the Freedom Healing Process©: *Codependency, Brain Structure and Functioning, Mental Health Diagnoses,* the Eastern system of the seven *Chakras,* and *From Chaos to Harmony. Bon voyage!*

VII

The Freedom Healing Process as a Means to Trancendence

The inner journey you have traveled so far began before your entry into this planet, with a gradual relinquishing of the original state of unconscious spirituality that characterized you in the womb, before it, and for several years after your birth. The two intermediate stages which followed —*childhood* (belonging need) and *adolescence* (self-esteem need)—bit by bit diminished that original spirituality and led slowly and unconsciously to *adulthood* (autonomy need), characterized typically in its early stage by a nearly total disregard of its original spiritual nature.

But just as the infant has that in him which directs him to grow out of his initial unconscious spiritual state into the "human" being of adulthood, so does the "adult" being have that in him which eventually directs him to grow out of his human being state and rediscover his original spiritual nature. Unlike the infant, the adult experiences this transition consciously. In the words of Tielhard de Chardin, "I am not a human being having a spiritual experience; I am a spiritual being having a human experience."[1] So we see that our growth, generally pictured as straight-up-vertical, is actually circular: we come from spirit (down?) into human, and the human returns again (up?) to spirit. A few examples of these concepts and experiences will be useful. The collective idea being put forth here is that we originate in a spiritual realm and are essentially, therefore, spiritual beings having to "make do" on planet earth. There is evidence that we have a hard time adjusting to it, a concept extensively discussed by Jenny Wade in her amazing book "Changes of Mind: A Holonomic Theory of the Evolution of Consciousness."[2] Wordsworth has similar ideas expressing the pain of relinquishing "the glories he hath known."[3] Walt Whitman vigorously brings his spirituality into mundane daily life and makes us see and feel its essentially ethereal nature: "I depart as air, I shake my white locks at the runaway sun."[4] I myself have had, at my level of spirituality, significant spiritual experiences, and so have many of my clients.

The first is about an extraordinary cat, calico with copper eyes, who had more love in her than she could handle in one lifetime, so she took it with her when she left this planet. I loved—love—her dearly. Perhaps because I rescued her, skinny and lost, from the streets, she decided when she had regained her health that it was her job to take care of me, so she greeted me profusely whenever I came in, and groomed me thoroughly. Her time to pass on came all too soon, and, ironically, from breast cancer.

Two days after her burial, I awakened very early, and had just opened my eyes to see the time—6:15—when suddenly I became aware that I was *suffused with bliss*, continuously expanding but unmoving. T.S. Eliot says "Erhebung (rising) without motion,"[5] that is, no cognitive activity, just *experiencing* and *being*. It was ethereally (not verbally or cognitively) clear to me that what I was experiencing was *her presence comforting me for my loss of her love by letting me know that it wasn't lost!* When I reluctantly opened my eyes, I saw that it was 7:30—an hour and a quarter I had remained in that state without motion or cognitive activity, just *experiencing the bliss*. What a gift!

A second experience, equally if not more amazing, occurred one day while I was listening—studiously—to a client. As his story was moving along smoothly, I suddenly felt a horizontal trickling sensation, like a television news strip at the bottom of the screen, starting at the top left of my rib cage and making its way to the right; then I heard my mentor (who had passed on three months earlier) saying, "Girl, when I've been taking care of you for twenty years when I was in the flesh, what makes you think I'm not still taking care of you?" I was too startled to speak—*thank goodness*, considering that my client was still talking, apparently unaware of my astonishing experience. Neither of these experiences has been repeated, but that doesn't invalidate their reality: I *experienced* them, and *what you experience you can't deny*.

I have three more stories, all from friends. The first is from a lovely, spiritually inclined young woman who related to me the following story. One day her son, just six, told her that "God lives in us all." Managing not to look startled or disbelieving (high marks for her parenting skills) she asked him matter-of-factly, "Where did you learn that?" His immediate reply—"When I was with God"—startled her even more, so she asked, "When was that?" "Before I was here," he said casually.

The last two stories I put side by side, so to speak, and you'll soon understand why. First, my grandson, up until about fifteen months (at which time his attention became immovably—so far—fixated on heavy machinery) every time we stepped outside, would look straight up, point his arm directly to the heavens, looking beatific, and say "Ga, ga."

The second story occurred as I was walking down a hospital hallway one day. I turned a corner and saw coming toward me a beautiful dark-complected woman carrying a gorgeous baby, surely, I thought, from India. As they approached, they came under a skylight, and the baby looked up, pointed his finger to the sky and, *no kidding*, said "Ga, ga" beaming with joy! Of course I stopped and told her about my grandson; she smiled and said matter-of-factly: "They remember where they come from."

The core of this Healing Process© both originates from spirit and generates growth into spirit. If worked thoroughly and consistently, it ultimately results in transformation of the human "you," whose needs (the first four) are those of dependency, into the spiritual You, whose needs are those of Being, that is, needing to express and outwardly demonstrate the wholeness within. Awakened by the Healing Process©, the spiritual You fulfills the needs of Your human self from that wholeness, freeing you from the bondage and frustration of depending on outside sources.

No agency or entity other than You can really do this for you. Fulfilling your needs is an *inside job*. By working through this chapter on the three spiritual needs, you can, with sufficient practice, achieve even higher states of consciousness, perhaps all the way to experiencing the ultimate merging with universal spirit that is known as *samadhi* or *nirvana*.

In the first two chapters we saw how the Freedom Healing Process© came into being, and why, when, and how to use it. The subsequent chapters on the four types took you into the Process© beginning at your particular level, and guided your growth through to the autonomy need. We are now entering the final chapter of the Process© which describes the three spiritual needs and how to use them to continue your development into the realm of spirit. The Freedom Process© leads you toward this transcendent state in two ways: first, *in the moment* and second, *over a period of time*.

1. *In the moment* refers to the individual Process©. Each time you do it, you experience a shifting of your individual consciousness from *you as human self* to *You as*

Spiritual Self. This inward turning to Your true identity relieves you of the obsessive outward turning and seeking typical of most of humanity and of your human self, all of whom act and react according to what they think other people think of them. Instead, when you act from You as Spiritual Self, you are freed from the compulsion to judge yourself as others judge you. Any *moment* you choose can bring you to remedy whatever need is lacking, simply by doing the Process©.

2. *Over a period of time* refers to the Process© as longitudinal: as you use it repeatedly, incorporating it into your daily routine, its effects accumulate and bit by bit propel your growth up the hierarchy of needs, from one level to the next. Because this longitudinal drive gradually overcomes the counter-pull of your human self to dig in and stay put at whatever level it's at, the Process© succeeds in carrying you through your entire development, from your beginning level to adulthood and beyond, to spiritual unity. We will now explore in turn each of these two avenues of growth.

"In the Moment"

Basic to the Freedom Process© is the concept of the two "I's:" first, the "I" we use when speaking from our human self ("i'm happy"), and second, the "I" we use when speaking from our spiritual self: "I said to My self..." The human "i" is the observed and receiving self, and operates the four dependency needs; the spiritual "I" is the Observing and Giving Self, and operates the three Being needs (further discussion of this on pp. 176–184).

These two entities, recognized and discussed and used since recorded history by poets, preachers, philosophers, saints, and avatars, exist in every moment in our thought and speech, whether or not we design to listen to them.[6] Most typically they are at odds with each other, or to say it more precisely, the human "i" has a difficult time agreeing with the spiritual "I"—it wants what it wants when it wants it, and has to try, seemingly, every long and winding road of its own imagining before it is willing to heed a higher voice, *i.e., ask for directions.* No less a teacher than St. Paul expressed this conflict in a memorable phrase: "…the good that I would, I do not: but the evil which I would not, that I do." (Romans 7:20). To which self in his statement does each "I" refer?

Robert Frost makes the point in two lines:

"We dance round in a ring and suppose,
But the secret sits in the middle and knows."[7]

A mundane example of this inner conflict happened to me once in the supermarket. Having completed my shopping list, I said to My self: "Bread." My self replied: "We don't need bread, "i" just got some the other day." "i" didn't get any, and when "i" got home, guess what? *No bread.* Because we spend about ninety-five percent of our time in our human self, our thinking and talking are inclined to dismiss the spiritual "I" if "It" doesn't agree with the human "i," when agreeing with the spiritual "I" is *always* the right thing to do. As the above anecdote shows, we are generally not conscious of the distinction.

So let's take time to explore it now. The following story about a king and his difficult servant, a brief parable told by Sai Baba, is adapted here to demonstrate more fully these two entities (the "I" and the "i") and their relation to each other.[8] The servant, so goes the story, excelled at his work. He was a model of the perfect employee, doing promptly and flawlessly whatever the king bade him do. However, when not occupied with work, he got into mischief of one kind or another, often upsetting his fellow subjects. Eventually, they had all they could stand, so they went together to the king to protest. The spokesman addressed their ruler:

Learning to Fulfill the Needs of Your Self

"O revered Majesty, we come to ask for your help. It is about your servant Ahmed. We see how good a worker he is, but when he is not at work, he amuses himself by making our lives miserable. He sings and dances outdoors all night long, making much noise; he jumps out from behind the trees at our children as they go to school and then they are upset and cannot learn well; he shouts threats to our animals so that they begin to tremble when they see us; he even interrupts our times of prayer. We humbly petition and beseech you to give us relief."

The king was moved, and calling his servant to him, spoke as follows:

"O my excellent servant, I know how well and faithfully you do the work I give you. But my other subjects tell me that when you are not working you get into mischief, which disrupts their lives. You are of course aware of the flagpole in front of the palace? Yes? Well, whenever you are in between jobs, I order you to climb it up and down. In this way your leisure time will be occupied harmlessly, and my other subjects will be relieved and happy once again."

The servant of course carried out these instructions with his customary diligence, and the kingdom returned to its customary peace. Perhaps you have discerned the application: the King represents Consciousness, the "Observing Self;" the servant represents the "observed self," *i.e.* the human mind; the subjects represent feelings; and climbing up and down the flagpole represents a mantra—that is, a spiritual phrase (or activity) that is repeated continuously to keep the human mind from wandering into dangerous territories such as fear, anxiety, doubt, hostility, envy, or negativity, in between the jobs You give it.

Just so with our inner life: we must, if we wish to create meaningful, positive lives for ourselves, work diligently to lift our identity bit by bit toward the Observing Self, while directing our human mind to follow Ahmed's example of obedience when not using it for some deliberate purpose or specific task. The story delineates the two entities and their relationship very clearly: "I" am the Director and Governor of My (human) self; My self is subject to My will. The concept of the "I" and the "self" occurs at the more mundane level of our everyday conversation, as the following examples show. See if you can detect the two entities:

1. I said to myself, "Be careful, that sidewalk looks slippery."

2. If I don't watch myself, I'll eat the whole cake.

3. Sometimes when I feel down, I lift myself up by playing Mozart's "Alleluia."

The distinction between these two entities is blurred by the fact that the word "I" is used for both. How handy it would be if grammarians had recognized this distinction! They could then have clarified the confusion by inventing a differential device say, for instance, using "I" for the Spiritual Self and "i" for the human self as demonstrated above. Lacking this, the best clue is what each "I" does: the "I"-as-Spirit acts on the "i"-as-human; the "i"-as-human does things it shouldn't do and the "I"-as-Spirit corrects it (reread St. Paul's statement above). The "Big I" is the subject and is always right; the little "i" is the object, and is right *only* when it agrees with and is guided by the "I," which is not very often. *This reluctance or inability of our ego to listen to and follow the inner voice accounts for virtually all the problems we have.*

Now let's return to the three sentences above: the two entities are clearly discernible when we apply the concept in the preceding paragraph. The first sentence makes a clear distinction between "I" and "my self": "*I* said to My *self...*" The subject of the sentence is "I," the Observer, and the object is My "self," the observed (evidently a possession of the "I"), who receives messages from "I" the Observer.

But in the second and third sentences, the word "I" is, confusingly, used to mean the *observed as well as* the observer, even though the "I" who may "eat the whole cake" is clearly distinct from the "I" who can "watch" and "lift up" the greedy eater. You cannot simultaneously be the subject and the object. The shift from one to the other in our everyday speech shows how we unconsciously identify with both the Observer and the observed.

"Well, so what?" you might say. "This is just fooling around with words, just a quirk of semantics!" But on the contrary, it is crucial to our true identity: anytime we use the "I"-as-Spirit to mean our human self we cut it (the human self) off from the source of power, and we become a fragment, like Kafka's "bucket rider," capable of operating only on the momentum of our ingrained pattern.

Examining these two entities more closely, we see that they have different natures, characteristics, and functions. *That which is observed* I refer to as My "self." It belongs to Me, and I have the authority to change, govern, direct, and correct its four human components: thoughts, feelings, behavior, and body. Any other elements of My self fit into one of these four categories. This observed self, as you no doubt have experienced, is subject to limits and frailties, as the above sentences demonstrate: I-as-human self exhibit illness, anxiety, anger, lack of restraint, and therefore have need of guidance, nurturance, comfort, and so on.

The observed self, then, is the *human being*—mortal, unconscious, fallible, powerless, incapable of meeting its needs, limited to and by the time-space continuum. Its job is to survive in the world and learn lessons from the experiences (growth opportunities) that come to it. It is from this human self that Jesus speaks when he says, "I do not speak on my own authority" (John 14:10). (This is unusual for Jesus, since He spoke almost always from the spiritual "I").

In contrast, we see that the other Entity is *that which observes and wills*. Its distinctness from Its human self is revealed in Its very ability to observe that self: if I can observe my hand, then "I" am not my hand, right? Likewise, if I can observe my thoughts, feelings, body, and behavior, *I* am not *they, I* am not *self*. *I AM* that which *has* thoughts, feelings, body, and behavior, and which can observe, love, govern, and change them. Speaking from this "I," My job is to meet the needs of My human self: "The Atman (immanent self) is the Witness (the Observer) of the human mind and its operations."[9] This "I" exists outside the time-space continuum and cannot therefore be subject to any of the "shocks flesh is heir to."[10] The following diagram to the right shows this relationship.

The diagram pictures the flow of energy-consciousness-information from the Spiritual Self to the human self. If, as is the case in pathology, this flow is blocked by negativity or defenses, such as stress, ignorance, trauma, drugs, alcohol, painful feelings, and so on, the human self is cut off from that energy and the vital messages it sends, and is left to run on the patterns of thinking, feeling, and behavior conditioned into it in childhood. Without listening to the guidance of the "I" (who is always present and available) the self, like a ship without a rudder, loses direction and power, and is left to run on momentum—the *illusion* of power—continually repeating those patterns unless stopped by a greater force.

To sum up, the "I" has a human self, made up of thinking, feeling, and behavior, that operates positively only when it connects with and listens to the "I." This "I" is pervasive, originates in the *unmanifest* or *implicate* realm, and is the origin and essence of everything *manifest* or *explicate*. It includes the consciousness of the human being and is the source of power, will, love, comfort, joy, compassion and, above all, of creation. All things that exist in the manifest realm—that is, all things that are visible, tangible, audible, olfactory, gustatory, kinesthetic—and therefore susceptible to pain—originate in and come from the unmanifest realm

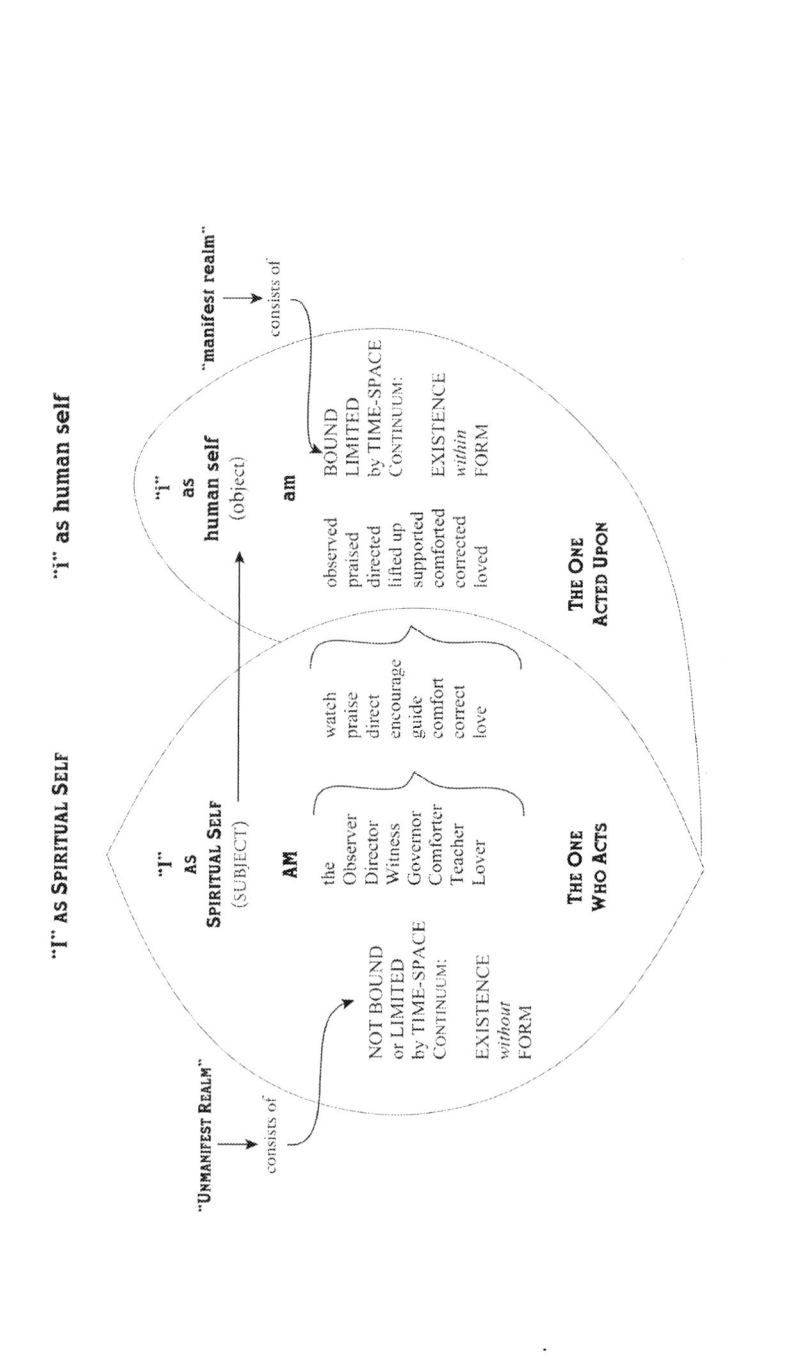

"I" as Spiritual Self   "i" as human self

"UNMANIFEST REALM" consists of →

"I"
AS
SPIRITUAL SELF
(SUBJECT)

AM

the
Observer
Director
Witness
Governor
Comforter
Teacher
Lover

watch
praise
direct
encourage
guide
comfort
correct
love

THE ONE WHO ACTS

NOT BOUND or LIMITED by TIME-SPACE CONTINUUM:

EXISTENCE *without* FORM

"i"
as
human self
(object)

am

observed
praised
directed
lifted up
supported
comforted
corrected
loved

THE ONE ACTED UPON

BOUND LIMITED by TIME-SPACE CONTINUUM:

EXISTENCE *within* FORM

"manifest realm" → consists of

where there is no pain, and which is the womb of creating, that is, *creating is its job.*

Our main purpose and job living in this manifest realm is to learn how to access or get back to the unmanifest, both *in consciousness now* and in the stage of life we pass into after this one. We thereby learn to live *from* that realm, "which taketh away the sins ("pain") of the world," (John 1:29) and, even while we still live "in the flesh" (Philippians 1:22) brings us into contact with the "glories we have known." (William Wordsworth: "Intimations Ode" st.VI).

Further, the spiritual "I" has the power to heal Its human self, to deprogram the belief system encoded in its feeling brain ("limbic system") by its childhood experiences. It does this in the way described in the four needs chapters by encoding into its human self new healthful patterns of thinking, feeling, and behaving. Since "I" can act on and change My human self, but My human self cannot act on or change Me (although, to its peril, it can and does, all too often, *forget* Me) it follows that I am, in the words of AA's second step, a "power greater than my self." (See Alcoholics Anonymous, Third Edition, p.59). This is a subjective expression of the second part of Jesus' objective statement: "Believest thou not that I am in the Father (*implicate*) and the Father (*explicate*) in me? The words that I speak unto you I speak not of myself: but the Father that dwelleth in me, he doeth the works." (St. John 14:10).

Jesus demonstrates the truth of this statement when, the night before the Crucifixion, "he took with him Peter and the two sons of Zebedee" (Matthew 26:37) and went to a special place to pray, signifying his need to move into his Spiritual Self (Matt. 26:38). That he is in his human self is shown clearly by his despairing statement: "My soul is exceeding sorrowful, even unto death: tarry ye here, and watch with me." (Matt. 26:38). He, the giver of comfort, now seeks it himself from his followers, fearing what he knows the next day will bring them.

Then "he went a little further and fell on his face and prayed, saying, O my Father, if it be possible, let this cup pass from me: nevertheless not as I will but as thou wilt." (Matt. 26:39). He returns to the disciples and, finding them asleep, his human self expresses resentment toward them for leaving him alone and comfortless in his humanity: "What, could ye not watch with me one hour?" (Matt. 26:40).

But ironically, their dereliction works to his benefit, since their seeming abandonment forces Jesus to continue his inner prayer work instead of codependently seeking solace from his followers. So Jesus goes a second time to the place of prayer and says, "O my Father, if this cup may not pass away from me, except I drink it, thy will be done." (Matt: 26:42).

Here we see him in transition from the human self of suffering to the spiritual Self of freedom from pain and fear. Then "he came and found them asleep again: for their eyes were heavy." (Matt. 26:43) This time he says nothing, showing that he has moved further in his understanding of the disciples, and thus further away from his own human fears toward his Spiritual Self. He goes away again and "prayed the third time, saying the same words." (Matt. 26:44).

When he next returns to the still-sleeping disciples his statement is dramatically different, indeed, it is 180 degrees opposite to the preceding two visitations: "Then cometh he to his disciples, and saith unto them, Sleep on now, and take your rest; behold, the hour is at hand, and the Son of man is betrayed into the hands of sinners." (Matt. 26:45) His composed, almost matter-of-fact acceptance of the inevitability of the next day's horrific event signifies the overcoming of his human fear and his transformation into a state of freedom from all suffering.

From human self, exhibiting resentment and anguish, to the Spiritual Self, exhibiting compassion and selflessness, in one brief night! Just so do our trials and tribulations work to our benefit if we read the message they bring us, that is, to do as he did: rather than turning outward to the circumference, he turned inward to the source and meditated, connecting to the implicate source for guidance, support and courage with which to meet his frightful explicate fate. From this example, we can say that the spiritual "I" has the power to heal its human self, to deprogram the belief system encoded in its feeling brain ("limbic system") by its childhood conditioning, and meet its needs Itself. Just how, then, is this done?

We will start by looking at the connections and parallels between the spiritual concepts we have been discussing and the structure and functioning of the brain in relation to the Observer (a subject discussed in greater detail in Appendix II, p. 1, diagram 1). Here we will just identify the four basic components: the basal brain stem (survival brain, heartbeat and breathing); the feeling brain (limbic system); and the two thinking brains, the motor cortex and the cerebral cortex. When these four brains are in balance and operating in harmony, they fulfill their objective of keeping the entire organism functioning healthily. But when they get out of balance, they (like Ahmed) create confusion in the organism and in its well being on all levels—cognitive, emotional, physical, and behavioral.

This unbalancing can happen in one of two ways. The first is that the feeling brain can flood the thinking brain with feeling messages, thus deranging its ability to function rationally and choose behavior in accord with its values. As a result, our behavior is dictated, instead of by our thinking brain, by our feeling brain, which may deliver negative opinions and ideas as well as positive, and thereby render us vulnerable and powerless over the consequences.

The second way the unbalancing occurs is when the thinking brain confuses old internal patterns or defenses, leftovers from childhood, with external information (reality), either by discounting or repressing feeling-messages from the feeling brain, or misinterpreting data both present and past. The result is self-defeating ("better not to say anything—they might fire me") or counterproductive ("that _____!

I'm gonna let him have it!"), undermining rather than promoting the welfare of the self. Either way, Your self ends up out of balance.

The question then arises: how can that balance be restored? Obviously, *neither the thinking brain nor the feeling brain can do it alone,* since each one can only, and must, perform its given functions and accomplish its characteristic goals. From the preceding discussion you no doubt have the answer: it lies in the Observing Self, that is, *You.* Only by moving into that Observing Self position can You coordinate all the components of Your self and will them back into balance so they can function productively together.

One way to bring that about is by doing the Freedom Process©: by observing, experiencing, and releasing feelings, and then fulfilling the need, You are restored to the position of governor of Your self. When instead You identify with Your human self (which of course ninety-nine out of a hundred of us do all the time) by thinking and speaking from it ("I'm sick, stupid, poor") Your self remains powerless and needy, because power does not reside in the human self.

Conversely, by speaking from You-as-spirit, for example, "I am now sending currents of healing energy into My body, mind, and circumstances," You restore and maintain harmony (presumably what the meditating did for Jesus), because power is a property of You-as-*Creator and Observer.* It is because of this overseeing function that the Integrating Consciousness is represented in the brain diagram as partly outside the brain and is delineated by a dotted rather than a solid line, to convey its incorporeal as well as its corporeal nature: it is pervasive—it exists without as well as within physical form (Appendix II, p. 207). One client refers to it as "the balcony," another as the "Mind behind the mind." Walt Whitman expresses the formless, limitless, non-material nature of the "I" in the following line from "Song of Myself":

> I pass death with the dying and birth with the new-wash'd babe, and am not contain'd between my hat and boots...(Stanza 7, l. 133)

This concept brings to mind a fascinating and relevant segment from Jenny Wade's book "Changes of Mind":

"Then all of a sudden there was this yellow room and these people. That's when I was beginning to figure out what was going on. Not very happy about it...I didn't realize right off that I could make noises [cry]—that seemed to just kind of happen... Starting to breathe was pretty strange, too...I had never done anything like that before.

"The breathing was just in bursts at first, every time I made a noise. Then I noticed every time I was doing it I was doing it in between the noises, so I was thinking about that, too. It kind of distracted me from being mad because I was concentrating on what was going on inside me. Listening to the way it sounded. Feeling the air go in and out. Making it go faster and slower—that was kind of a neat idea. I thought as long as I had to be in this place, I might as well have something like noise and air...

"I felt I knew a lot. . thought I was pretty intelligent. I never thought about being a person, just a mind. I thought I was an intelligent mind. And so when the situation [of being born] was forced on me, I didn't like it too much." (p. 51).

Deborah not only feels herself more intelligent and insightful than the hospital staff, but describes herself as a mind, not embodied...Deborah's identification of herself as a mind—and all the direct records showing two sources of consciousness—are corroborated by Helen Wambach's independent experiments (1981). Wambach regressed over 750 people and then had them describe fetal life phenomenologically. Eighty-nine percent of her subjects reported having two separate, simultaneous sources of awareness. They did not identify with the growing fetus or its stream of consciousness, although they accepted that the fetus was "theirs." Instead, they identified themselves with the physically transcendent source of consciousness and tended not to become involved with "their fetus" until six months after conception. In fact, many were extremely reluctant to join "their consciousness" with the body-bound awareness of the fetus. Wambach's subjects characterized themselves as disembodied minds hovering around the fetus and mother, being "in and out" of the fetus and having a telepathic knowledge of the mother's emotions throughout pregnancy and birth.

One-third of Wambach's subjects said they did not come into the fetus (join their consciousness with that of the fetus) until just before or during birth; 12 percent stated they attached to the fetus about the beginning of the third trimester (interestingly, when brain activity is first observed); and only 11 percent reported prior attachment to the fetus (1981). The rest joined within a day or two after the birth. Subjects ascribed their reluctance to join with the fetus to negative feelings about being born. Approximately 68 percent expressed antipathy and anxiety about being embodied. Their attitude was resigned toward physical life as an unpleasant duty they must perform in response to an unidentified imperative.

The regression research suggests that the transcendent source of consciousness coexists with physical source. While the brain lacks measurable coordinated activity until the third trimester, the transcendent source, with its mature, unchanging awareness may be present even before conception. It seems to be spatially and temporally limited to an area immediately around the fetal body or the mother from conception up to an extreme limit of two days after birth. At some point during the pregnancy or prenatal period, the transcendent source becomes "stuck" to its body, with less freedom to dissociate its quasi-independent selfhood from that of the fetus. To sum up the data on the transcendent source of consciousness, it appears to be distinct from fetal awareness...

The characteristics of the transcendent mode of consciousness appear to be remarkably like Arthur Deikman's *Observing Self* (1972, 1982):
It is fully mature and insightful.

It operates in a receptive mode, recording and processing its environment.

It registers thought, feelings, and actions but is not comprised of, or very attached to, these—the only exception being a revulsion for reincarnation.

It is a distinct self but has little ego.

It recognizes "normal" spatial and temporal boundaries.

It has no subjective experience of time, but seems to live in the moment.

The distinction between awareness and content of awareness tends to be ignored in western psychology; its implications for our everyday life are not appreciated.

Awareness is the ground of conscious life, the background or field in which all elements exist, different from thoughts, sensations, or images. "Behind" your thoughts and images is awareness and that is where you are.

Whatever you can notice or conceptualize is already an object of awareness, not awareness itself, which seems to jump a step back when we experience an object...Thus every day consciousness contains a transcendent element that we seldom notice because that element is the very ground of our experience. The word "transcendent" is justified because if the subjective consciousness—the Observing Self—cannot itself be observed but remains forever apart from the contents of consciousness, it is likely to be *of a different order from everything else. Its different nature becomes evident when we realize the observing self is featureless, cannot be affected by the world any more than a mirror can be affected by the images it reflects.* (pp. 51-56).

Every time we practice it, the Freedom Process© gives us the experience *in the moment* of identifying with this Integrating Consciousness that establishes us in our true identity. *That which we experience we cannot deny or disbelieve.* This means, among other things, that I-as-Observing Self am both the supplier and the supply of MY self's needs. I AM the source and the substance of the health of MY body, the clarity of MY mind, the nature and duration of MY feelings, and the rightness of MY self's behavior. I AM responsible for MY self. I AM that Power which can inform and reprogram MY self according to how I want it to be.

All this I can do by realizing *what I really am*. Whatever Your self needs at any moment, there is a limitless supply of it in the unmanifest realm, the realm of energy (spirit), the origin of everything manifest: in the words of the Nicene Creed, the "maker of all things, both visible and invisible." You, as Observing Self, fulfill the needs of your human self by talking to it along the lines indicated: "Wherever you are, I AM; You cannot be where I AM not. And where I AM there is an unlimited supply of whatever you need. I

AM now filling you with love, love, love. What I AM is the substance and supply of all things."

Unfortunately, we do not identify with our Observing Self very often, and generally not consciously. Most of the time we identify with our human self, as described above, and thereby disconnect from our true identity as Spirit. We then become wayward and impulsive like Ahmed, a mere fragment, cut off from the Power within us and therefore in a state of unmet needs. In consequence, we turn to other people to meet them, reverting to our familiar dependency, eclipsing the Higher Self and reducing us to its shadow. This leaves the merely human self, a condition of limitation and neediness, painful but comfortable because it feels familiar—*like home.*

In contrast, we can prevent or recover from this diminished state by regular use of the Freedom Process©. If you persist (and you can always do a process to release your resistance or discouragement) You will demonstrate the principle that You-as-consciousness create your reality: *What you hold in your mind*—unconscious as well as conscious— *will magnify and manifest.* The *invisible* (implicate) creates the *visible* (explicate) throughout the universe. *What you think about, you bring about.* It is therefore of the greatest importance that we release the negative patterns accumulated in our limbic storehouse, and consciously replace them with healthful concepts and memories so that we manifest what we want rather than what we don't want.

Through the transformation of My self by turning within, outer things are also transformed, from things which are separate from me and whose value "I" measure by their utility, to expressions of the same consciousness/energy/ substance that "I" am: a tree is no longer something that exists just to give me shade in the summer and fuel for my fireplace in the winter or the paper on which I write these words, but a beautiful, explicate form and expression of that same energy. The following passage from Wordsworth's "Tintern Abbey," expresses a similar sense of unity:

Learning to Fulfill the Needs of Your Self

>   And I have felt
> A presence that disturbs me with the joy
> Of elevated thoughts; a sense sublime
> Of something far more deeply interfused,
> Whose dwelling is the light of setting suns,
> And the round ocean and the living air,
> And the blue sky, and in the mind of man:
> A motion and a spirit, that impels
> All thinking things, all objects of all thought,
> And rolls through all things.
> *Lines Composed above Tintern Abbey*, ll. 93-103.

The concept of identifying with the Observer and speaking from It to one's human self is in contrast to the current practice of affirmations, an ancient spiritual activity that over the last several decades has gained great popularity in the self-help field. In the current way the affirmations are stated, the "I" is identified with the human self, as in the following examples:

> I am secure and protected wherever I go.
> —or—
> God protects me and keeps me secure wherever I go.

Since the Observer (God) cannot be subject to feelings of insecurity, it follows that the "I" in these examples can refer only to the human self. This negates the purpose of the Declarations, since the human self lacks the power to direct itself. Consequently, while that style of declaring will, like brainwashing, eventually have some effect, it has the drawback of keeping *You* identified with Your *human* self, the place of non-power. In contrast, if you identify with the Observer, the creative source, and speak *to* Your human self instead of *from* it, its needs will be met much more quickly and completely. Here are some examples:

The Freedom Healing Process as a Means to Transcendence

> You (human self) are safe and secure in MY care.
> I (Spirit) value you (human) and give you the courage to ask for a raise.
>
> Wherever you (human) are, I (Spirit) AM, and where I AM, all is well.
> There is nowhere you can be that I AM not.
>
> I AM with you and within you, at every moment ready to supply your need.

Saying your Declarations this way, although it may feel strange at first, gives you the experience of using your spiritual power, transforms your mood in a matter of minutes, and establishes a new mind-set in a matter of weeks.

You can confirm the effectiveness of this style of declaring by the following brief experiment. With your eyes closed, repeat the following phrase three times, intensely, as though you really mean it: *"God, please help me."* Take a few moments, eyes still closed, to experience and identify the feelings this statement produces. Now, repeat the following phrase, also three times, in the same manner, eyes closed: "*I (Spirit) Am* helping you (my human self) now."

Again identify and experience the feeling. If the first one made you feel anxious, and the second one reassured, you're right in line with most people; if the reverse, a little practice with the second way will reward you with a deep sense of safety and comfort. Evidence of the transformation will appear in spontaneous changes in your behavior: as your needs get met, they no longer drive your behavior, freeing you to choose it according to your values. Your self-esteem and self-confidence will spontaneously improve.

"Over a Period of Time"

We are now ready to discuss the second way the Process© generates spiritual growth, which is *over a period of time.* As it led you through the maturation process, from security (infancy) to autonomy (adulthood), you learned how to fulfill each need. Now you are moving to the spiritual levels, consisting of the need for your Being to develop spiritual qualities and, based on the inner work you have done so far, use them to help others grow on their path. As you continue working with the spiritual needs, you may find a second go-round on issues already worked on in the first four stages of your process, giving you a chance to work out and release more of the painful original feelings. You will, consequently, become more healthy, integrated, and wise.

The Process© operates cumulatively and inclusively, like links in a chain, or a relay race—each need supports and is incorporated by the one above it and each need is dependent on the one below it (except the security need).

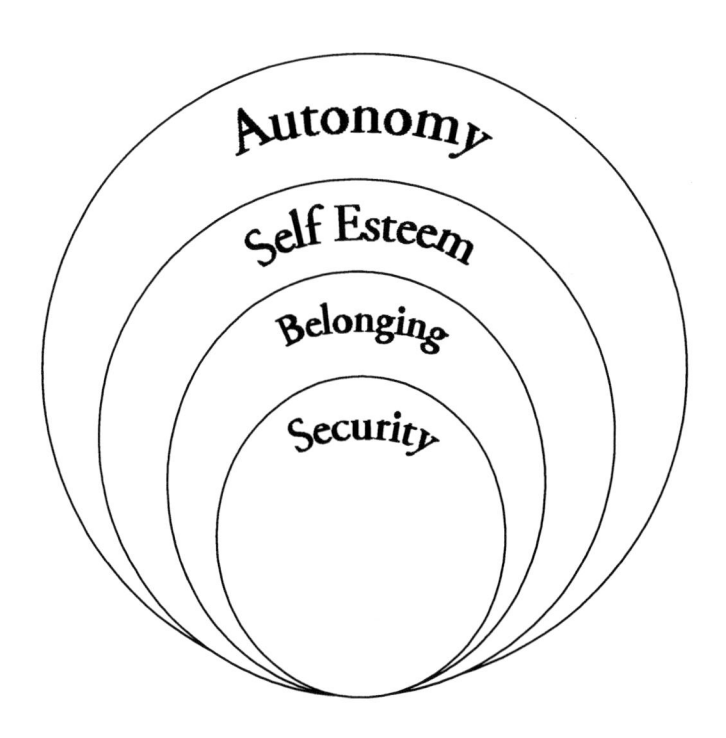

Autonomy

Self Esteem

Belonging

Security

The Chart© diagram of the needs as a sequence of stacked rectangles, while useful as a learning tool, does not adequately show their interconnectedness. The circular diagram above shows the relationship more accurately.

In both shape and function, this diagram is reminiscent, not surprisingly, of the four-fold brain, in which the successive layers function interconnectedly, as just described above, each one corresponding to one of the four parts of the brain structure: the *security need* (infancy), correlating to the basal brain stem, the governor of heartbeat and breathing; second, the *belonging need*, correlating to childhood and the feeling brain (the limbic system); third, the *self-esteem need*, correlating to adolescence and the emergence of the thinking brain (the motor cortex); and finally, the *autonomy need*, correlating to adulthood and the further development of the thinking brain.

We thus see how beautifully the structure of the hierarchy reveals the interdependence of the needs: because each step up the ladder includes and protects the need below it, we see that autonomy is ultimately as necessary to security as security is to autonomy. In other words, you can't get to autonomy without self-esteem, which you can't get to without a good strong sense of belonging, which you can't get to without security, and conversely.

To the degree that we systematically practice the psycho-spiritual workout described in the four type chapters, we succeed in developing a healthy, functioning, human self, giving ourselves what we didn't get growing up. The deficits in our dependency needs are fulfilled and we gradually become autonomous, capable of defining and governing Our human self, and of setting boundaries and fulfilling whatever needs occur in our day-to-day living. This is a major achievement, and it feels very good indeed to know who You are, that is, to have the ability to define and govern Your self.

But we have come only about halfway on our journey of evolution. While much of our culture consciously or unconsciously demonstrates the belief that to have arrived at the autonomy stage of development is the paramount human goal, what has been accomplished by this ascent is the establishment of a healthy self, an ego—an essential achievement, but not the end goal. Beyond this stage, there are three needs that, if not fulfilled, leave us in a chronic condition of profound disappointment, cynicism, separateness, alienation, egomania, and despair. To prevent this, that human ego we have so painstakingly achieved must be transcended: to realize our true nature and ultimate sense of being, "this mortal must put on immortality" (1 Corinthians 15:53). We will describe the three needs, and then outline the Healing Process© for all these together. For the autonomous self to develop its spiritual potential, it must incorporate what Maslow identified as "Being" needs, that is, the needs of the enlightened self to spread its enlightenment on all those who want it.[11] Continuing to do the Process© beyond the stage of autonomy carries the human self, *over a period of time,* into a transcendental merging with spirit, of which the fruits are unlimited joy and power.

For example, years ago when I was teaching in a university, counseling in the evenings, making preparations to move back home to Philadelphia from the southwest, sending out applications for a job, and grieving the loss of a very close and beloved relative, all at once, I did the Process© four times a day, thirty to forty minutes each. The results were amazing. Though in actuality I had two hours less time per day, I got more done than I would have believed possible, and certainly more than I could have *without* the Process©— the exact opposite of what I had expected. The frequent meditations kept me centered in spirit—peaceful, positive, and creative—and able to handle the grief.

The result was an ability to stay clearly focused for much longer periods of time than ever before. I was efficient and constructive in my actions in proportion to the degree to which I was mentally and emotionally secure and confident—

qualities that I gave to My self in the meditations. Evidently, I concluded, the time it takes to complete any given activity is not a constant, but is a function of the degree of stress involved, that is, the time needed diminished in proportion to the degree of my serenity and increased in proportion to the degree of my anxiety. *This must be how great people get so much done,* I thought: they have found a way to move into the Higher Self, though they might not call it that, and from that elevated vantage point remain focused and serene.[12] The remainder of this chapter discusses each of these three Being needs in turn and identifies their symptoms, then guides you through the Process© by which each can be met.

Self-Actualization

The first of the three Being needs Maslow calls *Self-Actualization*.[13] (See Chart© p. 186). By this he means making real or actual in the world the human self that develops from the four dependency needs being met. When the self-actualization need is thwarted, your growth stops at autonomy, and consequently you develop feelings of futility, emptiness, meaninglessness, boredom, apathy, frustration, depression, and demotivation.

Hidden from Your self by denial, they generate a personality characterized by defenses of cynicism; overworking and socializing to blunt the inner sense of futility; compulsive spending; obsessive indulgence in self-improvement activities, such as working out (with or without a gym), having a personal trainer, getting massages, taking up hobbies, taking courses, going to spas, giving extravagant parties that benefit the body and the ego, but that are essentially meaningless.

Such compulsive activities can be used to justify one's existence, to repress the nagging feelings of boredom and apathy, and avoid confronting the sense that one's existence is meaningless, "full of sound and fury, signifying nothing."[14]

They are *behavioral defenses*: they block the journey into feelings, thereby preventing you from identifying your unmet need, the source of virtually all your troubles.

In contrast, fulfilling the self-actualization need results in *congruency*, meaning that the outer behavior is a true expression of the inner nature. This profoundly spiritual concept is expressed in a sonnet of Gerald Manley Hopkins:

> As kingfishers catch fire, dragonflies draw flames:
>   As tumbled over rim in roundy wells
>   Stones ring; like each tucked string tells, each hung bell's
> Bow swung finds tongue to fling out broad its name;
> Each mortal thing does one thing and the same:
>   Deals out that being indoors each one dwells;
>   Selves—goes itself; *myself* it speaks and spells,
> Crying *What I do is me: for that I came.*
>
> I say more: the just man justices;
>   Keeps grace: that keeps all his goings graces;
> Acts in God's eye what in God's eye he is—
>   Christ. For Christ plays in ten thousand places,
> Lovely in limbs, and lovely in eyes not his
>   To the Father through the features of men's faces.[15]

"Each mortal thing" does the same thing: expresses in its outward form and action the being that dwells within.

A more down-to-earth but nevertheless revealing example of self-actualization was related in one of my counseling courses by a professor of Italian descent. His mother was an outstanding cook. As a child Joe was accustomed to her cuisine and rather took it for granted; having little to compare it with, he regarded it as standard fare.

But when he went away to college and had his first encounter with institutional food, his eyes were opened, and after a few weekends spent at his house, so were the eyes—and palates—of his college buddies. So great, in fact,

The Freedom Healing Process as a Means to Transcendence

was their appreciation for his mother's culinary expertise that by the beginning of the second semester they had developed a system of booking reservations for a weekend at his home. Joe was impressed—and very popular.

However, full understanding of the phenomenon did not come to him until graduate school when he encountered Maslow's concept of self-actualization. It led, in his words, "to a revelation":

> I saw that for her, cooking wasn't just an accomplishment or hobby: it was *what she was*. She'd start Sunday dinner on Thursday, planning the menu for nutritional value, preferences of the guests, cost of ingredients, balance of color and texture of the various dishes and courses, time and order of preparation, presentation, and most important, the mixture and balance of flavors.
>
> In addition to her culinary expertise, she had a genius for artistic organization: all the elements—candlelight, flowers, fine china and silver, the correct *placement*, herself serving each guest butler style (with the help of my sisters!) so that all could eat at the same time and the food remain hot...All was coordinated and so perfectly done, the entire event was beyond mere gustatory delight—it was an aesthetic experience, like a Verdi opera or a Michelangelo painting.

Through cooking, she *actualized* Her *self*: she expressed outwardly "that being indoors dwells." A lover of beauty, order, taste, style, precision, and generosity, it was her delight to delight others.

The story makes clear that self-actualization isn't only a matter of the person's profession, which may or may not be an expression of his true self. The true Self, in contrast, is the Inner Self demonstrated and made visible—just as the dinner is an idea brought forth into reality. As Hopkins says, "*the just man justices*: acts out that being indoors each one dwells."

Another example, told in the Book of Genesis, is the story of Joseph, the youngest of the twelve sons of the patriarch Jacob, and his favorite. Joseph's advanced spiritual state was signified in late adolescence by a series of dreams, and was demonstrated by his ability to interpret them accurately. Despite his being the youngest, the dreams pictured him in the position of authority over all his brothers. But the manifestation of that position comes about gradually, through a series of severe misfortunes that bring him to the lowest of states: he is sold into slavery by his jealous brothers, taken to Egypt, made a servant to Pharaoh, falsely accused of sexual assault by Pharaoh's wife, and put in prison—how the mighty is fallen!

Undaunted by this series of seeming disasters, he holds firmly to his inner sense of authority and demonstrates it by interpreting the dreams of his fellow inmates. Word of his remarkable talent comes to the attention of Pharaoh, whose dreams about seven lean and seven fat kine are troubling him mightily. So convincing is Joseph's interpretation—that there will be seven years of abundance followed by seven years of famine—that Pharaoh appoints him overseer of all his lands. How the fallen is mighty!

By always making the highest choice possible, that is, always actualizing his true Self, Joseph rises to a position second only to Pharaoh. When the famine he foretold comes about and his brothers come to Egypt to get grain, Joseph's interpretation of his youthful dream is realized: he is the authority to whom they apply. He is thus positioned to deal with them however he chooses.

His choice verifies his father's belief in him: instead of doing something horrible to them in retribution for their selling him into slavery, he uses the "law of retributive justice" in a higher way: "Fear not," he says when they discover his identity, "Now therefore be not grieved, nor angry with yourselves, that ye sold me hither: for God did send me before you to preserve life" (Gen. 45:5), or in other words, "You meant it for evil but God meant it for good." His experience demonstrates the concept that what we often experience to be bad or wrong is the pathway to our good. Imagine for a moment what it would take for you and me to achieve such a degree of conviction, determination, and complete trust that *whatever came our way* was God's will, meant for our good, and productive of good if we keep seeing it that way! Not all the tribulations *en route* to Joseph's exalted station were able to derail him from the conviction of his chosen course, and thereby "preserve life"—his own, his brothers, and even his enemies—which of course made them no longer enemies. *The just man justices, the spiritual man forgives.* Joseph's naturally righteous character actualizes in every situation, so that by acting according to his nature, he becomes God's agent in bringing good out of evil. His unfailing self-actualization to act what he is, not to allow His human self to be pulled off center by external events, thus prepares him for the sixth, and next, of Maslow's needs.

Self-Realization

Self-Realization is the recognition that this Inner Being, the Immortal Consciousness—the Self, Witness, Atma, Buddha, Christ—is one's true nature, rather than the human, mortal, transitory self of this lifetime that we commonly identify with. It is expressed most clearly in the Sanskrit phrase "thou art that" ("tat tvam asi")[16] that is, you, the named human being, are really that unnamed Spiritual Being, the Inner Knower and Guide, to be realized through the practice of turning inward, as in the traditional forms of meditation and the Freedom Healing Process©.

In such a state we experience our true identity as always the same, not subject to the mutability of the time-space continuum. Unlike our explicate, mutable, earthly condition, our implicate domain feeds us, like Joe's mother, joyously and without ceasing. Our needs are fully met all the time before we even recognize them to be needs, like our experience in the womb, only now we have conscious experience of it. Complete fulfillment means bliss and joy, a condition of non-cognitive beingness—"satchitananda" ("being, knowledge, bliss")—second only to Unification in uniqueness and wonder.

When the need for self-realization is not met, as is the case for most of us most of the time, we suffer from feelings of aloneness, disconnectedness, fragility, insufficiency, lack of fulfillment, a pervasive sadness or melancholy, and a sense of something essential missing that we can't quite put our finger on. (See "Being" Chart© on page i facing the Preface). These feelings generate such defenses as braggadocio, an attitude of superiority, and a pretense of happiness and satisfaction with one's life to cover up its futility and lack of meaning. Failing to heed or understand these signals, the person remains stuck at the level of Self-Actualization, typically feeling, *is this all there is?*

You can see that such defenses are common in our culture, an indicator that the vast majority of our population is still struggling with the four primary needs, despite the current interest in spirituality (not all of which is shallow or bogus). The statistics of my own caseload over the past twenty five years point in the same direction: during that period the most common complaints have been and still are anxiety and depression, both of which indicate a deficiency in security, the very first need.

We can therefore conclude that, since the remaining three dependency needs are also unmet, only an infinitesimal fraction of our population can have grown to the stage of self-realization, and only a handful even know what the word means. Without a spiritual awakening, the defenses at this level are self-reinforcing and therefore virtually impregnable. Offering to help or suggesting a change to someone

The Freedom Healing Process as a Means to Transcendence

thus afflicted is likely to be futile, because it arouses his defense of superiority. Since at this level of needs the Freedom Process© produces results more quickly than in the first four, his consequent resistance is doubly sad.

In his play *Saint Joan*, George Bernard Shaw creates a character who undergoes just such a transformation, an English priest who throughout the play has been the embodiment of the uncompassionate, unenlightened rabble lusting for Joan's destruction. But at the climax of the play, when his horrendous wish is fulfilled, the event proves much too much for him to handle. The atrocious sight of the flames engulfing Joan shatters his bloodthirsty mindset and rockets him into self-realization.

He later recounts this to the French bishop Cauchon, who had tried to save Joan, "It was not our Lord that redeemed me but a young woman whom I saw actually burned to death. It was dreadful: oh, most dreadful. But it saved me." Cauchon acknowledges the priest's transformation in an ironic question that demonstrates his already self-realized state: "Must then a Christ perish in torment in every age to save those who have no imagination?"[17]

The dramatic irony conveys a profound spiritual message: the priest's "sin"—his feral blood lust for the destruction of another human being—ironically brings about his salvation. While he meant it for evil, God meant it for good, a recurrent theme in theology and in our lives. The greater spiritual message, subtly delivered by Cauchon, is that few people "get it" without having some experience of it. If more of us were more able to "get it" in imagination, even second or third hand, how much less suffering there would be!

Likewise, another spiritual giant, one who in our time died for "those who have no imagination," articulated the principle underlying Shaw's words: "Unearned suffering is redemptive."[18] Through the realization of his Higher Self, Martin Luther King, Jr. brought forth the power to use his suffering instead of being destroyed by it, and therefore by spiritual means, like Joseph, generated societal and cultural changes in six short years that otherwise would have taken generations to achieve. Those around him knew he anticipated, and feared, being assassinated, but his self-realization gave him the power to stay the course.

We lesser folk may be encouraged by the example of those whose lives demonstrate that even partial, unconscious, or occasional self-realization brings forth good. The example of Princess Diana comes to mind. Her own suffering led her to identify with the suffering of others wherever she encountered it. Through that compassion and empathy, she awakened love even in the heart of strangers. A rare television picture, aired during the time of her funeral, showed the aborigines of Australia's outback, their heads hanging down and tears flowing freely, clearly heartbroken, grieving her death! How did they get the news?

Unification

The final need, and the ultimate stage of human development, is the need for *Unification*, meaning a state of complete fulfillment, bliss, joy, and of being one with the universe and everything in it, a condition of non-cognitive beingness, which the Hindus call "satchitananda" (being, knowledge, bliss). Those who have experienced it express it in various spiritual traditions. As the following examples show, Unification means the realization that:

> The Atman, or immanent eternal Self, is one with Brahman, the Absolute Principle of all existence; and the last end of every human being is to discover the fact for himself, to find out Who he really is. (While...God) "is present in the deepest and most central part of his own soul," He is also and at the same time one of those who, in the words of

Plotinus...sees all things, not in process of becoming, but in Being, and sees themselves in the other. Each being contains in itself the whole intelligible world. Therefore all is everywhere. Each is there All, and All is each. Man as he now is has ceased to be the All. But when he ceases to be an individual, he raises himself again and penetrates the whole world.[19]

The truth that is to be realized may be summarized simply as the Realization that no matter what is arising, no matter how many others are present, there is only one Being.[20]

All men are cells in the one divine organism, in the divine body.[21]

A derivative of this highest state of existence is the ability to participate in the consciousness of another being, to actively experience the truth that consciousness is one, "not contain'd between my hat and boots," (Whitman, "Song of Myself," st. 7, l. 133) and all things are imbued with it and participate in it, and it is immanent in all things.

Once you have had an experience of this sort, a veridical, if brief, incorporation into another's consciousness, there is no denying its authenticity. Just such an experience, involving of all things a snake, happened to me many years ago as I was on my way to a meeting in a school building. It was dusk, and the roof over the walkway added a bit more duskiness, making the thin brown elongated object on the pavement ahead of me appear to be a twig. But as I approached closer, it *moved*—indeed, it *wriggled*—evidence, I brilliantly thought, that it wasn't a twig, but must indeed be a SNAKE!

Despite my revulsion, the thought occurred to me that as it got darker and more people arrived, the snake, which indeed it was, stood a distinct chance of being trampled—a prospect decidedly worse than the revulsion; it galvanized me into action. Stepping around the little creature carefully, so as not to alarm it further (its vulnerability drawing me to it), I entered the building and began hunting rather urgently for something with which to move it off the pavement and into the safety of the grass (concerned though I was for it, I didn't yet have the courage just to *pick it up*).

When I returned with a piece of poster-board the snake was writhing frantically, searching for cover. Then, as I stood motionless, transfixed by its anguished survival dance, an amazing thing happened, quite difficult to describe and quite unlike anything I had ever experienced: I was caught up as by a mini-whirlwind into a frenzy, and *bodily experienced its panic* in "*my*" consciousness, or it could be said that *I was transposed into the snake's consciousness and was experiencing its fear—the feeling-experience that was happening to the snake was happening to me.* We were one in consciousness: "No matter how many others are present, there is only one Being." The moment passed, and with the poster-board I gently steered the agitated little creature to the grass, into which he wriggled happily away.

In contrast to such a fleeting experience of Unification, the mahatmas ("great souls") achieve this state continuously; they experience oneness with all life all the time. An example is the amazing story told about Lahiri Mahasaya, an Indian saint of the nineteenth century who was reputed to have attained universal consciousness. As Paramahansa Yogananda tells it:

> The master's omnipresence was demonstrated one day before a group of disciples who were listening to his exposition of the Bhagavad-Gita. As he was explaining the meaning of Kutastha Chaitanya or the Christ Consciousness in all vibratory creation, Lahiri Mahasaya suddenly gasped and cried out: "I am drowning in the bodies of the

many souls off the coast of Japan!"[22] The next morning the *chelas* read a cabled newspaper account of the deaths of a number of persons whose ship had foundered the preceding day near Japan.

Then there is the following wonderful illustration from the *Chandogya Upanishad*. A young man asks his father to impart to him "that knowledge, knowing which we know all." After stating it abstractly the father presents it through an exercise:

> "Pray, sir," said the son, "tell me more."
> "Be it so, my child," the father replied; and he said, "Place this salt in water, and come to me tomorrow morning."
> The son did as he was told.
> Next morning the father said, "Bring me the salt which you put in the water."
> The son looked for it, but could not find it, for the salt, of course, had dissolved.
> The father said: "Taste some of the water from the surface of the vessel. How is it?"
> "Salty."
> "Taste some from the middle. How is it?"
> "Salty."
> "Taste it from the bottom. How is it?"
> "Salty."
> The father said, "Throw the water away and then come back to me again."
> The son did so; but the salt was not lost, for salt exists forever.
> Then the father said, "Here likewise in this body of yours, my son, you do not perceive the True; but there, in fact, it is. In that which is the subtle essence, all that exists has its self. That is the True, that is the Self, and thou, Svetaketu, art That."[23]

Here is a final example, this one from a Hindu holy man still in the body, Sri Satya Sai Baba, believed by his devotees to be an avatar, an incarnation. He says lovingly to all:

> "I am you, you are I. There is no distinction. That which appears so is the delusion. You are waves, I am the ocean. Know this and be free, be divine."[24]

In the East, this concept of Unification, if not universally held, is at least a familiar one. But since it is not so widespread in our culture, some examples closer to home may be helpful. The following quotations, all from English and American poetry of the last three centuries, express the experience of Unification in various authentic and magnificent ways:

> All are but parts of one stupendous whole
> Whose body Nature is, and God the soul;
> That, chang'd thro all, and yet in all the same,
> Great in the earth, as in th' aetherial frame,
> Lives thro' all life, extends thro all extent,
> Spreads undivided, operates unspent,
> Breathes in our soul, informs our mortal part
> As full, as perfect, in a hair as heart...
>
> Alexander Pope, "Essay on Man," Epistle I, ll. 267-274

> And I have felt
> A presence that disturbs me with the joy
> Of elevated thoughts; a sense sublime
> Of something far more deeply interfused,
> Whose dwelling is the light of setting suns,
> And the round ocean and the living air,
> And the blue sky, and in the mind of man:
> A motion and a spirit, that impels
> All thinking things, all objects of all thought,
> And rolls through all things.
>
> William Wordsworth, "Lines composed above Tintern Abbey," ll. 93-102

> Why should I wish to see God better than this day?
> I see something of God each hour of the twenty-four,
>   and each moment then,
> In the faces of men and women I see God, and in my
>   own face in the glass,
> I find letters from God dropt in the street, and every
>   one is sign'd by God's name,
> And I leave them where they are, for I know that
>   wheresoe'er I go,
> Others will punctually come for ever and ever.
>
> Walt Whitman, "Song of Myself," ll. 1283-1289

These three quotations, from the early eighteenth, early nineteenth, and late nineteenth centuries, products of poets representing widely different traditions, express very similar concepts of divinity. First, rather than a personage, they all see "God" as a force that directs and informs:

> "A motion and a spirit, that impels all thinking things;"

> "All are but parts of one stupendous whole
> Whose body Nature is, and God the soul;"

> "Lives through all life, extends thro' all extent…"

Second, they all see God as immanent, the essential substance ("soul") of all things:

> "Whose dwelling is the light of setting suns,
> And the round ocean and the living air,
> And the blue sky, and in the mind of man."

> "Spreads undivided, operates unspent,
> Breathes in our soul, informs our mortal part."

> "In the faces of men and women I see God,
> and in my own face in the glass."

All these quotations make divinity something very similar to energy, energy that is benevolent, informative, intentional, and nondiscriminatory. Pope's formulation—"spreads undivided, operates unspent"—uncannily parallels the first law of thermodynamics: "energy can be neither created nor destroyed," but it can change in form: "Breathes in our soul, informs our mortal part, As full, as perfect in a hair as heart." These three expressions of the nature of divinity are echoed in the concept presented here, that unification of consciousness is our ultimate need and our true nature.

There is corroboration of this unification of consciousness in the animal kingdom, which if the concept is valid, would have to be the case. Researchers continue to find examples of long-distance communication and coordination of activities among animals, such as ant and bee colonies; the communal navigation of geese and ducks; the occasional lost pet who travels an astonishing number of miles to his new home; the unified, compassionate activity of elephants in caring for the young or hurt members of the herd, *etc.* For example, an animal television station showed a mother elephant and two of her friends figuring out the cooperative engineering needed to dig her squealing baby out of a mud hole, using only the equipment their bodies provided. Such examples clearly support the concept of the unification and interpenetration of consciousness throughout the universe.

When the unification need is deficient we experience characteristic suffering. The mindset of such a person, if it were put into words, would sound like the following: "I am the only thing that matters…I am a law unto myself…Other people and the rest of the creation don't matter…I have no interest in connecting with anything outside myself, nor any compassion for others…I can take care of my family myself…I don't owe anybody anything…I had to struggle, why should I help them?" *etc., etc.*

These phrases are all expressions of what the Greeks called "hubris"—a frame of mind consisting of such defenses as egomania, machismo, isolation, pride, and a sense of one's human self as the authority, ultimately superior and exclusionary to the rest of the universe. The attitude is summed up in the satanic phrase "Non serviam" ("I will not serve"),[25] the exact opposite of the self-realized person who achieves unification and thus serves everybody.

Hidden by these defenses are the feelings that cause them: alienation, fragmentation, incompleteness, uselessness, bitterness, and despair. All these are symptoms of a radical disconnect, of an absolute deficit in the need to merge individual consciousness with universal consciousness, thus realizing our oneness with all life—at least *a little bit some of the time*.

Actually, the phrase "individual consciousness" is an oxymoron, while "consciousness" is the name we give to specific forms of energy such as air, light, music, and love; it is limitless, not susceptible to boundaries, and "present everywhere at the same time all the time."[26] It cannot be individuated or divided; it is like Pope's description of God quoted above: "spreads undivided, operates unspent." (*How did he know that*? Modern physics has only just in the last century come to that awareness!). In contrast, the pull of hubris toward separation, exclusion, disconnection, and constriction reveals its core to be hatred and its energy negative, the opposite of the loving and compassionate energy that unifies, includes, connects, and expands.

Examples of hubris, alarmingly, abound in our culture: a moment's reflection brings to mind the many ways in which we collectively support egotism, machismo, pride, *etc*.; of many instances of groups that exclude other groups; of businesses that disrespect and alienate consumers; of corporations that disregard public welfare, not to mention the welfare of their own employees; of public and private disregard and abuse of animals and nature (upon both of which human survival depends); of religious or sectarian or ideological groups that, while supporting their cause, thoughtlessly, and no doubt sometimes willfully, damage another organization or nation and even the world altogether.

The prevailing ethic seems to be that what you get is at my expense, so I'd better hurry up and get all I can before you do, thus reinforcing the idea that there isn't enough for everybody and that each one of us is a separate entity "entire of itself."[27] This belief constricts, separates, and excludes, blocking us from achieving or even seeking unification, and making us actually afraid of it, as if we feel it would steal our identity.

The belief, if held to long enough and consistently enough, eventually brings about the very condition we fear and try to prevent. Only by reversing the belief and acting on its opposite, that "all are parts of one stupendous whole" and recognizing that the substance of all "spreads undivided, operates unspent," can we surmount our separatist, elitist, inhumane, and grossly unequal culture.

In terms of practising spiritually, our culture—indeed, our world—has "miles to go" before it learns that our only true safety lies in cultivating the three *Needs of Being*.

First: each of us must find our particular gift and purpose, and *actualize* it, that is, make it real and usable to the benefit of others as well as ourselves.

Second: each of us must *realize*—that is, *make real*—to ourselves and others our true identity as a spiritual being, and learn how to bring that into our daily living and interaction, both with those we love and *especially* with those we hate. In the realm of the spirit, there is no hate.

Third: arriving at the level of *unification* is an event rarely achieved nowadays, especially given the relative lack of true spirituality, individually and collectively, that characterizes our culture. There are maybe a handful of men and women alive today—predominantly in the Orient—who have reached this level and live it most or some of the time. What we will get from them, if we are regular in doing our

Process©, is the ability to give to the world what it so desperately needs—Self- Actualization, Self-Realization, and Unification—*both in the individual, the community, the nation, and the world.*

From this viewpoint of *unification*, what each one of us can do is to *give*: give in consciousness to those in need, not so much in material content, but in emotional and spiritual content; send out silent messages to those in distress and those in confusion, send messages of peace and harmony from your consciousness to theirs. *Talk to them in consciousness.* Do it daily, throughout your day; repetition is the key to achieving your purpose (so what you're broadcasting in consciousness must be positive, never negative). We need, *now,* to become givers rather than takers, and not stop until we have reached some degree of functioning at the level of the three *needs of being,* a trinity that is the product and hallmark of *unification of consciousness.*

In the preceding troubled century there are several notable examples of people who have achieved universal consciousness or some degree of it. In addition to certain holy men from various centuries whose actions and effect on humanity testify to their achievement of unity as a continuous state—in particular, Krishna, Buddha, Jesus, Mohammed, Ramakrishna, Muktananda, Paramahansa Yogananda, and Sri Satya Sai Baba—there are at least two lay people and one cleric of the preceding century who appear by their accomplishments to have achieved unification most of the time, if not continuously: Mahatma Gandhi, Nelson Mandela, and Bishop Tutu.

To achieve the liberation of his country by totally nonviolent means, to be unwilling to harm even those who had harmed him and his country by subjugating its people, ravaging its natural beauty, and exploiting its wealth for their own benefit, are astonishing, monumental achievements, and place Gandhi at a level of spiritual evolution and achievement beyond the ken of almost all the rest of us.

His life demonstrates a consciousness that saw "Each is...All, and All is each. Man as he now is has ceased to be the All. But when his ceases to be an individual, he raises himself again and penetrates the whole world."[28] Gandhi himself might have said these powerful lines. Through identification with his true Self and his sense of unity with all life, he achieved a state of love and harmony, principles that governed his behavior toward all, even his "enemies."

Declining the path of antagonism and using the principle of non-violence to "make the injustice visible," (his phrase) he brought about the double miracle of attaining India's independence peacefully while retaining the respect and friendship of the British Empire. He made his country's enemy its friend, the greatest kind of victory. (Even as I write this, Sunday morning, August 11/02, part of my mind wanders to the debate on television about whether or not to "take out" Saddam Hussein, and I shudder at the hubris of our country and the increase to the national karma it creates for us, and indeed, for the rest of the world).

An equally impressive example of unification, if not more so, is Nelson Mandela. To start with, the fact that he survived twenty-seven years in prison—a *South African* prison!—and survived *mens sana in corpore sano*, is so beyond the bounds of what seems possible to us mere mortals that we are inclined to see it as "miraculous" without giving that word any very specific meaning. But beyond that are two more accomplishments, both just as remarkable.

The first is his non-violent and successful revolution, which restored the government of his county to its native people and legally abolished apartheid.

The second accomplishment is his way of dealing with the former government that put his country through such hell. Co-fathered by Bishop Desmond Tutu, also unified in consciousness, the program may well be unique in all of history. Called "Truth and Reconciliation," the Program eschews any form of retaliation toward or punishment of any members of the former government. Instead, it operates

The Freedom Healing Process as a Means to Transcendence

to heal rather than punish, to save rather than condemn, to do for his "enemies" (he would probably not call them that) what they could never have conceived of doing for Mandela and his people.

What he did was to turn away from the human self, which is aggressive, selfish, and retaliatory, to the inner Self that loves peace and reconciliation. From this inner place the Program was born. It offers to members of the former government the opportunity to confess openly the acts of criminality and violence they perpetrated upon the population they oppressed. Participation is voluntary; no one is compelled to attend.

Those who show up are brought by their own conscience rather than by outside force. No punishment follows; repentance and a transformation in attitude and value system are the goal and the reward. It was evidently not enough for Mandela simply to regain his own and his country's freedom and start the healing for his own people: he must, in addition, have seen that he and his people could not be completely healed unless their adversary was also. Only by such a policy could there be any hope of achieving a unified and healthy state. Mandela, like Joseph, evolved through suffering to such a high degree of faith in spirit that he has become an alchemist: he has turned evil into good.

The policies and protocols of this venture reveal several underlying spiritual principles that flow from unified consciousness:

1. Coercion creates resistance and blocks the flow of intelligence and communication, and is therefore ultimately self defeating.

2. Refusal to engage in retribution opens the flow of energy and information, thereby intercepting the negative karmic patterns and generating positive karma.

3. Compassion and forgiveness keep the healing energy flowing and communicating, leading to unification of consciousness.

The results so far, while not perfect, are considerable: significant healing for a majority of the country and transformation for those who have chosen to confess. Not only does this have positive effects on them, it also makes them no longer inimical (or at least not *so* inimical) to Mandela and his government. As we saw with Gandhi, the best and greatest victory over an enemy is to make him a friend. However, some members of the ANC, not so highly evolved, disagree with the "Truth and Reconciliation" agenda and want to punish their former oppressors in the customary way of prosecution and imprisonment.

Nevertheless, Mandela and Tutu's program continues, the positive results so far achieved being testimony to *their unification of consciousness*. To see a national leader formulating official state policy according to *spiritual* principles, as opposed to expediency, self-interest, fundamentalism, religion, or fanaticism, is in itself astonishing, and an inspiring model for the evolution of human kind. Surely our espousal of armed force both toward certain of our own citizens and also toward those of other countries, such as Viet Nam and Korea, and now Iraq, have done much damage, both physical, emotional, and spiritual, with little to no visible good.

While few of us will be able to achieve fulfillment of these three Being needs, much benefit can come from working toward them. They are *"desiderata"*—"things to be desired,"—and a polestar by which to measure our progress and guide our lives. "We claim spiritual progress rather than spiritual perfection."[29] Making even small gains in meeting these needs can have powerful effects on our lives and relationships, and can be brought about by the same Healing

Process© you have learned to use for the four dependency needs. A review of the Process© follows.

The "Freedom Healing Process" For the Three Spiritual Needs

If you've done the "Freedom Healing Process©" after each chapter and used it frequently, it will by now be very familiar to you. Just to refresh you memory, here's a rerun.

I. Accessing Feelings: Pounding

This process is done by shaking or pounding, either with your fists, tennis racket, or bat, to loosen the feelings and start releasing them. As you do this, you may find some uncomfortable feelings surfacing, feelings you haven't felt before. The pain of the feelings at this level is very intense: you may feel that your existence is meaningless, that despite whatever human connections you've made, you are still alone, alienated, fragile, empty, despairing, lacking something you don't have a name for, can't even describe, and don't know how to get. Sometimes you wonder if you'll get it before you die! The solution is to do your breathing repeatedly, followed by more pounding and then pound again. Repeat until the pain—anger, frustration, loneliness, resentment—diminishes and you feel free and relaxed.

If the condition you are working on doesn't improve right away, remember you don't have to achieve it in one Process©. Nor should that even be a goal. Every waking minute we are subject to the ebb and flow of feelings, only some of which are pleasant. The rest, however, are just as valuable, maybe more so, since they are our signal of needs unmet, clamoring incessantly for fulfillment like baby birds chirping for food. And fed we must be, emotionally and spiritually, all day long. Hence the value in making the Process© an integral part of whatever activities you undertake throughout your day. The more often and the more thoroughly you do the Process© the sooner you will feel better.

II. Experiencing and Releasing Feelings: Breathing

This activity will be most effective if done for at least eight to ten minutes, or as long as You can direct Your self to keep it going. Remember how the breathing goes? Pull your abdominal muscles in toward your spine as you blow out through your mouth, then expand your abdomen as you breathe in through your nose. Let Your self experience the soothing rhythm of your body as it expands and contracts. You will gradually feel unified with that energy, merged into its flow, not engaged in cognitive reflection, just *being, experiencing,* much as you floated and rocked in the "oceanic bliss" of the womb, only this time you're aware of it. It's a wonderful feeling—comforting, soothing, an enriching sense of completeness, of needing nothing.

III. Meeting the Need: Infilling and Self-nurturing

Having released your painful feelings and cleared your mind of its obsessive chatter by the deep breathing, Your self will be able to experience the resulting state of profound peace and to focus, undistracted, on the messages entering Your consciousness from You as Higher Self. You can, of course, construct your Declarations your self according to your immediate need, always remembering to state what you need in the present tense, the only time frame in which you can get it. Examples follow on the next page in case you need a starter.

For these three Being needs, in addition to the method of talking to Your self, it's useful to add picturing Your self. To do this, stay in your Spiritual Self and picture Your human self as you wish it to be, focusing on one characteristic or quality at a time. You have complete jurisdiction in working on Your self, adjusting your message to whatever need of Your self is most deficient.

Following are some sample Declarations that you can arrange according to your need. At this stage in the Freedom Healing Process© they often emerge spontaneously, from a seemingly infinite inner space. The affirmations that come to you then will be clear and whole and perfect for the place you are in at that moment.

1. Self-Actualization

After five to ten minutes of deep breathing, repeat to Your human self any one of the following Declarations at least twenty times, and more if you want. Because the repetition impresses the content of the Declaration into the feeling brain, it's generally more effective to do one Declaration repeatedly and exclusively in any given meditation before going on to another. The goal is for the feeling brain to be filled with positive, healthful, and benevolent material because it dictates most of our behavior.

Picture Your self relating to people and situations, especially troublesome ones, with peace, acceptance, confidence, and compassion, and talk to Your self *ONLY* in supportive and loving ways. You may say the following declarations aloud or silently, or make up your own according to your present need, remembering that this segment deals with the need for self-actualization:

"What You do is what You are: Your true Self shines forth in all You do."

"You are now expressing Your truth, reality, worth, self, in the world."

Learning to Fulfill the Needs of Your Self

"Your actions express outwardly Your Inner Self."

"What You are is loving, peaceful, competent; You demonstrate outwardly what You are inwardly. You are congruent." (Remember to use the word "You," not "I," so that You are identified with Spirit).

Then picture Your self demonstrating Your inner nature, in all its actions exhibiting a sense of safety, acceptance, love, worthiness, and independence. See Your self relating to people and situations, especially troublesome ones, with confidence and compassion, and talk to Your self in supportive ways. Remember, you don't have to believe it to say it (if you already believed it you wouldn't be reading this); rather, you have to *say* it, and *keep* saying it, to believe it!

2. Self-Realization

This need is the realization that Your true self is a spiritual entity, not a human one, a very difficult concept to grasp. The following Declarations will help.

Say to Your human self:

"I AM what You really are: wherever You are, I AM."

"I-AS-Spirit support and fulfill you, My (human) self."

"I AM what you have been seeking all your human life. I AM the substance of all your needs."

"When you realize who You are, you will know who I really AM."

"When you realize who I AM, you will know who You really are."

"You are not what you think you are; You are what I think You are—and I think You are one with Me."

"I am your real Self."

Picture being on a balcony looking down at Your human self, and observe what it is thinking, feeling, and doing. Then move into that human self, so that You are integrating Your self into it and it into You. Observe Your self breathing the air You give it: You-as-spirit are infilling, shaping, and nourishing it, becoming one with it. You as a spiritual being are breathing the breath of life into Your human self, daily, minute by minute. Be still, and experience the amazing power that enters when you make this transition.

You are shifting into a vantage point 180 degrees opposite to Your usual one, the one in which you identify with your body and look from it to Spirit; instead, you now *look from Spirit to human*. It is generally about at this point in the Process© that Your human self (ego) begins to experience how impotent and separate and disconnected and alone it feels when it tries to be the center. In contrast, the more often You remember to speak to Your self from You-as-Spirit, the happier and more free Your self will feel, and the more "good works" You can do.

3. Unification

Speak from your Spiritual self to Your human self:

"You have no boundaries, are not limited by time or space."

"You are the same substance as the tree, the flower, the cat."

"You are not limited by Your body, but are one with all integrated beings everywhere."

"Your consciousness is not yours, does not start or stop at the physical boundaries of your brain; it flows into and through You, with all other living things, and all things are living."

Learning to Fulfill the Needs of Your Self

Picture Your self as light, flowing out into the immediate space which surrounds You, then into Your whole house, to all Your family, then outside into Your neighborhood, and gradually carry this vision as far as You can, to Your city, state, country, world, universe. See that You are an expression and a container of energy, like everything else. Or picture a city park, filled with people, and see rays of light emerging from a central point deep in the earth and connecting to each person, including Your self. Be conscious of the energy within you flowing to each one, and theirs to You. Let its message of joy and power fill You, and notice how good—indeed, *ecstatic*—you feel.

Or play Your favorite music (for this purpose, non-verbal jazz or classical is best) and experience Your self merging into it; feel the tingling as it radiates from Your arms and legs through your entire body, and becomes part of You—or, more to the point, you become part of it. One little segment of the universal creating and healing process has made its way through you, constantly creating, holding for a brief moment, then dissolving...and then repeating that pattern without ceasing.

Now that You have consciously practised the Creating and Healing Process© and have learned how to awaken it whenever you want to work it, You have discovered that you too are a creator, and in fact, a creator every minute of Your life. The remaining question then is, how and what are You creating? Because if you are creating unconsciously, whatever troubled stuff is still in You will take hold and the product You create will be impaired to some extent, and You will continue to cause and receive trouble to that same extent.

If, however, you are creating consciously, as You have learned from the Process© in this book, Your product will be positive and enlightening. Enjoy the sense of wholeness: the complete absence of any feeling of separateness, plus the experience of merging, connectedness, and oneness filling You. You are in a place of total peace, not simply the absence of discord, but a powerful, continuously intensifying and expanding inner state of harmony, safety, joy, and bliss. T. S. Eliot describes it as "a grace of sense, a white light still and moving/ *Erhebung* ("rising") without motion."[30]

This is *unification of consciousness*—that is, unification of the individual self with the Universal Self, or, as Emerson named it, the "Oversoul." Even a tiny taste will make You seek it again and again, and with each experience You will want to go more and more deeply into that feeling of oneness as You return to your original source, like a baby returning to the safety and comfort of the womb. The more often You do the Process© and the longer You work in each session, the better You will feel, the more You will enjoy the beauty of life and nature, the more help You will be to those you love, and with enough practise You will be able to love even the ones You never thought You could.

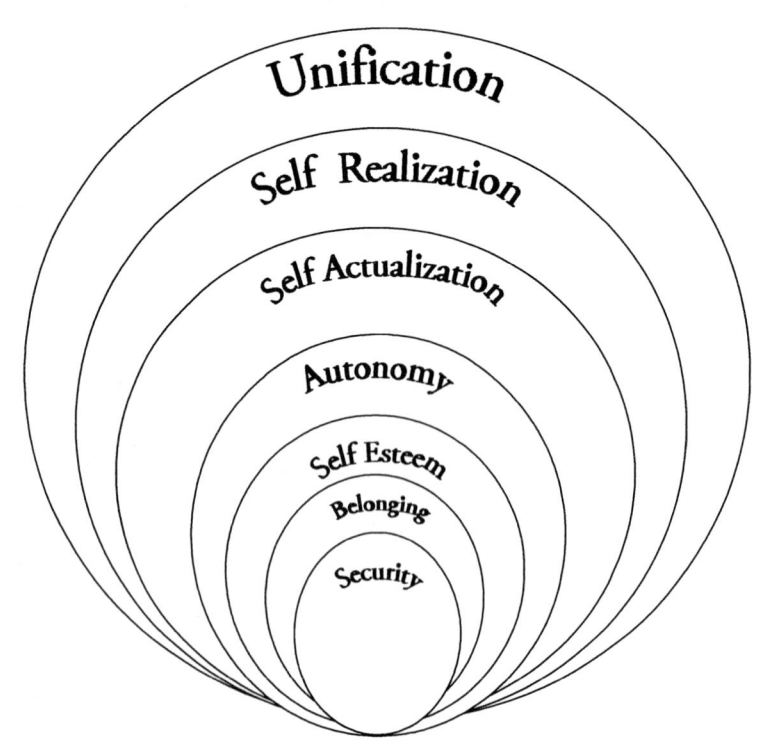

Unification
Self Realization
Self Actualization
Autonomy
Self Esteem
Belonging
Security

You have completed, for now, your journey of maturation, from the stage of needing to get, to the stage of needing to give. We can depict this by expanding the diagram of the dependency needs to include the three Being needs, as shown above.

The complete human being pictured this way is reminiscent of the concept popular in the Middle Ages, that the human being is a microcosm containing all the elements of the macrocosm, in which each part is essential to the whole and the whole to each part. As with the Universe, so with each of its elements, including the human being: we see that we can't get to *unification* without achieving *self-realization*, to *self-realization* without achieving *self-actualization*, to *self-actualization* without achieving *autonomy*, and so on down to *security*. We also see that you can't maintain *security* without having a sense of *belonging*, nor maintain *belonging* without *self-esteem*, and so on up to *unification*, which embraces and encloses all the preceding steps.

So while achieving *unification* depends ultimately on fulfilling all the needs that come before it, each of the needs below *unification* can't remain whole without it. The eighteenth century poet William Blake expressed a similar principle in the following brief poem:

> To see a world in a grain of sand
> And a heaven in a wildflower
> Hold infinity in the palm of your hand
> And eternity in an hour.[31]

By now you can see that beyond the psychological healing and evolution it generates, the Freedom Process©, practiced sufficiently, awakens and advances spiritual evolution as well, through the three stages just described. It is thus a true meditative process, with elements deriving from the world's major spiritual paths, such as Hinduism, Buddhism, Zen, and contemplative Christianity.

The Freedom Healing Process as a Means to Transcendence

In its own way, the Healing Process© will do for you, as you may have already discovered, what those profound systems have done for so many. First, it takes away the pain and frustration of trying to live successfully when one or more of your basic needs isn't met. Second, it confers upon those who practice it consistently the fruits of the spirit: serenity and bliss within, and limitless love and good will without. Such a person is eventually so unified with Spirit that self is eclipsed and love radiates from him as the sun radiates light—to everyone, all the time.

The person to whom this book is dedicated was—is—such a one. For someone who has not yet encountered a *guru*, or been around someone who has, the general reaction is how dull such a person would be—imagine, no personality! But the contrary is the truth. Somebody like Gandhi, Martin Luther King, Jr., or Mandela, is magnetically appealing, attracting those still working through their dependency needs and transforming them, not by meeting their needs personally and thereby perpetuating their dependency, but by surrounding them with love and "beholding the Christ in them," for "there in fact it is," inspiring them to undertake their own journey of transformation into Spirit.

The following chapter is an appendix: it presents and discusses five other systems each of which has significant correlations to the Freedom Healing Process©.

VIII

Discoveries & Conclusions

Appendix I

Codependency

Several years after I had been working with the Chart© on the four needs, I began to see parallels with several other major conceptual systems. The first discovery was the correlation between the contents of the Chart© and codependency: each of the four needs, when unmet, causes one of the four types of codependency, a perception that led to a process for healing it. The second discovery was the parallel between the content, functioning, and structure of the Chart© and the content, functioning, and structure of the brain. Third was the correlation between the mental and behavioral defenses of the Chart© and various diagnoses of the "Diagnostic and Statistical Manual."© The fourth similarity is the Chakras, in both structure and function, and the fifth,

"From Chaos to Harmony," was inspired by my friend and editor Ed Pratowski. This chapter discusses each of these five systems in relation to the Chart©.

A. Codependency and Needs

Before exploring the connection between the Chart© and codependency, it should be said that, despite a dramatic drop in public attention, codependency is still a very real, widespread, and painful disease.[1] You didn't cause it; you inherited it. It is Your *self,* not *You,* that is codependent, and only You can heal it. You are, essentially, *consciousness,* that is, a *spiritual* being; Your *self* is a *human* being, *codependent* variety. Understanding and developing the relationship between *You* and Your *self* is crucial to your recovery and central to the Freedom Healing Process©.

Codependency is caused by unmet needs. A "need" is something without which we get sick or die: just as our bodies need vitamins, proper nutrition, sunshine, *etc.*, to thrive, our minds and hearts need love, protection, security, to thrive. When these needs are not sufficiently met in childhood, they generate painful feelings which run our lives no matter what our chronological age.[2] If at thirty, fifty, or seventy, you are still needy and still (unconsciously) expect your needs to be met by other people, you are codependent. You only *look* grown up. Your feelings, thoughts, and behavior are need-driven rather than chosen: you live from your unconscious rather than from your conscious mind.

Trying to get your needs met from others keeps you emotionally a child, a victim. However, *met they must be:* they are not whims or luxuries, but necessities. The question then is, having grown up with a needs deficit, how do you, now supposed to be an adult, meet them in a way that is healthful, one that instead of fostering dependency and neediness fosters independence and self-governance? That is, how to we deal with codependency?

One answer lies in the Freedom Healing Process©. Initially it consisted of a dimly outlined shape that, early in my practice, I detected in the flow of my client's process—if I managed to stay out of its way. Its outlines got clearer the more I tracked it, until I was able to describe the pattern as follows: the client begins by (1) *narrating* a troublesome event or situation but doesn't mention the feelings it stirred up in him. His narration generally hides his feelings but reveals his (2) *thinking*, which shows cognitive patterns that are unclear, irrational, and defensive. His cognitive functioning is other-directed, analytic, critical, and interpretive, rather than inner-directed, expressive, and insightful; it moves his focus from *himself* to the *other*—who is in his mind always the problem. *When the group's or therapist's empathic response makes it safe for him to bring his feelings to the surface and experience and release them, his thinking and perception become clear, focused, rational, and about himself rather than the other person.*

Once his mind has cleared, it is open to the direction of the Process©, which next moves to the consideration of *behavior change*. This is often voiced by the client as a question: "What could I do different?" He then proceeds like Zeke did to explore how he could have handled the situation better, and how he could use this Process© in the future.

Discernible in this sequence are three distinct stages: (1) the release of feelings *(affective)* which (2) clears the thinking *(cognitive)* which leads to (3) behavior change *(behavioral)*, or ACB for short. In graphic form, the shape of the Process© looks like the diagram on the following page.

The client starts confused and distressed and dependent, and ends relieved and clear, having experienced a mood change, gained some self-knowledge and some choice over his behavior.

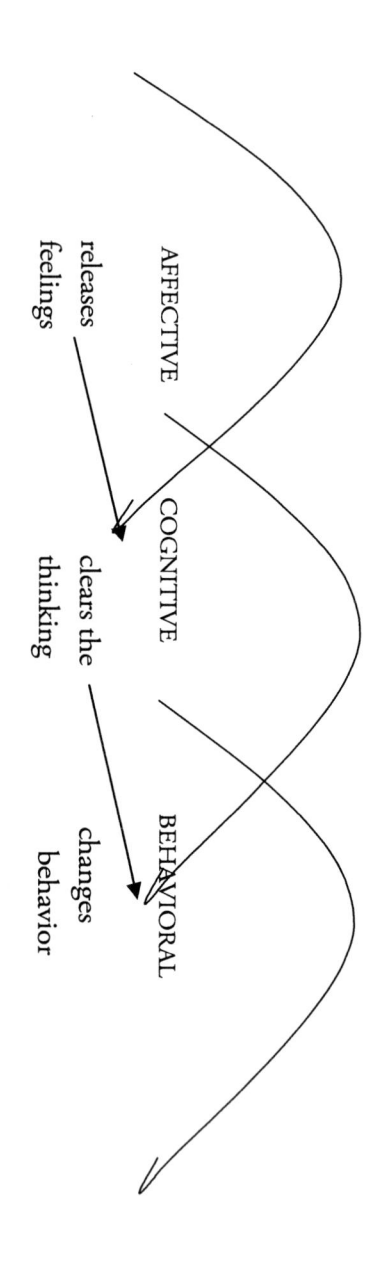

AFFECTIVE
releases feelings

COGNITIVE
clears the thinking

BEHAVIORAL
changes behavior

From these observations, I drew three conclusions about what I started to call the "Freedom Healing Process©." It originates within us, is self-directed, and flows from our center to our circumference. It thus exemplifies the universal creative process, which everything that creates or is created follows: it is generated in the (to us) invisible world of spirit (energy, virtual reality), and emerges into visible reality—from implicate to explicate, unformed to formed, intangible to tangible.

There are innumerable examples of this universal pattern: childbirth ("out of the nowhere into here"), thunderstorms, music, poetry, clothing, business deals, wars, murders, *etc.*, it could go on forever, the good and the bad together. An example that never fails to thrill me is when, while driving to New York, I've been looking and looking, straight ahead into the wild blue yonder to see the miracle...and then suddenly, as I'm approaching the Newark Airport, *there it is*, a tiny silver sliver emerging from the sky behind it, like a baby coming though the birth canal, growing as I watch, into a huge, sleek airplane! There was *nothing*, then suddenly there is *something*. Out of the implicate, into the explicate!

When you practice the "Freedom Healing Process©" you will experience this sequence. The Process© is the reverse of the pathological process of codependency, which as we have just seen, focuses on the outer and the other, thus avoiding the inner and the self—the only place true satisfaction can be found.

While the client experienced this process from inner to outer, I as therapist discovered that it worked equally well in reverse, from outer to inner: the visible, cognitive, external behavior and words of the client told me the painful thoughts and feelings that lay beneath and generated them, and at the deepest inner level, the unmet needs which caused the painful feelings and set the whole sequence in motion.

So the way I read the ACB Chart© was the reverse of the client's process, giving me a model by which to help my clients heal. "As within, so without," took on a new meaning, while "as without, so within" seemed equally significant: at the surface level, the codependent exhibits disturbed behavior and thinking, defenses that both hide and reveal the painful feelings that indicate unmet needs and therefore provide the entry to recovery.

Soon after I began practicing this model, an amazing experience occurred, which brought all these elements together and became the first step in the "Freedom Healing Process©" (and, in addition to various other uses, turned out to be a method of healing codependency). The experience arose from two totally unconnected events.

First, I had recently discovered Abraham Maslow's concept that behavior is motivated by needs, which seemed to me indisputable, and which became the core concept of my counseling.[3] Second, in the recovery groups I was running in a Salvation Army Alcoholism Recovery Program, the men repeated the same stories, in the same flat tonality, over and over. For a while I was unable to make any sense of this, or to see any benefit coming from it. The stories kept running around in my head like squirrels and I kept chasing them, scrabbling for an explanation.

Then, just as I arrived home one evening, without any warning, it *happened:* Maslow's needs concept and the men's stories suddenly converged, and with a sense of revelation and all the excitement of a fledgling counselor, I saw that the flatness of their narration was a *defense!—it protected them from having to deal with their severe underlying emotions.* (This was my first conscious encounter with defenses and how they function, and I was, as the men would have laconically said, *"mighty excited"*).

How, it finally occurred to me, *other than through a defensive style,* could a sixty-year old man recount, group after group, his father's almost daily beating of his mother, and in response to my horrified exclamation, "My God, Jed! How could you bear it?" reply with completely flat affect,

"Naw...Didn't bother me none. Got used to it." Defenses are *cognitive*, not *affective*, and though damaging and counterproductive in the long run, very comforting in the short run. What a lesson Jed taught me! However, my discovery, while extremely exciting to me, did nothing for them. I gradually saw that their defenses were unassailable and repelled all attempts to express appropriate emotion or discuss their universally heartbreaking individual stories more deeply in the group. The defenses were a bulwark against the fifty to sixty-year old pain that haunted their lives, preventing it from breaking out of their repression even the tiniest bit. Here are some examples (written in their vernacular):

> Denial: (completely flat affect):"He don't scare me none; I could beat him easy!" (*fear, bravado*).
>
> Self-justification (said with significant pride): "Always was a loner." (*Intense loneliness, fear of rejection*).
>
> Generalization: (said timidly): "It don't pay to be timid—you jes' get walked on." *(Sense of injustice; fear of self-assertion).*
>
> Excuse: "I tol' her she shoudn' feel hurt. I was jes jokin'."(*Guilt*).
>
> Rationalization: "I ain't never tol' him cause I didn' wanna' hurt his feelins'."(*Timidity, guilt*).

Suddenly, in the midst of my bafflement about the meaning of these phrases, a chart, detailed and complex, appeared in front of my eyes, in much the same way that the meaningless fragments in a kaleidoscope suddenly coalesce into a meaningful and beautiful pattern. It consisted of three columns. The column on the left listed Maslow's seven main needs, moving vertically from the bottom need to the top, each one in its own compartment, rather like an elevator. For each need, there were, in the column to its right, several words that defined the corresponding feeling when its need isn't met; and the third column, consisting of what I later learned were called "defenses"—ways of thinking and behavior that cover up painful feelings (col. 2) caused by unmet needs (col. 3).

I was, as you might imagine, more than astonished—I was *breathless*—from the numerous implications of this amazing appearance. Eager to capture as many of the phrases as I could, I grabbed a five-by-eight card and quickly jotted down one after another, careful to install each one in its designated place of arrival. As the words and phrases kept coming, I kept copying, trying to catch each one, and it gradually dawned on me, word by word and with mounting excitement, that the phrases, now fading more rapidly, were both *symptoms of the pain of unmet needs and also defenses against them*.

While I was astonished by the whole event—the way it just *appeared* and appeared *complete*, the precision with which all its elements fit together, the concept it presented—it was clear that its predominant significance was its diagnostic and therapeutic usefulness: it provides a direct line for the therapist from the client's surface *behavior* and *thought* patterns ("defenses") through his *feelings* to his inner *unmet needs*, the cause of both his pain and the key to his healing. The Chart© facing the deciation page is a replica, with more items added in all columns over the years.

Because the Chart© reveals the invisible (the unmet need) that underlies and causes the visible (feelings and defenses), it makes the *implicate* process *explicate*, adding a fourth component to the affective-cognitive-behavioral process described above: after you've released your feelings and cleared your thinking, you become aware of the unmet needs that are your inner guide in choosing your behavior. *When you are not conscious of your needs, your behavior will be dictated by your feelings,* which are quite capable of disregarding your values altogether and are not interested in editing. Feelings are completely amoral and unbounded.

But when needs *are* met, *behavior changes spontaneously and always for the better:* they become more compassionate and moral. "Bad" behavior is invariably a symptom of needs unmet to one extent or another, not of course an excuse to tolerate it, but rather a signal to get the need met. The result is that the *bad behavior will become good behavior.* As the four needs chapters amply demonstrate, *behavior cannot change for the better and stay changed without needs being met.*

This then is one of the most important elements of the Chart©: it shows which needs create which behaviors, both good and bad. For parents, teachers, doctors, day-care personnel, foster parents, *etc.*, this is exactly the concept and the "visual aid" needed, because the diagnostic process is right there in front of your eyes.

Several years later, as I was giving a lecture on the Chart©, it dramatically delivered another concept from its store of knowledge and amazed me again: it showed me the *cause of codependency.* It came about in the following way. In one of my evening groups I was listing and describing the defenses typical of the security need when suddenly, with a sense of revelation, I saw: "*Ah ha!*—It's the '*Clown*' type![4] All these defenses against insecurity *are the traits of the Clown type of codependency!*"

My next thought was even more exciting: what about the other three types—*did they match up with the other three needs?* One glance at the remaining levels of the Chart© gave me the answer—one by one, by gosh, they *did!* As I filled in the defenses for all four needs (Maslow's system), I saw that each one consisted of the characteristics of one of the codependent types (Satir's system). From this discovery I drew the following conclusions:

Discoveries & Conclusions

1. Each of the four types of codependency is caused by a deficit in one of the four needs.

2. Therefore, we can say that *codependency is caused by unmet needs,*

3. which means it can be healed by *meeting the needs.*

4. To meet the need, you have to know what your type of codependency is—which is precisely what the Chart© tells you.

This unsought convergence of these two systems, Maslow's needs concept and Satir's roles concept, an event of reciprocal validation, was and still is amazing to me. As I saw them connect, I experienced a sensation like the two parts of a seat belt clicking together, followed by a sense of completeness. The discovery of their connection provided a crucial concept and model for diagnosing, understanding, and healing codependency, consisting of the conclusions listed above.

By revealing the cause of codependency, this linking together of two separately developed systems made the Chart© even more useful.[5] It is immediately embraced by clients. Their first reaction is generally along the following lines: "That's *me*! That's *exactly* how I was as a kid!" And: "That's *right*, I was *totally insecure!*" The Chart© is also useful for diagnosticians, teachers, parents, spouses—any who want to understand themselves and others.

The key, then, to healing codependency (and almost everything else) is for you to meet the needs of Your self *from within.* The Freedom Healing Process© shows you how to do that. As long as you are codependently convinced that the core of the problem is that other people aren't taking proper care of you, your life will not work to its fullest. You will not be healed, happy, and free until you discover that you can incorporate security, acceptance, self-esteem, and autonomy from the external in direct proportion to how thoroughly You first fulfill *each one of these needs for Your self.* *It's an inside job*—and a daily, minute-by-minute job. You will draw to you from outside whatever the climate is inside you.

You can validate the truth of this metaphysical law from both angles: if you see Your self as acted upon rather than acting, the receptor rather than actor, you make Your self a victim. On the other hand, if You see Your self as the actor, the initiator, capable of meeting your needs from within, you can choose a more desirable result. If You are in charge of Your self, You can determine whether You get good or bad results in every area of your life: relationships, parenting, work, health, *etc.*

Therefore, whether you get *good* or *bad* depends on how aware you are. *What you think about, you bring about.* Whether you maintain a climate of sunshine and love and prosperity inside you, or you hold storms of fear, doubt, and anger within, you will draw the same to Your self: "For whosoever hath, to him shall be given, and he shall have more abundance: but whosoever hath not, from him shall be taken even that he hath." (Matt.13: 12)

The next section discusses the Freedom Healing Chart© in conjunction with the codependent (disease) cycle. The characteristic pattern is described in relation to the Chart©, followed by an explanation of how the Freedom Healing Process© intercepts the disease cycle and releases the codependent from his trap so that eventually he can achieve full recovery.

B. The Codependent Cycle and the Chart

Codependency qualifies as a disease because it has both definable symptoms and a predictable progression. There are three components in the cycle: needs, feelings, and defenses (both mental and behavioral), each of which generates the next.[6] As the four needs chapters remind us

Discoveries & Conclusions

again and again, when a particular need isn't met sufficiently, we suffer—and are motivated by that suffering to meet the need in whatever way we can. Unmet needs are thus our *inner guide to healing*: they signal us that we need emotional food. If we hear their signal and respond consistently, the toxic cycle is intercepted and codependency cannot develop.

However, if we ignore the signal, as is too often the case, the emotional distress triggers defenses—ways of thinking and acting (see any section three on the Chart©)—that repress the pain so that we are no longer conscious of it. The need therefore sets off another cycle. You can see, then, that codependency is not a disease that runs its course and ends of itself. On the contrary, it is self-perpetuating and chronic, characteristics typical also of chemical addiction.

The defenses warrant a closer look because *they are the disease*: thought and behavior patterns whose job is to hide any uncomfortable feelings and needs we encounter. Although in the moment defenses seem to help or even to be necessary, they are liars, telling us things are okay when they are not, or—more typically codependent—*not* okay when they *are*. In the long run they work against us: daydreaming (defense) can lose you a job; overworking (defense) can lose you a relationship. This is how most of us get by, without even noticing it: we live unconsciously in our defenses to prevent feeling the pain, as I learned so well from the men in my group at the Sally.

The result is that the pain accumulates bit by bit and becomes a permanent fixture in the unconscious (feeling brain), skewing and distorting how we see other people and the world in general. The more effective the defenses are, the more damage they do us. Until we find a way to release the pain, it remains repressed, encoded in the feeling brain (limbic system), which registers and stores emotionally charged memories and the behavior patterns created by them. If the defense goes off duty for even a second, the pain pops right up, and is a sure sign of codependency.

Defenses are thus a short-term gain, but a long-term pain. That's why some people you know are still complaining about something that happened ten years ago! Because we develop a tolerance to defenses (just as we do to alcohol and other drugs) their effectiveness is undependable. That is because we become habituated to the initial feeling of relief they provide, but sooner or later the defenses lose their potency and we therefore begin to feel the pain again. The defenses respond by strengthening proportionately, until from years of accumulation they harden and become a veritable suit of armor that other people cannot penetrate, and which they see as our personality, when in reality it is one of the types of codependency. We end up looking like steel when we're really butter inside.

Eventually, as the pattern of defenses *vs.* pain cycles over and over, the armor becomes too hard for any nurturance to get through. The consequence is that our needs never do get adequately met, leaving us susceptible to emotional distress that will become debilitating and chronic, and if not dealt with, susceptible also to physical illnesses and pain. What started as a temporary reaction or defense becomes a permanent condition; what started as protection becomes destruction. *To halt this toxic cycle the need must be met.*

The Chart© shows you how to intercept this cycle and start your healing process specifically for codependency. It identifies the type of codependency you have, the particular need that causes it, what is needed to heal it, and what stage comes next in your growth. Following is a description of how the Chart© works.

First, notice that it functions both vertically and horizontally. Second, when you read the Chart© from bottom to top, it lists the seven needs that define the stages of growth, beginning with the first four—security (infancy), belonging (childhood), self-esteem (adolescence), and autonomy (adulthood); then the three spiritual needs: *self-actualization, self-realization,* and *unification* (discussed at the end of chapter seven). When you read the Chart© horizontally beginning with the primary need—security—it shows in turn how each type of codependency develops, and lists the components of each, presented in sequence from cause to result.

So, starting at the bottom left-hand side of the first pyramid (just like you are reading this sentence) and reading left to right as usual, you observe that the *unmet need* (col. 1) causes *painful feelings* (col. 2) which in turn set off *mental* and *behavioral defenses* (col. 3) that constitute the *type of codependency* (col. 4). The sequence can be meaningfully stated in reverse, from result to cause: the *type of codependency* consists of *mental* and *behavioral defenses* that are generated by *painful feelings* caused by *unmet needs*.

This sequence provides a us with a very precise definition of codependency: codependency consists of an *aggregation of patterns of thought (which are obsessive) and patterns of behavior (which are compulsive) generated unconsciously by the pain of unmet needs. These patterns function both as defenses against that pain and also as signals to get the need met and to get it met from sources outside the self.* The short version is: *codependency consists of defensive thinking and behavior generated by painful feelings caused by unmet needs*—which in turn instinctively seek out other codependents, caretaker variety, to get those needs met *that you think you can get only from outside yourself.*

But since these defensive patterns are typically indirect, manipulative, or aggressive, they almost always end up backfiring. That is, the system of defenses is a treacherous friend, unable to fulfill in the long run the comfort it provides in the short run. By blocking the pain, it obscures the cry of the unmet need, and so prevents it from being met, in turn causing more pain, thus arousing more defenses, and so on and so on...Thus ironically do the defenses keep alive the pain they were created to alleviate.

The Chart© shows what happens if you aren't aware of what you are feeling: the feeling, instead of you, will determine your action, and your repressed feelings will be acted out in behavioral defenses, such as teasing, attacking, retreating, *etc.* These unhealthful behaviors in turn create consequences for both you and others. All too often it is only by being faced with the consequences (which you can't predict or control) and having to live through them that you realize you're caught up in a codependent cycle.

Many of us live like this without any awareness of the toxic pattern we are creating, or of the inevitable karmic returns. Thus we abdicate responsibility for our own life and behavior, and call our difficulties "God's will" (a phrase used only about something we don't like, never about something good). In contrast, events we experience as bad, painful, harmful, unfair, *etc.*, when looked at as opportunities to learn how to remedy the things in ourselves that create distress and thereby block our growth, will eventually be seen in retrospect as good, as Zeke's story shows. "The past is perfect." *How we deal with what we consider to be adversity determines the course and quality of our life.*

As you continue to practice the Freedom Counseling Process©, you will find that you gradually begin to intercept your codependency cycle at successively earlier stages. For instance, instead of letting it get all the way to the stage of consequences, you will register trouble at the stage of behavioral defenses. A good example of this is catching Your self doing some kind of acting out: driving too fast, forgetting to take the trash out, yelling at your kids, *etc.*, all behaviors which conceal your feelings from you and reveal them to others.

Next, you will catch your cycle at the stage of mental defenses: worrying, analyzing, interpreting, *etc.* Each time you notice the cycle at an earlier stage, you intercept its momentum and save Your self that much pain. *Consequences signal defenses, defenses signal painful feelings, painful feelings signal unmet needs.* The ultimate goal is to become aware of your feelings *as they happen*, so that you can release them on the spot (privately, of course). The next step is to notice your need when it happens and feed it appropriate declarations, repeating them until you feel what they are saying to be true. Thus you defeat codependency and achieve wholeness.

The codependent disease cycle is, like addiction, both progressive and chronic; left to itself it always gets worse, never better, and once you have it, you have it forever—unless something or someone enlightens you. Moreover, you can see that working on one component alone, such as your thinking or behavior, is non-productive, since you can't get rid of that component so long as the one that precedes it is still operating. This would be treating the symptom and ignoring the cause: while the pain is suppressed, the thing *causing* the pain is still there, sending out its call for help. In contrast, the Freedom Healing Process© deals with all three components of the disease—feeling, thinking, behavior—and does so in that order, from cause to effect, as we saw in the ACB process described earlier in this chapter.

You may find that you have characteristics from some of the other need-levels as well as your main one. Two factors account for this. First, because each need must be met sufficiently before the next need can be, it follows that the lower your type on the Chart© the more unmet needs, and therefore the more pain, you have.

For example, if security is your primary need, you will also have deficits in belonging, self-esteem, and autonomy, and will suffer, respectively, feelings of abandonment, low self-esteem, and shame, as well as insecurity. Being focused on the insecurity, you will not be consciously concerned with the pain signals of the other three, but they will nonetheless affect your mood and your behavior. To sum it up, the lower your type on the Chart©, the more distress you will experience and the more defended and less free you will be, and therefore the more you need to practice the Process©. (If you've forgotten it somewhat, reread enough of Chapter Two to refresh your memory).

The second factor, following from the first, is that the needs of course do not exist in us as fixed entities, the way they appear in the Chart©. Since most of us have more than one deficient need, our feelings fluctuate among the levels as we go through our day. Even when our needs are mostly met, we can at any given moment undergo an experience that causes a drop in the level, like a plunge in the stock market.

In each of the following situations consider which need is primarily unmet, and therefore what your feelings would be: a good friend forgets your lunch date; there is talk at work of "downsizing;" the boss chooses somebody hired *after* you to chair the committee; you have an argument with your mother and she says you always had a hard time standing up for yourself.

Any one of these will cause your consciousness to be flooded with feelings and defenses of different kinds that are in constant motion, volatile, fluid, shifting in and out of each other, like clouds on a windy day. *By attending to your defenses you can identify your feelings; they in turn will tell you what need is deficient.* You-as-spirit can then fulfill that need *from within* by going to the chapter on that need and using the declarations given there or, even better, ones You create for Your self. Once the need is met, You are free to choose Your behavior consciously.

When your feelings are repressed rather than expressed and you can't therefore experience them, you lose your inner signal of a needs deficiency. This exactly describes the codependent's plight: you are at the mercy of your feelings, and instead of hearing their message, your only concern is to get rid of them. You are like the driver who suddenly sees a warning signal on his dashboard. He pulls into a service station and rather than asking the mechanic to identify the problem and if possible fix it, he says, "This red light is driving me crazy. Could you take a hammer and knock it out?"

Our obsession with stopping the pain makes us lose sight of the fact that the only effective and lasting way to "fix it" is to *meet the need.* But you can't do that if you don't know *what the need is,* and *how to meet it.* In that case, the anger and whatever other painful feelings you have take over and determine your behavior. For example, yelling or saying something sarcastic, or slamming the door, *etc.* is counterproductive and will of course make you (and anyone else within earshot) feel worse, setting off yet another defense to cover up that feeling and keep the destructive process going.

On the other hand, when you are conscious of your anger, you can (if you choose) take control of it and then decide what behavior is appropriate in the circumstance. *That's* being autonomous! By listening to the anger and heeding its message, You free Your self from the humiliation of acting out your feelings, and also from consequences— the "law of retributive justice" (that is, *karma*)—and you are made whole again.

To sum it up, living in a condition of repressed feelings guarantees the continuation of the disease, that is, of mental defenses: the unclear, negative, obsessive thinking we call the "old tapes," "stinkin' thinking," "yama-yama," "the committee," "the internalized, punishing parent." Always obsessive, this defensive thinking has a tendency to metastasize, obliterating healthful, rational thought and self- awareness, reviving our old codependent patterns and perpetuating the disease cycle. In contrast, when toxic feelings are discarded, the defenses are no longer needed and so fall away, leaving the mind clear and reversing the cycle shown in the codependency diagram.

As you keep using the Process©, releasing defenses whenever you're aware of them, taking care of your feelings when they call you, and doing the appropriate Declarations, you will soon notice a decrease in the number and intensity of defenses and an increase in positive feelings. The result is greater ability to govern and nurture Your self, the goal of the suffering codependent.

It's an inside job.

Appendix II

Brain Structure & Functioning

The effectiveness of the Freedom Healing Chart© derives in part from the fact that it is grounded in our physiological and neurological structure (as well as our spiritual nature). The *Process* of the Chart© is a spiritual and psychological twin of our physical and ontological system, and of our phylogenetic development. The stages of the Chart© and their sequence parallel the stages of our individual and evolutionary development and functioning.

A brief review of the structure and evolution of the brain will make the parallels clear. Both evolutionarily as well as structurally, we human beings have four brains:

1. The *survival* brain, which correlates to the basic brain stem that governs heartbeat and breathing ("R-complex") in one-celled animals and newborn babies. It corresponds psychologically and emotionally to the first level of the Freedom Healing Chart, which is *security*.

2. Next is the *feeling* brain, or "limbic" system, the seat of emotion, which correlates to the child-mammal brain, and corresponds to the second level of the Chart, which is *belonging*.

3. The third stage is the "old" *thinking* brain (the motor cortex) which correlates to the primate/adolescent brain and corresponds to level three on the Chart which is *self-esteem*.

4. Finally, we come to the fourth stage, the "new" (meaning "latest") thinking brain, which correlates to the human adult brain and corresponds to level four on the Chart, which is *autonomy*.

Discoveries & Conclusions

We will discuss each of these brains in turn: its history, development, and functions. Together, they form a structure like the one below, a diagram from Richard Restak's book, "The Brain," p.35.

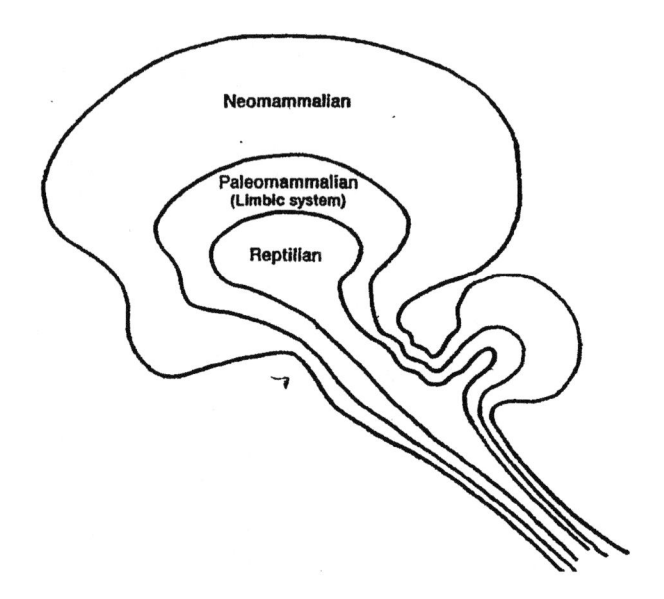

The first brain to appear in the history of the species was in ocean creatures and reptiles; it consisted of the "basic brain stem" that generates the heartbeat and breathing, and is scientifically identified as the *reptilian* or *R-complex* brain. (It is also the first brain to appear in the conception of each individual human being). In the above diagram, you can see its position deep inside the cranial structure, surrounded and protected by the second, third, and fourth brains because its viability is essential to their physiological and eventually their psychological development (as well as its own) and, most important, the continuing development of the species.

The second brain, developing from the structure and functioning of the first brain, is the "feeling" brain, scientifically called the "limbic system" (meaning simply the brain in between the first brain and the third). It is the buffer for the "R-complex" which it surrounds, protecting it from invasion or injury. It also has a role to play in terms of feelings—it is the "area of the brain most concerned with emotion" and therefore inevitably with behavior.[1] At this early stage of evolution, behavior is automatic, programmed, and irreversible. As the limbic system continued its evolutionary process, it created many more functions, such as the development of feelings, music, war, poetry, memory, *etc.*

The third brain to develop is, in scientific jargon, the *motor* cortex (or *neocortex*, meaning the "new brain"). It surrounds and envelops the limbic system (correlating to childhood), and defines our being as "early" human (correlating to adolescence). It is the next-to-last brain, inhabits the frontal lobe and, "can be thought of as a computer; the premotor cortex, its computer program. The result is an increasingly controlled sequence of muscle movement rather than an isolated and chaotic discharge" such as we experience in infancy and childhood (Restak, p. 28, ll. 5-8). In position, function, and activity, this description parallels the third level (adolescence) of the hierarchy of needs, *self-esteem.* "The outlet channel for action is the *motor cortex*" (Restak, p. 27, l. 34), which signifies the transition from an earlier level of progression to the next—and final—stage, while indicating the characteristic intensity, curiosity, and drive of adolescence.

The fourth and final brain, the adult thinking brain, occupies the outermost cranial layer, is the latest brain to which evolution has taken us, and correlates to the fourth level of the hierarchy of needs. This "thinking" brain supports the three neurological structures we have just discussed, and defines our being as "late" human. Dr. Paul MacLean describes it in Restak's book as "somewhat like an archeological site, with the outer layer composed of the most recent brain structure, the cerebral cortex [as distinct from the *motor cortex*] which is highly developed in primates and reaches its greatest level of complexity in humans" (p. 35, ll. 11-14).

Restak continues, quoting MacLean: "...reptiles display countless behavior patterns commonly observed in human beings. This should not be surprising, according to MacLean, since we still carry around with us, like forgotten luggage, the brain structures of our reptilian ancestors" (p. 37, ll. 10-13).[2] "Reverting to our computer analogy, it seems reasonable to suppose that this ancient brain structure is contributing its own 'program' for influencing our behavior. Thus, MacLean postulates that such human characteristics as ritualism, awe for authority, social pecking orders, even obsessive-compulsive neuroses, may be partially caused by our reptilian brains" (p. 37, 16-19).

Restak sums up his concept: "At the most anterior part of the brain are the prefrontal lobes, which play a decisive part in firming up intention, deciding on action, and regulating our most complex behaviors (p. 28, ll. 10-12)... .*The principal role of this area of the brain seems to be the regulation of background tone necessary for behavior. It is, in fact, a superstructure that energizes all the other parts of the cortex and is an overall regulator of our behavior.* If we had to describe the prefrontal lobe in one word, it would be *purpose. Goal-directed behavior is lost after destruction of the prefrontal areas"* (p. 28, l. 20-26). (Italics mine).

From this brief description of the functions, characteristics, and sites of the four-brains-in-one we can see an amazing parallel: *each individual human brain develops on the same pattern as the evolutionary model,* or as the scientists say: "ontogeny recapitulates phylogeny," meaning that the development of the individual replicates the development of the species. Thus we can say that the history of the evolution of the human race *is contained in the brain of each human being*—an astonishing concept and theory, which we will now explore more fully.

While the basic brain stem is functional at conception—has to be to keep the embryo alive—and the feeling brain soon becomes functional, the thinking brain, which consists of both the motor cortex (the "old" brain) and the prefrontal or cerebral cortex (the "new" brain), is present only in structure, not yet in content or function. Its continued development after birth (not completed until about the age of *thirty-five*) is directed both by genetic inheritance and by the experiences it goes through. It directs the elements and successive stages of our cognitive and physiological development, including speech, consciousness, cognitive memory, reasoning, judgment, *etc.*

Surrounding and enclosing the feeling brain (to protect it and perhaps to keep it from running rampant), the thinking brain corresponds at the species level to "human" and at the individual level to adolescence and adulthood, which correlates on the Healing Chart to the need for *autonomy*. Its characteristics are predominantly masculine: it operates on reason, stability, logic, even-temperedness, fairness, seeing all sides of a situation.

In contrast, the feeling brain (the limbic system), whose characteristics and functioning are more feminine, and relate to *belonging* (the second level of the Healing Chart), registers and stores sensory data, feelings, and emotions. It corresponds at the individual level to childhood, which on the Healing Chart is the *need for belonging* and at the species level to the mammalian stage of evolution. Among other duties, it encloses the basic brain stem, which corresponds at the individual level to the prenatal and neonatal stage, and at species level to the reptilian stage of evolution, which correlates to the *need for security.* That the oldest/first brain in the development of both the individual and the species is positioned in the deepest and most protected part of the four brains is profoundly moving and reassuring: nature's way of underlining and insuring the primacy of survival. Combative in content though it often is, the thinking/adolescent brains structurally protect the feeling brain and the feeling brain in turn structurally protects the survival brain.

Discoveries & Conclusions

While the thinking/adolescent brain and the feeling brain are structurally sympathetic, functionally they are antipathetic—husband to wife, parent to child, boss to employee, teacher to student, coach to team, governor to governed, and so on. It seems that the older of the two prevails most of the time, but that's just your feeling brain trying (as usual) to highjack your thinking brain. Neutral, logical, factual, and absent of animosity or dishonesty ("just the facts, ma'am"), the thinking brain at its present state of evolution is no match for the feeling brain, which is amoral and operates on *whatever works to win*, abandoning scruples, disregarding consequences, and lacking consideration of the other peoples' feelings.

From the above description of the feeling brain you may be thinking I have a negative view of our limbic heritage. But when I tell you of the joy I experience from a delicious dinner; a well-performed drama; a magnificent concert in our new state of the art concert hall; a new exhibit of Cézanne at our spacious and rich art museum; a walk on West River Drive to experience the rapture of a brilliant autumn afternoon, the trees displaying their crystal gold and red clothing; a poetry reading in one of our universities—surely you will not accuse me of holding a grudge against our limbic nature. This is what makes the limbic system so fascinating: when it is good it is *very, very good*, but when it is bad it is AWFUL—indeed, one might say at times even *diabolical*.

Thus we see that the limbic system spans the universe neutrally, creating and absorbing the good and the bad alike without opinion: "nature without check with original energy."[3] It is amoral, unintellectual, and unrepentant, focusing its energy on *getting what it needs/wants* and getting rid of what it *doesn't* want *by any means necessary*. In a disagreement between the feeling brain and the thinking brain—the impulsivity and intense energy of the feeling brain opposed by the rationality, logic, and morality of the neocortex—the winner in any given instance is the *one who stops talking—or crying, wheedling, accusing, threatening, throwing a tantrum*—last.

This is, more often than not, the feeling brain: the old formula "intellect over emotion" is more something to be achieved than something by which to operate. Think of it like this: your three-year old asks for some candy (feeling brain); you say "No, not before lunch" (thinking brain). This, of course, has no effect whatever on his request, because he doesn't yet have the neocortical functioning to understand the meaning of your response. What he *does* know is *repetition,* which wins about ninety percent of the time and which leads us to one of its most important faculties, our *memory.*

Without memory, where would we be? Even the three-year old knows, instinctively, its power. It stores our feelings and experiences (every one we have) at the unconscious level and reminds us of them when an event in the present is similar enough to call them up. Freud named it the "unconscious," a term now completely part of our everyday conversation. It is also amoral, making no moral boundaries or judgment, thus allowing it to include all kinds of different things without comment (a limbic function). It is therefore the storehouse of emotions, unconscious memory, and artistic inspiration, including the fun, laughter, joy, and ecstasy we feel from the art the universe creates and the art we human beings create in its image. The limbic system is generous in giving us these joyous elements through which we define our humanness and elevate ourselves to spirituality. But it also has a dark side (discussed later).

It's therefore quite obvious, if we are to ensure the continuation of the species and promote its further growth, that we must find something with the ability and clout to reconcile these two different kinds of operating. That "something" is represented in the diagram of the brain (p.214) as a dotted line slightly above and around it, and represents what we might call the "Abiding Consciousness."

To discuss this concept with maximum meaning, a look first at the dark side of the limbic system will help us understand its nature in depth, and show us how to reign in our "demiurge," with a view to keeping the good side of the limbic system good.

Discussion of the evolution and functioning of this part of the brain starts with what the Greek philosophers referred to as the "demiurge" or "Dionysian" (as opposed to "Apollonian") nature of the human being: that is, that part of the feeling brain which, being older than the thinking brain (both historically and individually), has neither brakes nor scruples and therefore has done horrendous things throughout recorded history (the ancient Greeks should see it now!): Oedipus unconsciously—we might say "limbicly"— unknowingly marrying his mother, then when he discovered the truth, putting out his eyes; the fall of Troy and the injustice done to Cassandra; the crucifixion of Jesus and the two thieves with him; the invasion by Julius Caesar of what we now call Europe, including England; the eradication by the Christians, no less, of an entire culture—the Druids, who inhabited Wales, Scotland, and Ireland from pre-Christian times well into the "Dark Ages"; the fall of the Roman Empire to the Huns; the many murders and wars throughout the middle ages; and, finally, to the bloodiest of all, the nineteenth and twentieth centuries: the Civil War, the "Great War," the second World War, the tragedies of Korea and Viet Nam, the "cold" but none the less frightening war with the Soviet Union, and now, as I write, the unimaginable horror of the possibility of nuclear war of dimensions able to destroy the entire planet.

Such diabolical activities of the human being do not come from the thinking brain that, without the limbic system's occasional demonic outbursts, would maintain life at a steady and reasonable, if unexciting, pace. But the neocortex is no match for the dark side of the limbic system: at some time every single one of us human beings has "lost his temper"—that is, our feeling brain overwhelmed ourthinking brain—and we acted out out grudge, anger, fear, revenge, panic, *etc.*

The time in which we are living presents just such a perilous challenge, with our government talking and sounding bellicose and Iraq being inscrutable. A one-word substitution in a poem by Andrew Marvell describes our present fear: "at my back I always hear, [Armageddon] hurrying near."[4] In such a state, in which the path of our own government, seeming to operate from its thinking brain, but in fact from the dark side of its limbic system, is as frightening, if not more so, than the supposed opponent, the need to understand ourselves and learn to investigate our own motives and visceral urges is of paramount importance. Indeed, it may be all we can do, in our present state of evolution, to avoid Armageddon— thus bringing us to the diagram of the brain with the dotted line above it, back on the first page of this chapter. (p. 214)

The dotted line represents our spiritual nature, which, as you probably have guessed, is the answer to the limbic-neocortex conflict. By doing the "Freedom Process©" daily, we learn to reside more and more in the "Abiding Consciousness," our Spiritual Self that exists, so to speak, above as well as within the level of the human being and its propensity to conflict, and never directs us wrongly. This Consciousness, operating continuously "without ceasing," reviews the messages of the limbic system and the neocortex and mediates between them; then provides the power to moderate and comfort the limbic system, while energizing the neocortex to take appropriate action. It would be interesting to see what might develop if, say, five thousand people all did this Process© daily for a month! There was, in fact, just such an experiment in several American cities a few years ago, and the results were quite startling: in all of the cities the crime rate dropped by over fifty percent.

We are now ready to look at the parallel between the structure of the Healing Chart© and our neurological and evolutionary structure and development. The four sections of the Chart© parallel the four segments of the brain chart. The first column of the Chart© is about *survival* and *security* ("things without which we get sick or die") which relate to infancy (the first three years) individually and the R-complex brain evolutionarily. The second column is about *feelings and belonging* and therefore correlates to childhood individually and the limbic system evolutionarily. The third column is about the development of *self-esteem* and therefore correlates to *adolescence* individually and the *motor cortex* (the controller of movement and behavior) both neurologically and evolutionarily. The fourth is about *autonomy* and therefore correlates to the *cerebral cortex*—thinking, rationality, logic—both neurologically and evolutionarily. Thus the Chart© is an *archetype*: its components and their sequence replicate the components of the brain and the sequence of their development. We human beings value so highly how we are made that we keep making things—sometimes unconsciously—in our own image, as we are told God did in making us.

This parallel explains why the Process© that the Chart© embodies is so effective: practising it exercises and integrates the four fundamental components—*security, belonging, self-esteem, and autonomy*—of our embryonic, psychological, and cerebral makeup. It is thus holistic, each component operating in ontogenetic/phylogenetic sequence as it contributes its essential function to the well being of the whole.

For instance, the limbic system and the neocortex, complementary components whose job is to integrate and maintain the operation of the entire system, are very different in function, and often oppose and at times attempt to overcome each other. The limbic system "concerned principally with self and species preservation," operates on conditioning and, unless it is consciously reprogrammed, on the earliest conditioning in its life (Restak, p. 41, ll. 21-22). That is, the particular sensory, emotional, and belief patterns that surround the child in his first years of life, stemming of course from his family's gestalt, are imprinted in his limbic system and contained throughout his body, and become physiologically and biochemically, as well as psychologically, part of him.

These belief patterns create the template on which the child's values, habits, talents, likes and dislikes, *etc.*, develop as he grows, indiscriminately presenting him with the good and the bad—the limbic system doesn't play favorites. In this non-judgmental and amoral manner, however his caregivers relate to him will be implanted and permanently recorded in his limbic system—his "unconscious." Whatever their input and caretaking are, so will his be.

We can say, then, that the limbic system represents the past and the unconscious. Its function is to insure the retention of all emotional experience, by whatever patterns or defenses it has developed, whether they remain effective or become destructive. Parents take heed! If you want to raise a good, moral, intelligent, and happy child, you have to: (1) demonstrate those qualities yourself (he does and thinks what you do and think) and (2) relate to him only with positive statements. No scolding, yelling, negativity, hitting, or "punishment." All these create pain, fear, anger, and distrust, a template he will act out the rest of his life unless you adopt a different approach. Your child repeats your behavior—what else does he have to model on?

Here's an example: if you heard Mom humiliate Dad almost daily by reminding him how little money he made, your limbic system, which records everything it hears, would have encoded a sense of shame relating to your manhood, and fear and resentment relating to women. Many years of hearing these negative and hurtful comments would incorporate them into your sense of self, components of the artificial persona that conceals your real Self. By the time you reach adulthood that old emotional pattern, embedded in your limbic system, will be activated by any correction or even suggestion directed to you by either men or women,

Discoveries & Conclusions

and will cause you to react most typically with aggression, to cover the pain.

In addition, in relationships with women, you would either be cautious, ambivalent, passive aggressive, or dominating and hostile. For you, they are dangerous (though desirable) creatures. Clearly, you are operating on patterns from the past that most likely have little or no relevance to present reality, but instead are destructive leftovers from your childhood trauma, keeping you alternately seeking and running. Your limbic programming is dictating and confusing your cortical functioning, or, in other words, your child brain is running your adult brain.[5] You are not living in the past; the past is living in you.

In contrast, the thinking brain (neocortex) operates on data rather than feelings, observing facts, events, and information from both outside and inside itself, reasoning about them and drawing conclusions from them. It represents the present and the conscious mind. Having by nature no affinity for feelings, and oriented to logic and linear thinking, the neocortex reacts to emotions as it does to external data: it tries to make sense of them, to keep them in line, to make inferences and develop theories based on them.

But it must constantly deal with its *sister*, the *feelings*—these foreign things that conduct the needs messages sent out by the basic brain stem—and interpret whether they are legitimate signals of externally created problems, or messages of internal discomfort, since the job of the neocortex is to straighten out such mysteries. Most of us go at this job with our feeling brain, forgetting or neglecting what we really are, "a Power greater than the self."[6] The result is that we get tangled up and worse off than when we started. As the child's feeling brain has the power to upset the parent's thinking brain, so the limbic mind in each of us can derange our adult mind, dissolving it into the confused thinking that makes up our mental defenses—and illnesses.

When in this state, the thinking brain is dysfunctional, and its attempts to deal with feeling messages are like trying to cut hot taffy with a pair of scissors—the scissors get all gummed up and useless, and you get nowhere with the taffy. Thus the two brains, designed to complement each other, often end up in a battle that the feeling brain generally wins because it doesn't have scruples, common sense, consideration for its partner, and so on. It is *amoral*—so it "gets away with murder." Whether between the two parts of the brain or adult and child or husband and wife or boss and employee, the conflict typically goes like this:

Parent Brain/Thinking Brain:
"Get ready. We have to go to the Post Office."

Child Brain/ Feeling Brain:
A strong surge occurs, inaudible, invisible, non-verbal, somewhere in the region of the abdomen which, if it had words, would say something along the lines of: "*Please* could we eat lunch first?"

Parent: "No! It's income tax day and it will be very crowded! We have to get there *right away*!"

Child: (translation of feeling messages): "PLEASE! You know what happens to us if we wait too long for lunch!"

Parent: "You can make it. We have to go now!"

So they go and, waiting in line, the child passes out and has to be carried home—or, the adult's thinking brain doesn't listen to his feeling brain, which has a low-blood-sugar attack from standing so long, and he passes out and is taken to the hospital.

The conflict between the thinking brain and the feeling brain is outpictured also in the relations between men and women, and accounts for some of the major differences, difficulties, and frustrations each experiences with the other.

For example, Dr. James Ballenger says that "the pathways from the cortex, which is the thinking part of the brain, to the amygdala (the feeling part) are weaker than those from the amygdala back to the cortex. So thought has to use back roads and dead ends to get to the amygdala to gain control over it, but the amygdala has superhighways to get back to the cortex."[7]

Given that men are typically more defined by the neocortex and women by the limbic system, Dr. Ballenger's neurological finding helps explain why men typically have a harder time being empathic and why women typically have an easier time integrating thinking and feeling. We therefore might conclude that since *thought* (male) has a harder time moving back ("regressing") to the amygdala, while *feeling* (female) has "superhighways" to the cortex, feelings (emotions) are the more powerful and dominant element in the current stage of the evolution of "homo sapiens."

Practising the Freedom Healing Process© resolves this imbalance: experiencing and releasing the toxic feelings and chemicals by deep breathing restores the flow of blood to the neocortex, moving out the obsessive, defensive thinking so that the mind becomes clear, or as the Buddhists say, "empty," meaning "uncluttered." In that state it can hear the need-signals sent out by the brain's survival system, and think rationally how best to meet the need. Both systems being then satisfied, neither any longer seeks to dominate the other. By working with each component of the neurological structure, the Freedom Process© reverses the pathological sequence, and balances and integrates the entire mind/body system.

If you grew up with your needs mostly met, your neocortex learned how to read the limbic signals, and to provide whatever was necessary and appropriate to keep the developing brain safe and secure. If, however, you grew up with your needs insufficiently met, your thinking learned to be habitually defensive—irrational, negative, obsessive, critical, abusive—a caricature of healthy, rational, cortical functioning, and therefore useless or even toxic, unable to perform its job of getting your needs met in a healthful way.[8] The neocortex becomes easily overwhelmed by the limbic signals, as the neat, rectilinear houses of Fargo were flooded by the raging formless waters of the Red River in 1998. If the volume of this defensive chatter gets so loud it obliterates the limbic signals, their cry for help is blocked (the adult, out of touch with his feelings, is repressing the child), and the same result follows—the needs don't get met.

In this eventuality, for most people a very common state, the whole organism remains stuck in survival mode: all its behaviors will be some form of fight or flight. In other words, destructive behavior such as rage, panic attacks, tantrums, violence, acting out of any kind ("fight" type of behavioral defenses) is what happens when the feeling brain dominates the thinking brain. On the other hand, repression of feelings and absence of empathy, also resulting in unmet needs and compulsive behavior—such as silence, withdrawal, isolating—are what happens when the thinking brain dominates the feeling brain (not very often, incidentally).

To summarize: the proper functioning of these two brains consists of balancing and supporting each other. The thinking brain must hear the messages of the feeling brain and provide appropriate and timely remedies (the adult taking proper care of the child). Conversely, while making sure its message is heard, the feeling brain must follow the guidance of the neocortex (the child obeying the adult). It is the obligation of the thinking brain to bring the internal state of the feeling brain into proper relation with the conditions of external reality, adjusting the individual's inner functioning to the outer conditions and exigencies it encounters.

Example: I'm driving a bit too fast (because I didn't leave on time) to get to an important interview. I see the traffic light about half a block away just about to turn to

Discoveries & Conclusions

yellow. I can either put the "pedal to the metal" or slow down, preparing to stop. *Question 1:* what would the thinking brain tell me to do? *Question 2:* what would the feeling brain tell me to do? And what decision *should* the feeling brain make? One of them is what you *want* to do; the other is what you *ought* to do. To coin a saying: doing what you *ought to do* paves the way to a long life.

When this job is done successfully, the child, whether our offspring or our own inner child, will be naturally well behaved. But if the thinking brain is not healthy (which means that the feeling brain is also not healthy) and its decisions or policies are therefore ineffective, unfair, or destructive, the feeling brain in the adult and in the child will rebel, either passively or actively. Practising the Freedom Process© restores the balance between these two systems, and lays the foundation for successful parenting.

Another area in which brain structure plays a significant part for the Healing Process© is its connection to the newborn infant in whom the thinking brain is not fully developed—in fact it hasn't even started its developmental process. It consists at this stage of a mere physiological structure containing a jelly-like substance that eventually will wrap itself around every cell in the body. This differentiates each cell and its ordained function from all other cells, the purpose being that when we want to walk we can walk and when we want to draw a picture we can draw a picture, *etc.*

This process of differentiation that makes the child grow and develop properly is gradual and not completed until about *thirty-five* (which is why our children should not be allowed to drive until twenty-five *at the very earliest).* The purpose and the effect of this process is to keep the function of each cell clearly delineated and functioning correctly in its own space so that it doesn't slide around into a different cell, a process accomplished by the myelin sheath. (The deterioration of the myelin sheath, the material that differentiates one cell from another, is the genesis of multiple sclerosis, a degenerative disease that operates regressively, reversing the process described above and gradually eliminating the cells that define one part of the body from another, so that the body parts gradually lose their ability to do their particular function).

The implications of this physiological fact, that development of the neocortex isn't complete until about thirty-five, can hardly be overestimated. It accounts for a significant amount of the customary difficulties between parent and child. Because they are functioning at birth first from the basic brain stem, then gradually from the developing feeling brain, babies and young children are *different in kind, not just in degree*, from grownups, who function from both the thinking and the feeling brain. Conversing with children from adult-brain functioning as if they are miniature adults or younger siblings is confusing to them and frustrating to the adult, who quickly learns that he must accommodate to his little one if he wants peace, and not expect the little one to accommodate to him.

From the newborn to the beginnings of adulthood, children must be met where they are at, a state, first, of *survival:* eating, sleeping, and adjusting to living in an environment characterized by the pull of gravity rather than by the floaty support of the amniotic fluid. As they develop both mentally and physically, they continue until about the beginnings of adolescence (11 to 12) to operate on and from imagination, play, creativity, and feelings. In Wordsworth's "Immortality Ode," there is a description of this state that sheds light on its function and purpose:

> Behold the Child among his new-born blisses,
>   A six years' Darling of a pigmy size!
>   See, where 'mid work of his own hand he lies,
> Fretted by sallies of his mother's kisses,
>   With light upon him from his father's eyes!
>   See, at his feet, some little plan or chart,

> Some fragment from his dream of human life,
> Shaped by himself with newly learned art;
> A wedding or a festival,
> A mourning or a funeral;
> And this hath now his heart,
> And unto this he frames his song...*St. VII*

A darker consequence of the fact that the child operates from a not yet completed cerebral cortex is that he only gradually develops the ability to edit and filter experience. He therefore has insufficient rationality to evaluate reasonably what life brings him, or to reassure and guide himself in times of real or imagined injury or danger. He needs his parents' neocortex until his own is developed enough to sustain him. This statement has several implications.

First, it means he should not be exposed to frightening situations, whether real or imaginary, including violence on television, the street, or inside his house, which is the worst. His feeling brain will take it all in and store it like a computer, and it will stay imprinted there at an unconscious level, affecting every relationship he has for the rest of his life (unless he's lucky enough to get some effective therapy).

If a later event occurs that bears even a small resemblance to his early experience his feelings will respond the way they did in the original situation. However, since the trauma got planted in his feeling brain (his unconscious) he will not remember it consciously, that is, cognitively. But his behavior will demonstrate it. The result is that it pops up whenever an experience in his present life triggers it...and *he doesn't know why!* So it stays there forever, continuing to affect his behavior.[9]

Second, if he is so exposed, he should be encouraged to vent his feelings, privately, in whatever way he can— talking, crying, drawing, throwing bean bags (at the floor, not, of course, at people), pounding pillows, or deep breathing. None of these activities is harmful to others (of course, you have to guide him as to where and what to pound or throw) and none of them make him violent. On the contrary, by releasing the rage inside him, they make him violence-free and give him an invaluable tool to use for the rest of his life whenever he gets frustrated or angry.

The child should also be comforted and reassured, and *his feelings heard by his caregivers*. For instance, if he says at age three, "I scared of doggie...doggie scary," DON'T say, "No, the dog isn't scary." Having *experienced* the fear, this confuses him because "Daddy knows everything, so I must be wrong." So to be in sinc with Daddy, he has to repress his feelings. They aren't going to be the same as his, and they can't be, because the two of them are operating from different parts of the brain: Daddy from the neocortex and baby from the limbic brain. If, instead, you validate his feelings and allow him to have them, he will feel sane and acknowledged. Because his mother's brain operates more, and more easily, in her feeling brain than does Daddy's, she is more likely to be the one baby runs to in such situations. Thus we see that Freud's superconscious, conscious, and unconscious are actual neurological entities that have specific places and functions in the brain and correlate to the male, female, and child.

By these means his emotional security in the moment is insured and he learns eventually from the example of his caregivers how to comfort and reassure himself. If, however, his chief caregivers aren't functioning from a fully developed thinking brain and a healthy feeling brain, the child's needs won't be sufficiently met and his thinking brain will not develop properly: he will be twenty years old physically but only six or seven in his thinking and reasoning. This leaves him to run on his limbic system—a risky guide, as we have seen earlier: it can and will tell us to do some pretty stupid or antisocial things and *we blindly follow its lead* and most likely get into some kind of trouble. But then it can turn around and tell us to do something nice for somebody else and we agree but keep putting it off until we've forgotten all about it. These storms in the feeling brain undoubtedly explain much of the immature and frequently alarming and illegal behavior of our culture.

Only gradually, as the thinking brain grows, do children develop—though not always use—the full range of human functioning: conscious memory, reasoning, self-restraint, problem solving, conscience, compassion, empathy, *etc.* One of the most important activities of the caregiver is to track this progressing development, and to do so with sensitivity, so as neither to over-stimulate nor under-stimulate the child's cognitive functioning. When we force—or cajole or bribe or even encourage—the child to cortical activity beyond his developmental stage (even though he may, in an effort to please his parents or teachers, actually do it) we increase his anxiety and sense of inadequacy, a case of the thinking brain causing trouble for the feeling brain. The resulting damage to his self-confidence can lay the foundation for codependency or addiction or even mental illness in adulthood. If, instead, we make available a sufficient supply of appropriate toys and activities, and allow him to explore them without interference, he will proceed at the rate comfortable to him and will consequently strengthen his sense of security and self-confidence.

The developmental inability to edit and filter mentioned above causes the child to take in everything to which he is exposed. The adult cliché "he's too young to notice" or "to remember" is a truth only if the word "cognitively" is added to it. In fact, the child's feeling brain records every situation fully and there it remains throughout his life, determining reactions and dictating behavior, unless consciously recognized and released by some such process as the one described in this book. The later in childhood the experience happens, the more easily it can be mitigated by the editing and filtering of the thinking brain.

Conversely, the younger the child when the trauma occurs, the less developed the prefrontal lobe and therefore the greater the potential damage. So the reality is exactly opposite to the adult assumption: the *younger* he is, the *more* he absorbs. He has no filter, no sunglasses. The implication of this for good parenting is: don't fight in front of the kids—*especially* the baby! In fact, don't do or say anything scary, age-inappropriate, harmful, or in any way detrimental to any of the four psychological needs within earshot of a baby or a young child. The limbic system at this early stage doesn't distinguish between persons—or, rather, not yet having boundaries, it is inclusive, and simply absorbs and registers whatever its environment provides, regardless of the subject. And, since he doesn't yet have language, he can remember events at this age only as feelings.

The limbic system is what unites us as human beings; the neocortex is what separates and divides us. At the neocortical level we differentiate, debate, and reason; at the limbic level we assimilate, harmonize, and agree—and fight, argue, kill. A child typically wants the people around her to be in accord, that is, everybody happy and safe; unsafety to another is unsafety to her. She is like the string of a violin that resonates when its counterpart an octave higher is sounded: "If Daddy hits Betsy, if teacher yells at Bobby, if Mommy screams at Daddy...they might do it to me." Living in such conditions generates constant fear—and adrenalin—in the child, producing the mental and behavioral defenses shown on the Chart© at level one.

Knowledge of the child's neurological development and of his corresponding psychological needs as just outlined provides the basis for a simple and dependable guideline to parenting: track your child's limbic development, which comes first and has to do with play, imagination, creativity, *etc., as closely as you track his cortical development* (which comes last) so you can respond appropriately to his emotional as well as his cognitive needs. While a highly functioning neocortex is based on a well-developed limbic system, it is not more important to full neurological functioning than the feeling brain. Each must learn to cooperate, to lay down his/her arms of mass destruction, and each find a "power greater than themselves"[10] in the best interest of the client.

Further, track and meet your own needs, so you can refrain from any behavior you would not want his limbic system to record. Your child's emotional growth is thus supported, an accumulation of feelings of anxiety, rejection, unworthiness, and shame is prevented and codependency averted. Moreover, his intellectual progress will be strengthened by a sound limbic foundation.

In contrast, we as adults, if we are to be truly adult, must not only make the shift into cortical functioning, but learn when to stay there and when to become limbic in dealing with our offspring, whose predominantly limbic functioning unsettles us and often pulls us back into our own old limbic patterns.

For example, did you ever experience frustration or puzzlement as to why, when you tell your child to do something, he will time after time not do it? You give a command such as "go clean your room," "go get ready for bed," "go set the table" (interesting how many common parental communications are imperatives, and how many of them begin with the child-unfriendly word "go!"). To this he will respond by pretending to do it, doing some of it, making an excuse why he didn't do it, attempting to bribe an older sibling to do it, or coercing a younger sibling to do it in his place. Frustrated, you holler at the child "*What's the matter with you?*" becoming a child yourself. "Don't you understand *English*? Are you *deaf*? If you don't finish, you'll be punished!"

What is happening here? The answer, and the remedy for his "bad" behavior, lies in the neurological difference we have just discussed: the child's thinking brain is not yet developmentally capable of figuring out how to do the job when presented in adult language. Punishing or yelling at him for not doing something he doesn't know how to do— or doesn't yet have the experience or cognitive ability to do—is not only useless; it is abusive. It damages his self-esteem—and yours, too! Only gradually does a child develop sufficient neocortical functioning to identify or reason out the sequence and components of a whole process, such as those mentioned above, let alone to break it down into smaller component processes and then order them in a rationally meaningful sequence. (Also, he doesn't like the word GO)!

While the adult brain will not need the experience to know that dusting should be done before vacuuming but can arrive at it by logic and reasoning, the child has neither the experience from which to learn it nor the neocortical functioning to figure it out. So how to proceed? To learn properly, which means successfully, egosyntonically, fearlessly, the whole child must be included. By this means the child's emotional growth (security, belonging, self-esteem) will not be neglected in favor of his cognitive learning, as it is so often today.

So do the job *with*, not *for*, him: he will get "how to" from your experiential model, and if you do it pleasantly and consistently, someday you will have a very happy daughter-in-law. The time to be "limbic" is in the directive stage, *e.g.* "I really like it when we clean your room together;" the time to be "neocortical" is in the connecting: "I see you didn't quite get it all done. Let's work on the bookshelves a little more."

Playing, imagining, creating, as Wordsworth beautifully describes, are the child's work as well as his joy, and they lay the foundation for intellectual growth: security and belonging come before and provide the foundation for the components of self-esteem and autonomy. It is the heart of parenting to walk the child through all his early learnings, so that he experiences the process and the sequence of its components with a loving, patient guide. By this means, the parent teaches the child not only *what* to learn (content) but, more important, *how* to learn (process) so that he gradually and naturally lays the foundation for becoming a self-teacher. Most important of all, he learns that learning is enjoyable, and that his parent is supportive, understanding, and kind.

This essential parental function obviously cannot be successfully accomplished by a parent still carrying his own childhood traumas and the behavior patterns they generate. He will act out on that conditioning and automatically do to his offspring (and wife) what his parents did to him, or its opposite. This may be just as destructive, since his adult behavior will reflect the feelings generated in him when a little boy. It is therefore essential that the parent spend some time daily practising the Freedom Process© to release his old patterns, insure that they stay inactive, and reprogram his limbic system.

The quality of our lives and our survival as a nation—indeed, as a world—depends on good parenting. The fabric of our society is at stake: much of the current venality, greed, violence, and crime we perpetrate and suffer, and the utter lack of compassion we exhibit, are caused by the trauma, neglect, and abuse—emotional as well as physical—installed in us as children.

Adults who were mistreated or abused as children create dysfunctional families (meaning those in which the four basic psychological needs are not met sufficiently) whose children will grow up to create their own dysfunctional families, a process which increases geometrically. When the number of dysfunctional families reaches the majority, the obvious result, now clearly discernible, is a dysfunctional culture.

We have already more than arrived at that stage, and are therefore inevitably insuring multiplication of the dysfunctionality of the next generation. While some children who grow up in situations of loss, abuse, neglect, poverty, *etc.* not only survive but by some means—an inspiring teacher, a protective older sibling or grandmother, a therapist or school counselor, a wise and compassionate man of the cloth—become healthy and raise healthy children, the majority do not.

To expect children who have been abused and treated carelessly, by society as well as by parents, to grow into honest, highly functioning, responsible, non-criminal, compassionate, productive adults, is the most flagrant nationwide case of denial since a white male slave owner told his slaves that they were only three-fifths of a human being. Unhealthy parents raise unhealthy children and create an unhealthy culture; healthy parents raise healthy children who develop a healthy culture as they grow up.

Further, it is outrageous to be outraged when children who have grown up so wounded become dysfunctional or dangerous teenagers and adults. What other outcome could be expected??? The fact that so many of us are to some extent one or the other or both is the clearest evidence of the failure to put into practice the values people, preachers, and politicians talk about so endlessly. The primary unpracticed value is *that of real concern for all life including animals and the environment,* concern real enough to put money and self-rehabilitation behind it.

Crisis is too mild a word for what is happening in and to our country; *catastrophe* is more accurate. Improved understanding of children, of how they grow and how to meet their needs, is the *crucial element in halting and reversing the decline of our culture,* and should be a required part of the curriculum of every institution of learning in this country, from kindergarten through graduate school. Occasional private efforts in that direction are too little and too late. Only concerned, enlightened public effort can avert the disaster gaining ground daily, *the same fate for the next generation having been already determined.* We are commiting national genocide. The Process© described in this book, designed specifically for healing dysfunction, would be one means, if used widely enough, to halt the continuing deterioration and provide the foundation for a healthy, functional society, one which cares more about people than about profit.

Appendix III

Mental Health Correlations

While reading descriptions of the four needs, you may have noticed, perhaps more than once, that some of their defenses are similar to certain mental health diagnoses. When I came upon this parallel, it was hard not to draw the conclusion that in many cases the mental health diagnoses are the *same thing* as the defenses (third column in the Needs Chart©), and therefore stem from the same needs-deficit in childhood. More important, it was clear after several trial runs that the mental health diagnoses also could be healed by the Freedom Process©. In this chapter we will explore how the MH diagnoses correlate to the four needs and therefore how they respond to the same healing process. The Chart© facing p.i includes these MH correlatives; discussion of each one follows.

The most severe diagnoses are those associated with the first two needs—security and belonging—because they occur earliest in our development and therefore cause the greatest damage if not fulfilled.[1]

1. The Security Need/The Clown Type

We begin with the *Security Need/Clown Type*. Some of its *fight* defenses, such as agitation, hyperactivity, hypermntation, teasing, joking, practical joking, scattered thinking, and aggressiveness and inability to focus, correlate to symptoms of the currently popular "ADD" (*attention deficit disorder*) and "OCD" (*obsessive compulsive disorder*) including rituals, obsessive or fragmented thinking, compulsive neatness or cleaning, organizing self or house or yard or office or extreme activity of any kind. There is also a correlation to "ODD" (*oppositional defiant disorder*) including inappropriate aggressiveness, stubbornness, non-compliance, defiance, physical or verbal abuse or violence.

The usefulness of this correlation is that when a client comes to my office with, say, a diagnosis of ADD, the fact that his symptoms are identical to the defenses of the security need tells me that, probably since he was a baby, he has suffered from chronic feelings of insecurity, causing him to act out in a variety of ways. The route of recovery, therefore, is apparent: release the pain and meet the need.

Another example is the client who comes in with no diagnosis, but exhibits jumpy, obsessive thinking, incessant worrying, short-temperedness, and cracks a joke after every sentence, signals of *obsessive compulsive personality disorder*. All of these are defenses against insecurity, originating almost always in early childhood.[2] Whether diagnosed as a mental health disorder or an unmet need, an event in the present has reopened an old wound that was in some way damaging or frightening to the child, and the "adult" now has to deal with it. Unless the person has had some therapy along these lines, it is more than likely that he won't be able to a remember the event or condition, which of course makes him feel crazy. What the Freedom Healing Process© can offer him is first, that to recover he must recognize and learn how to meet his needs, and second, a method by which to do that.

The earlier the insecurity started, the more deeply it is embedded, and therefore the harder it is to dislodge: how we are treated in childhood stays with us as we grow up, hidden in our feeling brain (the "unconscious"), and unless dealt with directs virtually all of our behavior as adults. It is therefore essential to release as much of the childhood trauma as possible; consistent use of the Freedom Healing Process© will bring about recovery in each person's time frame.

Once the need is fully and consistently met, the condition gradually diminishes and eventually disappears, if events don't occur that stir it up. There are plenty of examples from my practice alone of people who have been free of their trauma for many years, and then suddenly life brings a situation they find too hard to handle, reawakening the original wound. We apparently carry the template of our dysfunction permanently: once installed in the amygdala it's there forever. The limbic system doesn't know or operate in time.

Among the *flight defenses* (see third row of security need on Chart©) the predominant correlative MH diagnosis is *depression*, arguably the most frequently diagnosed and widely discussed mental health condition of the last five decades. Its symptoms are forms of the flight defense, either literal or symbolic: sleeping excessively or not at all, loss of appetite and libido, despondency, irritability, shutting down, isolating, demotivation, gloom, apathy, and at its worst, suicidal ideation or action. When someone thus afflicted starts releasing, the feelings that surface are fear, anger, and anxiety, all of which are symptoms of a deficit or impairment in the security need, most likely from some childhood trauma. As the Healing Process© releases these feelings, the depression gradually lifts.

We can therefore draw the conclusion that depression is actually a *defense against those painful feelings* and *unmet needs,* a conclusion validated by the permanent (so far) recovery of many of my clients suffering from lifelong depression for whom other methods of recovery had been unsuccessful. The discovery, brought about by the release of their repressed anger and fear, that the cause of their depression was insecurity (either past or present), was confirmed when they did the third part of the Healing Process,© the self-nurturing. That this Process© actually *released their depression* was astonishing to them, since nothing they had tried before had helped consistently. They subsequently discovered that releasing their depression had also released not only their underlying anger and fear but also the root cause: *insecurity*! Finally, the real culprit was discovered and sent packing for good by the Process.

In following and supporting my clients' processes, I also made some discoveries, perhaps the most important of which was the teaching tool the Freedom Process© gave me. Thanks to the Chart©, once I heard a client's story—often just his opening sentence—I knew immediately which of the four needs was his primary deficiency.

As my clients became proficient in releasing their painful feelings and instilling in themselves a sense of inner security, I taught them how to reprogram their limbic system by talking to it as though it were a child, directing them away from depression and toward a positive and happy frame of mind. Freed from the grip of permanent, continuous depression, they transformed themselves into people who experience occasional depression (a normal condition) but are able to bring themselves out of it reliably.

Now that you have learned the Freedom Process©—releasing your painful feelings and giving Your self the support and nurturance it needs whenever it is upset, discouraged, or angry, *etc.*—you can transform Your self in similar fashion. As the Process© releases these feelings, the depression gradually lifts, a clear indication that it was caused by repressing such feelings and was therefore a defense against them (as well as a signal of their original presence).

A second MH diagnostic category that correlates to the *flight defenses* is *dissociative disorder*. The defenses are from mild to severe: checking out, mental vacuity, daydreaming, absent-mindedness, demotivation, fantasizing, wandering thinking, detachment, disengagement from the body.

The extreme of the flight defense is *multiple personality disorder*. When the anger and fear caused by insecurity reach unbearable intensity, the unconscious creates another identity to flee to, and continues creating others ("alters") when any existing one is too threatened. It is most likely to originate in very early childhood, before the thinking brain has

Discoveries & Conclusions

developed fully enough to balance and protect the feeling brain against constant damage such as: being chronically beaten; frequently locked for extended periods in a closet or basement or out of the house, sometimes in cold weather; shuffled unpredictably back and forth from one family to another; housed at Grandma's and visited by Mom three or four times a year; deposited in an institution such as a religious orphanage and not visited at all (all of the these were real events, drawn from my caseload). While MPD does benefit from the Freedom Process©, it carries such a frightening intensity of dysfunction that its treatment requires additional specialized techniques.

Another correlative MH diagnosis that also originates in early childhood trauma combines the two varieties of the Clown defense. Look again at the third section of the security Chart©, the one that has two different columns: in the fight column you see "manic" and in the flight column "depression." As with *multiple personality disorder*, *manic depression* derives from extreme insecurity at such an early age that the child has no ability to defend himself, so whatever painful feelings—such as fear, anxiety, anger, insecurity—are encoded in his limbic system become incorporated into the development of his personality.

Since one variety of defenses proves insufficient to mask the pain, its opposite is used. Now referred to as "bipolar disorder," manic depression is characterized by alternation, for extended periods of time, between *fight* and *flight* defenses: hyperactivity, hypermentation, grandiosity, and unrestrained, aggressive thinking and behavior on the one hand; and on the other hand, withdrawnness, fantasy, hallucination, introversion, depression, non-activity, and psychosis. The Freedom Process© is effective in cases of MD in which the client is capable of accessing his feelings (even just a tiny bit), and is neither actively delusional nor still in need of psychotropic drugs. Along with MPD, the complexity of the illness requires additional treatment modalities.

The distinction between the Clown Type of defenses and the mental illness of manic depression should be noted. The Clown Type is distinguishable from the manic depressive in three ways: it is characterized by being more often distinctly fight or flight rather than both or alternating; by the absence of delusion or psychosis; and by the defenses typical of both conditions being less severe in the Clown Type. The two conditions exist on a continuum of which MD is at the extreme end. But the Clown Type occurs much more often than MD and, in my practice, more than any of the other types, a statistic echoed by the prevalence in our society of the ADD diagnosis.

The implications of this statistic for our country are alarming. When a society is not capable of meeting its security needs (or isn't willing to), the three other needs can't function with full effectiveness either, so they too remain deficient. The security need is primary: without the base, the middle and top are insecure. The lack of sufficient security in many areas of our lives—professional, economic, domestic, marital, educational, criminal—goes a long way to explain the increase in the disorder just discussed; folks are "mad as hell" because they are insecure and scared in too many areas.

The economic disparities in our supposedly democratic nation could be paralleled to France at the time of Marie Antoinette ("let them eat cake"): the rich get richer by eating up the life savings of the workers whose dedicated and faithful efforts made them rich in the first place. The Enron executives got away with millions—enough for one of them to spend six thousand dollars on a *shower curtain!* And the faithful workers got away with *nothing*—a good many of them lost their life savings. This still unresolved scandal has, inevitably and understandably, resulted in a tremendous drop in the sense of security of thousands of Americans, and that insecurity will spawn anger, fear, depression, envy, *etc.*

2. The Belonging Need/Forgotten Type

The *Belonging Need/Forgotten Type* comes second. There are several MH correlatives to the belonging need, including, in order of increasing severity, avoidant disorder, separation disorder, panic disorder, and agoraphobia and schizophrenia. In all of these we can see the defenses of aloneness and isolation typical of the Forgotten Type ("I always was a loner," "I have to be alone so I won't get rejected").

The first four defenses show in increasing degrees the reluctance and sometimes actually the inability to socialize or to venture out of one's home or immediate surroundings, either altogether or conditionally, "only if I have a couple of drinks first," "if you pick me up," "if the house is on fire" (from a client who still had her sense of humor). The result, if the person is pushed too far, is the thing they fear the most, an anxiety or panic attack. The compulsive isolation, added to the abandonment, neglect, and rage they generate, leads eventually to a state of psychic compression similar to and often mistaken for depression, but characterized by two factors not generally present in the latter.

The first is the tension arising from the intrapsychic conflict between the inward-turning grief and the outward-moving rage. The second factor is a by-product of the first: a potential for explosiveness not typical of the Clown type of depression, in which the anger is more likely to be sarcastic and hyper. This state of compression is aggravated by the predominating defense of isolation that makes the condition especially intractable. You can't reach the person—literally as well as figuratively.

That there is a continuum in these disorders is clear. As the Forgotten Type or the agoraphobic stays in her house, and the avoidant personality stays in her room, so the schizophrenic stays in her *self*—*way* inside, like a super-shy turtle, not reachable, living in a primitive inner space of her own creation, as forgotten as she can get. All these defenses, some obviously more severe than others, are caused by insufficient nurturance and connectedness in early childhood. The evidence for this is when a client with such defenses or with one of the above diagnoses is able to uncover the hidden feelings, they are all ones which are caused by a lack of belonging: a sense of loneliness, rejection, abandonment, neglect, *etc.*

The schizophrenic, like the manic-depressive, is at the extreme end of this continuum, where these feelings are at their most severe. They are, however, so deeply repressed (due to the intensity of pain they generate) that he has no awareness of them: his mental activity consists almost entirely of defenses. Like electricity, his feelings are known only by their effects. Adult experiences of loss or lack, even very small ones, that restimulate the original trauma cause regression to the limbic (child/feeling) brain and relative disconnect from the neocortex (adult/thinking) brain, as well as from the outer world.[3]

This view of schizophrenia is very different from the current concept, which sees it as a thought disorder of genetic or biochemical origin. But because its symptoms, taken to the extreme, are the same as the characteristics of the Forgotten Type, I perceive it, instead, as essentially a defense against an extreme early and severe childhood lack or loss of bonding and nurturance, consisting of two main components: (1) total or nearly total psychic disconnection, whose job is to bury the (2) intense, rigorously compressed, explosive rage.

This repressed rage, that for the Forgotten Type or agoraphobic is difficult to access, is for the schizophrenic generally impossible. The inability to access, feel, and release rage is the major impediment to recovery for both diagnoses: it acts like a lid pressing down the unbearable feelings of abandonment and lack of belonging. Unless it is removed and the feelings released, the need cannot be met, and so long as the need remains, the disease is perpetuated.

The schizophrenic eventually, and of course unconsciously, sees virtually every event, public ones as well as his own, from the vantage point of his repressed trauma. As his repressed rage magnifies, it sets off norepinephrine (a brain chemical) to a degree correlating to the degree of fear caused by his abandonment. The functioning of the neocortex is thereby diminished further and the amygdala (the "survival button" of the brain) is activated. The result is that, without sufficient capability for sustaining rational thought, the schizophrenic remains locked into the defenses imprinted in his limbic system that become, like the turtle's shell, impossible to penetrate. Unless he dies or commits suicide, the mounting pressure of his internally repeated rage will eventually burst forth in some form of violent destruction, either on himself or another, an ultimate and tragic statement of a mind not able to heal itself.

A good example is Ted Kaczynski, the alleged Unabomber. His mother, as she told the story on *60 Minutes*, bravely talked about her son's tragic illness in infancy and what caused it: he was, she said, a remarkably happy, bouncy baby, until at nine months he got sick and had to be hospitalized. "It was about fifty years ago," she said, "when parents weren't allowed to stay with the child as they are now. I, of course, visited whenever I was allowed, but every time I left, he became frantic. I would remember how he'd grab the bars of the crib...and he'd scream and hold out his arms and I'd have to go out the door."

It must have been as unbearable for her as for the baby. She continued: "When I finally came back to take him home, what they handed to me was not this bouncing joyous baby, but a little rag doll that didn't look at me, that was slumped over, completely limp and non-responsive, and he never recovered.[4] He remained quiet—we called it "shy"—and stayed in his own room most of the time. Since he was a good student, and he was not discourteous or disruptive, we didn't think of him as being in trouble. But he became more and more reclusive."[5]

This is a classic, and terribly painful, case of schizophrenia stemming from abandonment in early childhood. Since his neocortex wasn't yet functional, the separation from his mother caused a severe panic reaction against which he had no defense (at the mammalian stage of evolution, separation from the mother is death), and the daily reenactment of the trauma conditioned his limbic system to expect separation and loss whenever his mother appeared. Such reactions are encoded chemically in the limbic system, and are strengthened rather than dissipated with time. A causal loop is thus created: the conditioned pattern affects perception, so that the pattern is subjectively seen where objectively it does not exist (=paranoia), and each such subjectively induced experience (=regression to the earlier trauma) adds another layer, so to speak, to the harmful conditioning.

Consequently, with every visit the trauma was reinforced, because his mother's coming was always followed by her leaving. Any subsequent explanation to him that Mom's repeated absences were hospital policy and not her choice would have no power to reverse the damage, since his neocortex wasn't sufficiently developed to effect a change in the limbic imprint. (In any case, as discussed before, the neocortex, even at its greatest degree of clarity, is no match for a raging limbic system). Not yet having learned how to comfort himself ("Oh, goody, Mommy's coming again tomorrow"), he would start crying the minute he saw her: every visit she made conditioned his feeling brain to expect separation and loss instead of love and protection.

He therefore came to associate his mother with danger, perceiving her as something inexplicably threatening that must be avoided at all costs. Combined with his overwhelming longing for her, the fear, frustration, and rage, repeated daily, created a disastrous intrapsychic conflict. It is no wonder that this week of frantic yearning-plus-dread-followed-by-desertion (eight times repeated!) left him limp and apathetic, "all passion spent."[6]

There would have been no way to resolve such a conflict; all he could do was avoid it. Hence his isolation, noticeable even in childhood, eventually became total: "he'd go upstairs...he became a very sober sort of child," his mother noted. Imagining this baby's inner state is painful enough; the actual experiencing of it must have been excruciating beyond endurance. The repressed rage that lay dormant all his life became the motivating force that finally propelled his tragic acting out. What a huge and painful tragedy, from such a preventable cause!

Surprisingly, it is not unusual for the schizophrenic to be able to acknowledge the fact of his abandonment, even though he is unable to access his feelings about it. I ask: "Did you feel, or were you, alone a lot when you were a kid?" The answer is invariable: "Always—I always was a loner." But if I say, "You must have felt enraged that they abandoned you," it is just as invariably denied, and denied coolly and convincingly. Apparently even *mention* of the abandonment is sufficient to cause a withdrawal into his shell and consequent diminution of neocortical consciousness, wherein lies the capacity for self-awareness, and consequent regression to the limbic system. Thus trapped in his child brain, the schizophrenic cannot be conscious of his feelings since the organ of awareness (the neocortex) is itself significantly diminished or shut down altogether. Consequently, like a child or an animal, he acts out his feelings. *We* can tell what feelings are in him but *he* cannot.

Although my present caseload doesn't include patients who are psychotic, I worked with several schizophrenics and manic-depressives as a member of team psychotherapy when I was doing agency work. Several of them made significant progress using this method, the criterion for its effectiveness being whether the patient had a minimal capability of accessing and expressing feelings, rage in particular.

My own caseload has included several clients with schizoid characteristics, all of whom had experienced moderate to severe abandonment in early childhood. In each case, the mother had difficult conditions of her own that took her away either physically or emotionally from her children, preventing her from being able to care for them adequately.

The theory presented here is not about blaming mothers; it is about finding the cause of the condition so that present and future distress can be prevented. The best way to state it is this: while childhood abandonment (either emotional or physical) by the caregiving parent may not always lead to adult Forgotten Type codependency, PTSD, or schizophrenia, every patient I have treated who suffered from any of these disorders had experienced severe abandonment, criticism, and rejection as a child.

The same phenomenon happens with alcoholics and addicts. The mood-altering substances they use also impair neocortical functioning, so they too operate from their limbic brain rather than from their neocortex. This accounts not only for their childish behavior, but also for the not uncommon misdiagnosis of them as schizophrenics, which underlines the impossibility of an accurate differential diagnosis prior to a thorough (5-7 days minimum) detoxification process.

To conclude this section, we can say that the symptoms of avoidant, panic, and separation disorders, and agoraphobia and schizophrenia are markedly similar to the characteristics of the *Belonging Need/Forgotten Type*, indicating a similar cause and a similar treatment. They both stem from a deficiency in the belonging need that diminishes the functioning of the neocortex to whatever degree, thus leaving the limbic system to run the show to whatever degree, but many can be effectively treated by this Process© with obviously greater success possible in the less severe cases.

3. The Self-Esteem Need/Perfect Type

Next is the *Self-Esteem Need/Perfect Type*. The correlative mental health diagnosis is obsessive-compulsive personality disorder. Its symptoms echo many of the characteristics of the need for self-esteem: overworking, excelling, perfectionism, preoccupation with detail to the exclusion of product, control of every activity to insure that it will be "done right," over-concern about being seen as respectable, correct, moral *etc.*, and lack of awareness of or concern for other people's feelings, including an apparent inability to grasp the hurtful effects on others of the rigidity of his focus.

Like the *Perfect Type*, the obsessive-compulsive personality is an absolutist for whom a perfect result is not what matters most—it is what matters *only*. The landscape of human history bears testimony to this phenomenon: we see in the foreground many marvelous works of art and scholarship, political accomplishments, scientific discoveries and achievements, and in the background many broken relationships, crazed spouses, and neglected or forgotten children.

The sad example of Martha Stewart comes to mind: the Empress of the domestic realm looms large in the foreground, while in the background, according to an article in McCall's (Oct. 1996)[7] she was "left by her husband" in 1987 and has a "complicated" relationship with her only child, Alexis (36, unmarried, no children) which will "never... appear warm and fuzzy to the public." It is a "major regret" that she never had another. The "house beautiful" lacks the essential ingredient of a home—a family.[8]

In addition to all these characteristics, the obsessive-compulsive is, like the Perfect Type, frequently appointed substitute parent. His caretaking is done, however, not from a base of compassion or concern, but rather from self-serving motives such as getting praise or approval from parents, relatives, teachers, coaches, the public, *etc.* or from a sense of obligation ("someone has to do it") or from his characteristic drive to be able to do anything and excel at it. Focusing on taking care of others carries the implication that the caretaker is okay, thus camouflaging his low self-esteem. His readily expressed loyalty to and pride in his siblings ("my brother's the best on the team;" "I'll beat you up if you so much as *look* at my sister") are thus projections of his own need to achieve and excel.

An excellent example is "Hannah" in Woody Allen's movie *Hannah and Her Sisters*. Her *Perfect Type*-lieutenant role, underlined by the fact that only she is named in the title, is gradually and cleverly shown to be ego-driven. That is, instead of arising from disinterested love or concern, her role comes from the need to preserve/promote her self-image as the OK one, the one who advises, not the one who gets advised.

In contrast is Elizabeth Bennett, in Jane Austen's *Pride and Prejudice*. That her care is disinterested and genuine is demonstrated in two ways: first, she dispenses it discriminately only to the worthy Jane and not automatically also to her two frivolous younger sisters, and second, that she maintains it when doing so necessitates relinquishing the man she loves (a relinquishment that she has no reason to suppose will not be permanent, but which, as it happily turns out, is only temporary). Were her caretaking not from genuine selfless love but from the need to be the obsessive-compulsive director, she would extend it to all her sisters equally, merely because they are hers. Moreover, such self-interest would compel her to withdraw it from Jane (regardless of the cost to her sister and their relationship) in order to retain Darcy.

Once again we see the symptoms of the MH diagnosis as similar—indeed, identical—to those of one of the types, leading us to conclude that the thought and behavior patterns of OCD are a defense against feelings of unworthiness and inadequacy. Given these similarities, we can conclude that the cause of OCD is the same as the cause of the Perfect Type: a deficiency in the self-esteem need, most likely originating from a traumatic climate of criticism and disapproval in childhood. Hence the purpose of the defenses: to make the person's value and capabilities indisputably visible to all.

The defenses of the Perfect Type and the OCD diagnosis appear similar to those of the Clown Type and its correlative MH diagnosis of obsessive-compulsive personality. But actually they are different in both source and goal. In contrast to the Perfect Type and OCD just described, the goal of the Clown type is to defend himself against the fear caused by insecurity. When the security need is not met, the needs of the three types above it cannot be met either, nor can the OCD symptoms be adequately dealt with, which is why the Clown is the most distressed of the four types.

4. The Autonomy Need/Trouble Type

Last but not least, we come to the MH correlatives of the *Autonomy Need/Trouble Type*. They are all personality disorders: antisocial, passive aggressive, and narcissistic. All of them have symptoms that indicate damage to the autonomy need in childhood or adolescence.

The first of these, anti-social personality disorder, has the most similarity to the characteristics of the Trouble Type. The symptoms or traits they have in common are: difficulty observing other people's boundaries or establishing their own in an acceptable and effective manner (neither too submissive nor too aggressive); disregard for other people's feelings and needs; non-compliance with societal, legal, and moral norms (*e.g.* from mild to severe: butting in line, running red lights, lying, stealing, mugging, and more serious forms of crime and violence); being blamed, made wrong, criticized, seen as the "identified patient," the "cause of all our troubles," *etc*. Like the Trouble Type, the anti-social personality shows neither compassion nor compunction, nor an appropriate sense of guilt or remorse on his own. If called to account, he becomes defensively aggressive and blames the victim, *e.g.* "she was asking for it;" "he should be more careful how he talks to me;" "I been hurt all my life;" "the whole damn family is crazy—why should I be the one who always catches hell?"

It is readily apparent that this resistance to acknowledging and accepting guilt, and taking responsibility for one's actions, is the Trouble Type's block to emotional and psychological recovery. Also true but not so easy to see is that, ironically, to him, resistance is the safeguard of his autonomy. Were such a person to admit he did it and it was wrong, he would be agreeing with their definition of him.

Such agreement would in his mind constitute capitulation and loss of autonomy. Both the antisocial personality and the Trouble Type may carry this so far that they cannot even accept praise or compliments. His negative and aggressive response in any given situation is magnified by the fund of resistance already accumulated in him from being blamed and punished over the years for many things he *didn't* do, as well as things he *did* do.

What is the source of this dysfunction? The similarity of symptoms indicates that the source for antisocial personality disorder is the same as for the Trouble Type: in each such case I have worked with, the person's autonomy, his ability to define and govern himself, had been consistently squelched throughout his childhood (a sure indicator of dysfunction in the autonomy or self-esteem need of the caregiver as well). The result is that he focuses aggressively on his rights, often at the expense of others, and acts out his resentment, outrage, hurt, and defiance of authority any way he can.

On the other hand, a Trouble Type may, like the Clown Type, unconsciously choose flight rather than fight defenses with which to resist the invasion or oppression of his autonomy. But the MH diagnosis—*passive aggressive personality disorder*—that matches this Type consists of defenses similar to the Clown (flight) Type, only more slick and sophisticated. Here

Discoveries & Conclusions

we find such symptoms as: (1) evasiveness and non-compliance, *not* doing things routinely and legitimately expected of him, *e.g.* homework, bathing, brushing his teeth, calling if he's going to be late.

Then come somewhat more oppositional behaviors: (2) procrastination, covert stubbornness and subtle sabotaging of activities or tasks he doesn't want to do (*e.g.* "Uh-oh! Mom! The vacuum cleaner broke! I can't fix it now! We're out of—and the stores are closed!"). A good example is a young lady who bore extreme resentment toward her charming and sweet but very dominating mother. Her one-liner was spoken in a kind of slow emphatic snarl: "When the b— makes me clean the kitchen, I do it, but *I take...my... sweet....time!*" (That such symptoms often occur in the years from thirteen to nineteen makes it tempting to think of the word *adolescence* as a *diagnosis* rather than a stage of growth). These defenses, although most common during these years, are not inherent in adolescence, but are symptoms in adulthood as well.

Such behavior, whenever it occurs, drives other people crazy. Parents, spouses, teachers, even peers become extremely frustrated, and go through a predictable sequence of responses, from mild requests, cajoling, and subtle manipulation, to nagging, abandonment, and sometimes even physical attack, aimed at getting the passive-aggressive/flight-type to produce, cooperate, carry out commitments (such as *homework*), or just plain *function*.

All such reactions are to no avail. He remains dug into his unproductive position, exhibits touchiness and surliness, often extreme, at even mild suggestions, and is critical and contemptuous of people who are, as he puts it, "trying to control" him. The requester is left with his frustration and anger intensified, while the perpetrator manages to present himself as an apparently innocent and abused victim. It is as if the Trouble Type/passive aggressive personality stuffed his hurt and rage and resentment into a football and flipped it to his oppressor (as he sees it)—and now that person is left holding the outrage, while the Trouble Type/passive-aggressive walks away *cool.*

From much practice over the years, this type/diagnosis develops sufficient skill at his *modus operandi* (all, of course, unconscious—defenses aren't from the conscious realm) to thwart even the most severe coercion or abandonment.[9] Threats of confinement or actual confinement, either domestic or legal, or withdrawal of beloved possessions (stereo, car, beeper) or privileges (staying out late on a week night, having friends sleep over) or, at the relationship level, threats of separation or actual separation—all these in many cases only harden the resistance. The more he experiences the damage to his autonomy—and all such stratagems feel like threats to it—the stronger his resistance. Short of willingly undertaking therapy to release his repressed feelings and learn how to meet his needs from within, the Trouble Type/passive aggressive cannot change unless life reacts so undesirably to his defenses that he is forced to see them as the consequence of his own behavior. It may be that the resulting shock is what is needed to jolt him into treatment.

Here's an example (it really happened): a man threatened by his wife with divorce, delays filing their joint mortgage payment in order to spite her. Her unavailability to him enrages him further, so he delays longer. Eventually, of course, his stratagem boomerangs and he has to pay a significant late fee. He was aware that his could happen, but his anger overrode his caution. This is the degree to which he had to resort to discover that he needed therapy.

There are two factors that indicate a deficiency in the autonomy need as the cause of the Trouble Type's anti-social defiance. The first factor is the similarity of autonomy symptoms to the TT's characteristics, in both cases caused by the thwarting of the natural growth of self-definition and self-governance. The reaction of the passive aggressive to this need-deficit is opposite to the aggressing defense of the anti-social personality: the passive aggressive/TT withholds what is required or expected, while the anti-social character raises hell. Both diagnoses are elaborations of the basic fight/flight defense.

The second factor is the similarity in effectiveness of the Freedom Process© for those suffering from this disorder. The same transformation occurs that we saw with the TT: the symptoms are reduced in frequency and intensity, and the person who emerges is happier and freer and, although he will occasionally have some passive reactions, he will no longer meet life with that mindset.

The third mental health diagnosis that shows some similarities to the TT is *autonomy need/narcissistic personality disorder*. Following are symptoms that correspond.

First is lack of empathy. This not only causes hurt to other people (which returns to the sender) but also distorts his concept of relationships. Instead of the basic reciprocity of companionship and affection, the narcissist operates unilaterally, using the relationship for his own purposes almost exclusively.

The second symptom is automatic expectation of attention and adulation for whatever he achieves, whether climbing Mt. Everest, sailing around the world alone, donating the funds for a new football stadium, giving his art collection to the local museum, funding a chair in a particular department in one's alma mater—all of these, of course, to bear the name of the donor and bring adulation, recognition, and publicity.

Another characteristic of narcissistic disorder that corresponds to the TT is a strong, sometimes vindictive or violent reaction to criticism or rejection. This aspect of the TT and the narcissist is exemplified in the aggressive spouse or adolescent whose right to rule the family is questioned by nobody. His exercise of authority is entirely self-interested and without regard (though it is sometimes feigned) for the feelings and needs of other family members. Consequently, they feel continually oppressed, resentful, and intimidated: "I feel like I have to walk on eggshells." They know that if they stir up the monster, or in any way challenge his rule, he will blame, shame, and even attack them either verbally or physically or both. They end up ashamed of themselves for feeling scared and reacting passively. The essential purpose of the relationship is thus damaged.

What is the cause of this disorder? Over-indulgence (generally by the mother) or over-dominance (generally by the father) on the autonomy need can lead the child to behaviors like the ones discussed above, especially when it's the first child and especially when it's a boy.

In the first case, overindulgence by the mother, due most likely to an unmet need for at least minimal attention from her father when she was growing up, the child is seen as perfect and treated as a law unto himself, with no boundaries or limits, and no requirements to modify "His Majesty" to accommodate others. He becomes his parent's boss. Failing to learn consideration for others, he grows up not knowing how to take their needs into account in his behavior, activities, and relationships.

The idiom "he's full of himself" is apt: the image gives us a way of actually seeing that there is no room in him for the feelings or concern of others because his mother didn't require it, even for herself. A consequence of this is that other people and their feelings and needs are not real to him. Without empathy, he can look out only for himself: he has little-to-no capacity or desire to develop interest in or compassion for others. His life is entirely about himself.

In the second case—over-dominance by the father— he gets the message of *total* boundaries: *i.e.*, he must obey, conform, bend the knee, *etc., but only to the parent who is doing the dominating.* Because his father's message is not about the child but about himself, the narcissistic parent, it is opposed tyrannically to the message from his mother, and is therefore abhorrent to the child. It implants in the child's feeling brain the idea that any action by another that feels controlling to him must be met by defiance or payback.

This diagnosis is arguably the most intractable of non-psychotic disorders, and can sometimes be more intractable even than some mild psychotic cases. This is because neither the narcissist nor the TT thinks anything is wrong with him, since his view of the world is the "objective" one (a favorite narcissistic word). His defense, therefore, is either *accusation:* "you made up the problem to push my buttons;" *blaming:* "it's your fault—you shouldn't talk to me like that;" *denial:* "nothing is wrong—it's all in your head;" or *justification:* "you *know* I have to have the radio on at night to help me sleep." He can be very charming and sincere and convincing (since he's completely sure he's in the right) in the face of irrefutable evidence (*e.g.*, OJ!). Only the most severe crisis can propel him into treatment and very often keeping him there is a lost cause.

However, if the unlikely miraculously happens, the Freedom Process© can be as effective for this disorder as for the antisocial or the passive aggressive personality disorder. The effectiveness is augmented if the therapy is presented as a primarily cognitive investigation, with particular focus at first on what causes his characteristic dislike of people who stir up his anger. Because this anger reaction covers up his resentment and loss of self-respect at not being the one in control, it is the key to opening up his feelings. (These fears are typically presented as motivations of the other person rather than feelings of his own, *e.g.* "he just has to control me;" "she wants to see how far she can push me").

If delicately and persistently approached, the narcissist will gradually let you in, and what is 99% likely to be uncovered in therapy is the bipolar nature of his childhood, alternately autonomous and dominated, although there are plenty of narcissists who got that way without the bipolar parental dysfunction. (I've known several narcissists in my twenty-three years of counseling *both* of whose parents spoiled them). While he enjoys the intense focus on himself—indeed, considers it appropriate—it also begins the process of pulling him out of himself, or, to speak more accurately, pulling himself out of him. Seeing that these patterns developed in early childhood relieves him of enough of his deeply buried guilt to allow him to begin looking at the effect of his behavior on others and why they react to him as they do.

Heretofore he probably has not been conscious of how his conversation sounds to other people, so when some brave person disagrees or confronts him he reacts with surprise and outrage. Indeed, just the realization that the actions of the other person may be reactions to his is a big step. From this base he can gradually come to see that, ironically, his pattern of narcissistic domination actually alienates the other person and thereby depowers and victimizes him. But when he relinquishes his dictatorial ways, they respond positively. So by giving others their freedom from his dictatorship he finds freedom for himself.

Based on the fact that these MH symptoms are so similar to the characteristics of the four types when their needs are not met, I suggest four hypotheses that anyone interested can further investigate and test: (1) Certain mental health conditions develop from the same cause as do the types: *i.e.* a deficiency or distortion in the intrapsychic needs stemming from childhood.[10] (2) These "disorders" are actually defenses, generated by those unmet needs. (3) It follows that these conditions can be healed by *fulfilling the need*—and cannot be fully healed *without meeting the need*. Therefore, (4) we can say that the Healing Process© for the four needs is appropriate therapy for the MH diagnoses as well. In my experience it has been effective for anyone who practises it consistently, often healing people for whom traditional methods, including medication, have been unable to do more than alleviate symptoms, and that briefly.

Appendix IV

Hierarchy of Needs & the Chakras

This appendix, the Chakras, came to me as I was finishing the book, bringing yet another spiritual system that correlates to Maslow's Hierarchy of Needs and the Freedom Healing Process©, and perhaps the most beautiful of all.

Those of you who are familiar with the Eastern system of Chakras (invisible "energy centers, gates and transformers")[1] will understand that they are our connection to the energy and web of the universe, in much the same way that the pump at the gas station is the conduit of energy to our cars (though not, perhaps, for very much longer), and the electrical system is the conduit of light.

So parallel are these two systems (the Hierarchy and the Chakras) to the universal one we might even say that the structure and functioning of each constitutes a mini-verse of its own: they replicate in our individual mini-energy systems the macro-energy of the universe. Likewise, each of us is a microcosm of the Macrocosm, a miniature of the whole ("a part of the main"),[2] sustained and nurtured by the energy-spinning Chakras in our neurological system. Just as the history of the development of the human species is contained in the brain of every human being, so is the universal energy/electrical system replicated and contained, through the Chakras, in the neurological system of every single human being.

This unseen essence (Bohm's "implicate order") that generates and sustains the whole universe, apparently likes its original model very much, since it keeps replicating it throughout the universe. We see this not only in the uncanny parallel, in both concept and content, between Maslow's hierarchy and the Chakras, but also in the correlation of both of those with Brain Structure and Functioning—which only dawned on me as I was writing this chapter. The two Charts follow.

Hierarchy of NEEDS

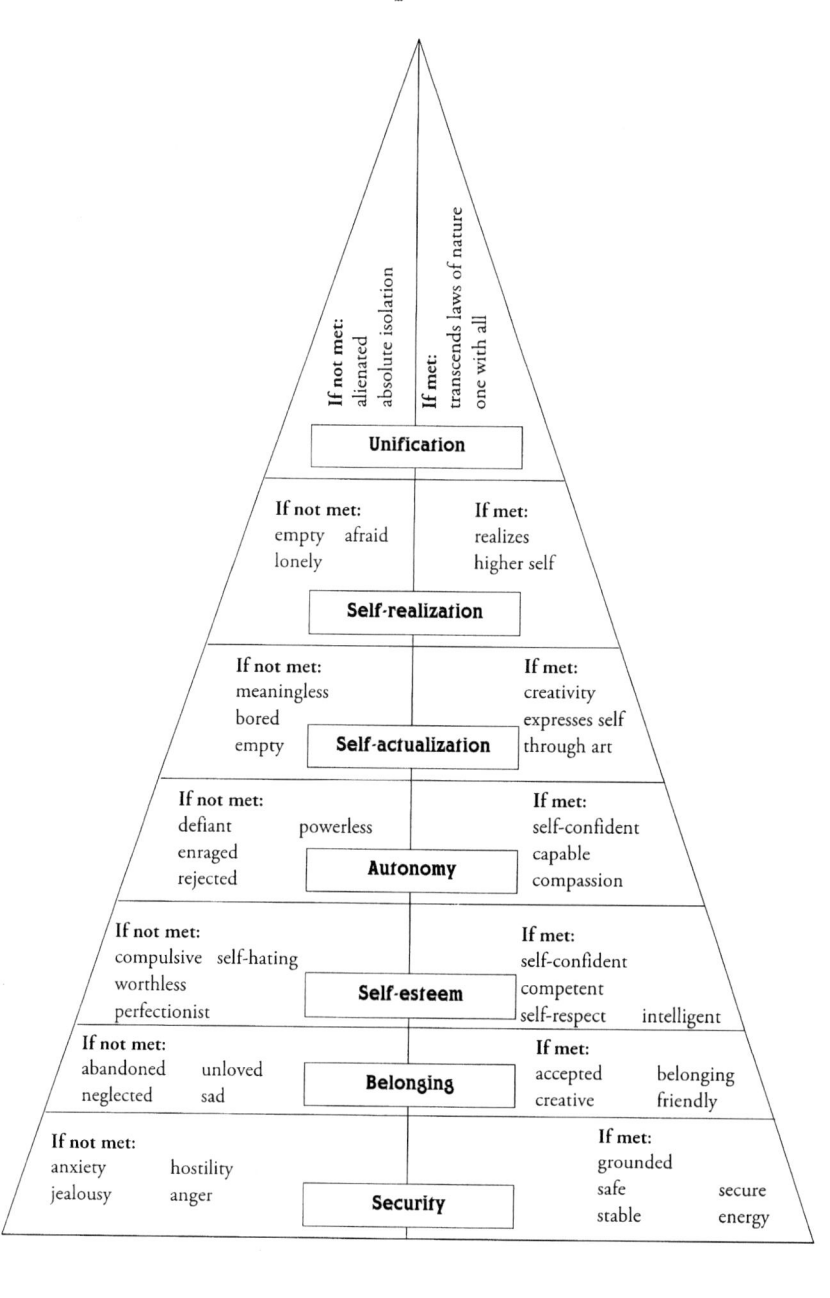

If not met: alienated, absolute isolation
If met: transcends laws of nature, one with all

Unification

If not met: empty, afraid, lonely
If met: realizes higher self

Self-realization

If not met: meaningless, bored, empty
If met: creativity, expresses self through art

Self-actualization

If not met: defiant, powerless, enraged, rejected
If met: self-confident, capable, compassion

Autonomy

If not met: compulsive, self-hating, worthless, perfectionist
If met: self-confident, competent, self-respect, intelligent

Self-esteem

If not met: abandoned, unloved, neglected, sad
If met: accepted, belonging, creative, friendly

Belonging

If not met: anxiety, hostility, jealousy, anger
If met: grounded, safe, secure, stable, energy

Security

CHAKRAS

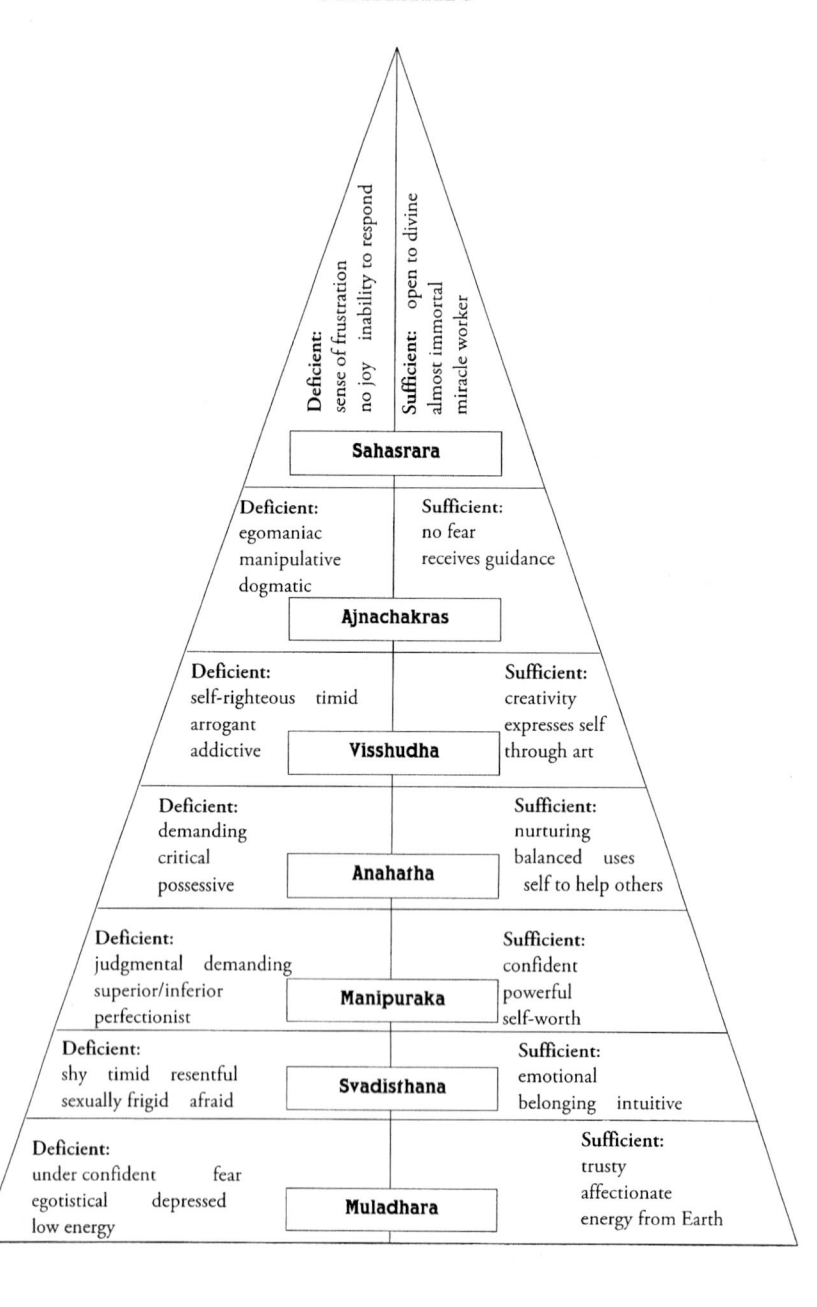

Deficient: sense of frustration, no joy, inability to respond
Sufficient: open to divine, almost immortal, miracle worker

Sahasrara

Deficient: egomaniac, manipulative, dogmatic
Sufficient: no fear, receives guidance

Ajnachakras

Deficient: self-righteous, timid, arrogant, addictive
Sufficient: creativity, expresses self through art

Visshudha

Deficient: demanding, critical, possessive
Sufficient: nurturing, balanced, uses self to help others

Anahatha

Deficient: judgmental, demanding, superior/inferior, perfectionist
Sufficient: confident, powerful, self-worth

Manipuraka

Deficient: shy, timid, resentful, sexually frigid, afraid
Sufficient: emotional, belonging, intuitive

Svadisthana

Deficient: under confident, fear, egotistical, depressed, low energy
Sufficient: trusty, affectionate, energy from Earth

Muladhara

Hierarchy of Needs	Commentary	Chakras
Unification	Unification	Sahasrara
Self-realization	Self-realization	Ainachakras
Self-actualization	Self-actualization	Visshudha
Autonomy	Autonomy	Anahatha
Self-esteem	Adolescence	Manipuraka
Belonging	Childhood	Svadisthana
Security	Infancy	Muladhara

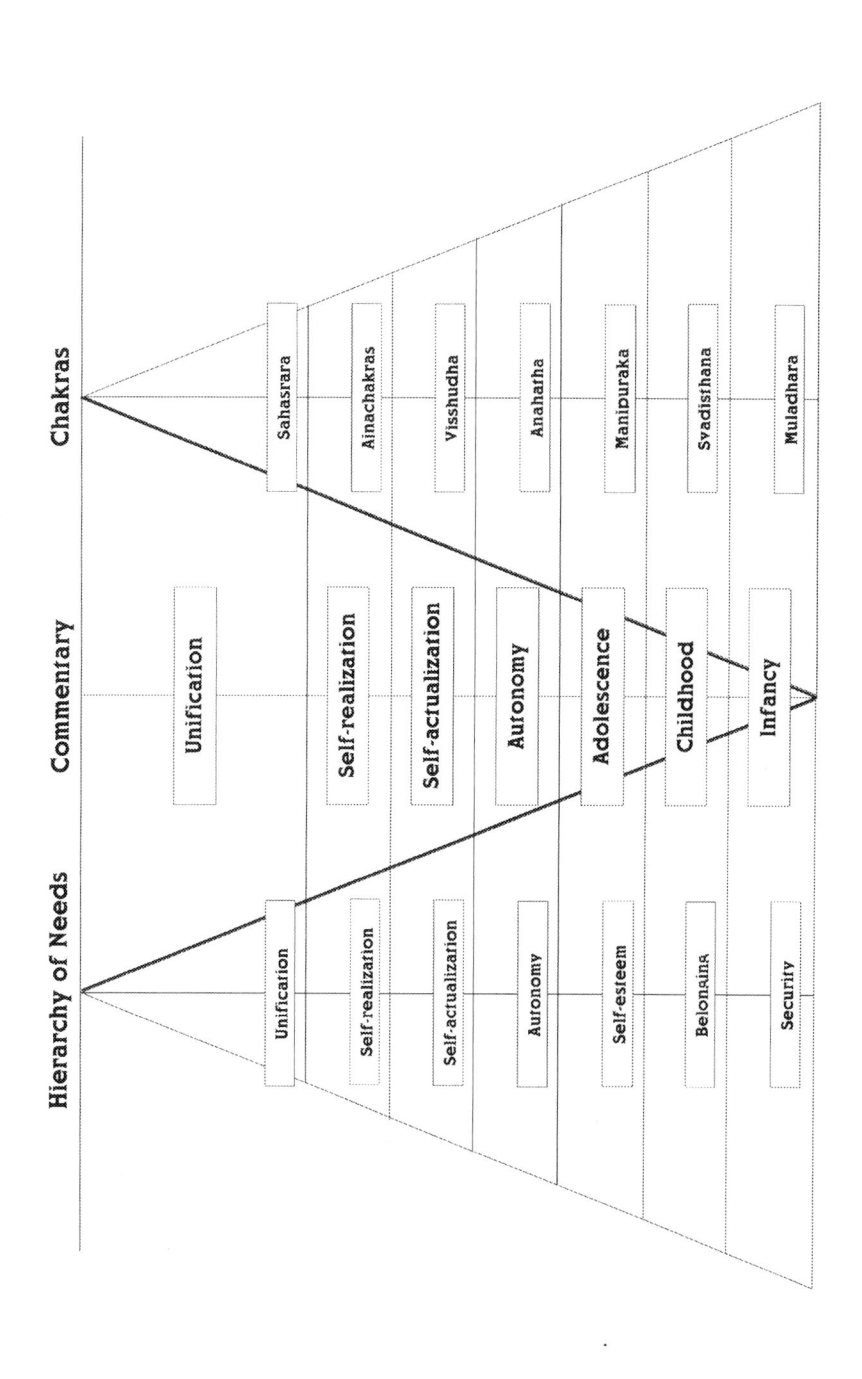

Discoveries & Conclusions

Appendix V

From Chaos to Harmony

To fulfill your needs and realize higher levels of self-actualization, we can add another dimension to The Process. As one part of the Process involves pounding pillows, you may instead pound on a drum. You may start with a pillow and graduate to a drum. As another part of The Process involves deep breathing (including a strong exhale), your outbreaths may involve into chants.

In advanced levels, the pounding on a drum (or drums) may become less random—developing a rhythm. Breathing and chanting may evolve into singing. Articulating your needs may lead to "singing the blues." Other sorts of venting, breathing meditation, and articulating may lead to playing a horn.

During a radio interview in Jamaica, the disc jockey asked Bob Marley how he got started [in music, activism, *etc.*]. He responded, "Started out crying...started out crying."[1]

The musical dimension may even fulfill unconscious needs, thus leading to higher levels of enlightenment and transcendence.

[Discussion on this topic will develop further].

—Edward R. Pratowski

Summary & Closure

The benefit of the healing method described in the introduction and demonstrated throughout this book may be summarized here: it is natural and inate, neither contrived nor invasive. We come equipped with it. It costs nothing, and can be done as often as you wish, without "side effects" (*i.e. harm*) or lessening of its effectiveness. Indeed, to the contrary, the more you do it, the more effective it becomes, and the longer lasting the results.

It creates not just alteration or suppression of symptoms (as with drugs), but *permanent transformation*—as long as you practice it regularly: by removing the old toxic programming from childhood and instilling new healthful programming, it gives you the freedom to meet any or all of the four needs at any moment, and therefore to govern your feelings, choose your thinking, and direct your behavior. It costs you nothing, feels good to do, and whatever your needs level, makes you feel better the more you do it: there is no limit to how high you can go. You will be transformed, "in the twinkling of an eye," and *you will be set free.*

Discoveries & Conclusions

To the Reader

From My Heart to Yours

Question
What's the difference between a "drug" and a "prescription"?

Answer
Where you buy it.

When you buy Valium, Xanax, Ritalin *etc.* from the pharmacy it's *medication*. When you buy it on the street it's *dope*. But the bottom line is, there is no difference in its makeup or its effect on you. *All mood-altering medications are drugs; all drugs are mood-altering.* Just calling them *medication* doesn't change their composition or what they do to you, only their legal status. All drugs make you feel better in the beginning, but all drugs alter and even damage you permanently if you do them long enough.

If you currently use either a street or prescription drug, the effectiveness of this method of healing will be diminished in proportion to the amount and frequency of your drug use. The reason for this is that all mood-altering chemicals sooner or later *depress or interfere with the functioning of the feeling (limbic) system and thereby impair your ability to experience your feelings*—and feeling your feelings is, as you have seen in Zeke's story, the key to recovery. This is true regardless of what they are, how few you take, who sold them to you, what you've been told about them or why you think you need them: *"they aren't addictive;" "you have a chemical imbalance;" "you need these the way a diabetic needs insulin;" "you'll need to be on them the rest of your life,"* etc., etc., etc.

The way out of this, and the key to recovery, is first, of course, to detox from the drugs, not hesitating to get medical help if needed. (If you're in doubt which way to go, *definitely* choose to get help: detoxing is, and should be, a medical process). Next, start the Healing Process© you've learned from this book, with special attention to your feelings, and do it on a regular basis: the more frequently you do it the sooner you'll begin to feel better and become happier and more functional.

Of course, it is precisely the reduction in feeling feelings that most people are seeking, because the natural system of dealing with feelings they were born with has been conditioned out of them. When emotional pain happens—and every day brings its share—we don't know what to do with it. Our culture quickly tells us that if you're down, take an upper (*e.g.* Elavil, Librium, Imiprimine, Prozac, speed, cocaine) or if you're up—*too* up—take a downer (*e.g.* Xanax, Ativan, Valium, Serax, alcohol, Dilaudid, heroin). If you're bored or dissatisfied, take anything available, beginning with pot or alcohol.

Unfortunately, in the long run, such "solutions" often become problems, in at least three ways: 1) they hide rather than heal the painful feelings, so you have to keep taking the drugs or the pain will resurface; 2) to whatever extent they do alleviate your distress, to that same extent they diminish your motivation to deal with the underlying problem therapeutically, so you don't rid yourself of the condition causing the pain; and 3) because the body builds up a tolerance to the drugs you feel that they are no longer helping, so you—or the doctor—increase the dose. All three of these consequences will inevitably lead you right into addiction if you take your drug-of-choice long enough.

This book offers a different approach, as by now you know very thoroughly. It teaches you a Process© for dealing with your feelings that is opposite to drugs/medication in every respect:

Discoveries & Conclusions

1. It is one hundred percent safe, because it's an innate process—you were born with it.

2. It is always effective, and it gets more effective, not less, the more you do it. You can't build up a tolerance to it.

3. It has no undesirable effects (what the medical/pharmaceutical industry euphemistically calls "side effects.")

4. It is free.

5. It is available to you anywhere anytime.

6. It is legal, and presents no difficulties or dangers to obtain.

7. You can't overdose on it.

8. It is holistic: it benefits all the elements of your mind/body system as well as your feelings.

9. It takes effect in one to five minutes—more quickly than a drug, even those that are mainlined or snorted—and the effect intensifies with each additional minute.

10. It can be used to get off drugs, after which its effectiveness will greatly increase, and you will be able to live drug free—as you were meant to do. Unless you have been brain-damaged or are psychotic, you have in you all the chemicals and chemical processes needed to function healthfully, though some of them may be impaired by chemical or emotional trauma.

The Freedom Healing Process© presented in this book has by now helped you to heal those impaired areas. Clients who come to this Process© drug-free progress rapidly, and of those who are still using chemicals, the majority eventually get off drugs altogether (under medical supervision) and consequently become able to live less restricted, fuller, healthier lives.

A passage from the book *Worst Pills, Best Pills* (Sidney M. Wolfe M.D., Rose-Ellen Hope, P. Ph. Public Citizens Health Research Group, 1993), written specifically about the elderly, applies as well to the general population in reference to this issue. The authors quote a British physician, Dr. George Carruthers:

> "Unfortunately, for a variety of reasons, medications are often used to treat the physical, psychological, social, and economical problems associated with aging (read "living"), even when there is scientific evidence that drugs are the least appropriate way of managing some of these problems. Rather than having the quality of life improved, the elderly (read "any age") patient may actually suffer adverse effects of drug intervention that was initiated, presumably, with the best intentions. Overuse of medications in the elderly (read "any age") may result. (*Overview*, p.2).

Further, in reference to the two most frequently medicated (and frequently *overmedicated*) psychological complaints, the authors state: "Anxiety is a universal emotion closely allied with appropriate fears. No drug is useful for the stress of everyday living. Try non-drug therapies for anxiety first. Drugs may control *but do not cure anxiety*." (p. 224). "The length of time it takes an antidepressant to work can overlap with the time of spontaneous recovery especially if the depression is situational—caused by a death or other external circumstances. The majority of people lift themselves out of depression with friends or activities, such as exercise, work, reading, play, art, travel, and spiritual resources... Antidepressant drugs should be reserved for depression that is major and does not respond to psychotherapy alone." *Worst Pills, Best Pills II.* Sidney M. Wolfe, M.D. Public Citizen Research Group. (p.244).

To summarize, here are the words of Dr. Peter Breggin:

"Anxiety sometimes can be *temporarily* alleviated by a variety of sedative drugs, including minor tranquilizers, barbiturates, opiates, alcohol, and perhaps antidepressants. But the effects are short-lived, with little or no evidence of sustained relief, and the hazards are considerable, including addiction, withdrawal, reactions, rebound anxiety, mental dysfunction, and lethality...Both alcohol and minor tranquilizers accomplish the same thing—a brief escape from intense feelings by suppressing or sedating normal brain function...As physicians or psychotherapists we should empower our patients to trust themselves and their capacity to triumph over frightening emotions. We should help them overcome anxiety through self-understanding, improved self-control of their minds and actions, more courageous attitudes, and more successful principles of living." See *Toxic Psychiatry*, p. 265.

In her book *Molecules of Emotion*, Dr. Candace Pert states the following:

"The tendency to ignore our emotions is oldthink, a remnant of the still-reigning paradigm that keeps us focused on the material level of health, the physicality of it. But the emotions are a key element in self-care because they allow us to enter into the bodymind's conversation. By getting in touch with our emotions, both by listening to them and by directing them through the psychosomatic network, we gain access to the healing wisdom that is everyone's natural biological right.

"And how do we do this? First by acknowledging and claiming all our feelings, not just the so-called positive ones. Anger, grief, fear—*these emotional experiences are not negative in themselves; in fact, they are vital for our survival. We need anger to define boundaries, grief to deal with our losses, and fear to protect ourselves from danger. It's only when these feelings are denied, so that they cannot be easily and rapidly processed through the system and released, that the situation becomes toxic*...And the more we deny them, the greater the ultimate toxicity, which often takes the form of an explosive release of pent-up emotion. That's when emotion can be damaging to both oneself and others, because its expression becomes overwhelming, sometimes even violent... By letting all emotions have their natural release, the "bad" ones are transformed to "good" ones, and, in Buddhist terms, we are then liberated from suffering. When your emotions are moving and your chemicals flowing, you will experience feelings of freedom, hopefulness, joy, because you are in a healthy, "whole" state." *Molecules of Emotion: Why You Feel the Way You Feel,*" pp. 285,286. Candace B. Pert, Ph.D, Scribner, 1230 Avenue of the Americas. Copyright by Candace B. Pert.

Discoveries & Conclusions

So, if you want short term relief, at the risk of becoming addicted, go for the legal drugs; if you want healing, a way to deal with painful feelings that not only does the job, but carries you—every time—into a state of fulfillment and bliss, try the Freedom Healing Process©.

Notes
Notes for Appendices
Bibliography

Notes

Chapter I
Zeke's Story

1. In order to preserve confidentiality, names of all people used in examples have been changed, and elements of their stories that have no bearing on the meaning of the example have been altered.

2. This technique, now fairly common in experiential therapy, is used in many rehabs to release feelings, especially anger. Because it is done by conscious choice in the therapy setting, it is entirely safe, and very effective. I first encountered it in "Reevaluations Counseling" about 1980. Over the years I have myself experienced its benefits, and have seen it benefit others. Chapters II through VI describe it fully. Children instinctively do it when frustrated or angry. It is holding painful feelings in, instead of releasing them, that makes us—and our kids—crazy. A "Miss Manners" note: if this exercise is disturbing to those around you, be considerate and wait till you're alone.

3. Throughout the book, the word "Your" is capitalized when used with the word "self," to make the point that we are essentially spiritual beings and as such the Guide, Director, Teacher, *etc.*, of our human self.

Chapter II
The Freedom Healing Process

1. Johnson, Samuel. *Rasselas*, ch. XVII, p. 1036. *Eighteenth-Century English Literature*, ed. Geoffrey Tillotson, Paul Fussell Jr., Marshall Waingrow, with the assistance of Brewster Rogerson. Harcourt, Brace & World, Inc. 1969.

Chapter III
Security Need

1. Abraham Maslow: *Toward a Psychology of Being*. Second Edition. Van Nostrand Reinhold Company. New York, 1968.
2. State University of New York Press, 1996. Chapter 2.
3. The story was a segment in the ABC show "20/20." It is recounted from memory, since ABC was unable to find it.
4. Each unmet need has a correlative chemical addiction defense (see "Needs Chart"). To someone suffering from the pain of chronic unmet needs, the mood altering capability of chemical substances is in the majority of cases irresistible.

Chapter IV
Belonging Need

1. "*The Death of the Hired Man*," in Adventures in American Literature. Rev. ed. Edited by H. C. Schweikert, Harcourt, Brace and Company, 1936.
2. Clancy D. MacKenzie,MD and Lance S. Wright,MD, *Delayed Posttraumatic Stress Disorder from Infancy: The Two Trama Mechanism*. Harwood Academic Publishers, Australia, Canada, UK. 1996 by the American Health Association (AHA). Published in the Netherlands by Harwood Academic Publisher GmbH. pp. 26, 29, 34, 42, 51-59, 116-117, 133.

Chapter V
Self-Esteem Need

1. Andrew Marvel, "To His Coy Mistress," Norton Anthology of English Literature, Revised. Vol. 1, pp. 987-8. M. H. Abrams, General Editor. W.W. Norton, 1968.

2. The fact that ulcers are now known to be caused by a particular bacterium doesn't remove stress as a factor. Since the bacterium is a common one carried by all of us, the question arises, what sets it off in some and not in others? Here's a possible hypothesis: the high energy and perfectionism of this type may contribute to depleting the immune system—which otherwise keeps the little germ harmless—and thereby creating the condition for the bacterium to be activated.

3. See Carolyn Myss, *Anatomy of the Spirit*, Three Rivers Press, 1996, *passim*, for discussion of the effect on the body of emotional and spiritual imbalance or illness.

4. This is a neologism. Consider the difference between the following two sentences:
   a. This weekend I have some letters to write.
   b. This weekend I have to ("hafta") write some letters.

The first is an observation or casual intention; the second is an imperative, that is, I am compelled to do it. When this is meant, "hafta" is the invariable word, and its meaning is correctly understood by the listener.

Chapter VI
Autonomy Need

1. The use of a similar phrase—"Trouble Man"—in Black argot, meaning in reference to that ethnicity pretty much what the term "Trouble Child" means for the dysfunctional family, suggests that the four types concept is as applicable sociologically as it is individually.

2. James Baldwin: "This country will accept Blacks only to the extent that they become white." I have been unable—so far—to find its source.

3. Listing these varied organizations together and under the label of "counter-culture" is not meant as a comment on any of them.

4. Whitehead, Hector. *Cairn Terriers*. W. Foyle, Ltd., 119125. Charing Cross Road. London, W. C. 2.

Chapter VII
The Freedom Healing Process
As a Means to Transcendence

1. Perhaps my favorite quotation of all time, I heard it first from a friend and haven't yet been able to find it in any of Tielhard de Chardin's books.

2. State University of New York Press, 1996, pp.50-54. This astonishing, precise, scientific study of the stages of growth shows, among other things, clear evidence of our existence before conception and after death.

3. "Ode: Intimations of Immortality from Recollections of Early Childhood," St. VI, l. 84, p. 511. *World Masterpieces*, 3rd. ed. Maynard Mack, General Editor. Vol. 2. W.W. Norton & Company, Inc. New York, 1973.

4. "Song of Myself," St. 52, l. 169, p. 64. *World Masterpieces*, 3rd. ed. Maynard Mack, General Editor. Vol. 2. W.W. Norton & Company, Inc. New York, 1973.

5. *Four Quartets*. "Burnt Norton," l. 174, p. 16. A Harvest Book. Harcourt, Inc. San Diego New York London.

6. For a wonderful exposition of this concept, see Arthur J. Deikman, *The Observing Self: Mysticism and Psychotherapy*, Bacon Press, Boston, 1982. My concept, which is very similar, derives from my own spiritual practice, initiated by Lloyd Butler, my amazing mentor, Emilie Cady's three books (see footnote 9), and *The Impersonal Life*, C.A. Willing, Publisher. P.O. Box 51. San Gabriel, California. Copyright renewed 1969, Sun Publishing Co., Tonawanda, N.Y. 14150. Deikman's bold and delicious book provided confirmation and validation at certain crucial times when I felt that what I was experiencing and knowing, while experientially valid to me, would be laughingly rejected by J.Q. Public and the world of professional psychology as well. My concept differs only slightly from his but in an important (to me) way: I see the "Observer" as immanent divinity, while Deikman sees it more as a human component.

7. *The Poetry of Robert Frost*, ed. Edward Cannery Lathem Holt, Rinehart and Winston. N.Y. 1967, p. 362.

8. The original story is found in *Sai Baba: The Holy Man and the Psychiatrist*, by Samuel Sandweiss. Birth Day Publishing Co., San Diego, Calif. 1975, p. 69.

9. Aldous Huxley, in *The Perennial Philosophy*, quoting Shankara. Colophon Books, 1944, p. 6. The following writers are some of the many who express this concept: (a) Emilie Cady, *The Collected Works of Emilie Cady*. Unity Books. Unity Village, Missouri, 1995. (b) Da Free John, *The God in Everybody Book*. Dawn Horse Press, Clearlake, Calif. 1983. (c) Arthur J. Deikman, *The Observing Self: Mysticism and Psychotherapy*. Beacon Press, Boston, 1982. (d) *The Impersonal Life*. See note 6. (e) Samuel Sandweiss, *Sai Baba: The Holy Man and the Psychiatrist*. Samuel H. Sandweiss, M.D. Birth Day Publishing Company, San Diego, California, USA.

10. Shakespeare, *Hamlet*, Act III, sc. I, l. 62-63.

11. Abraham Maslow, *Toward a Psychology of Being*. Ch. 3. Second Edition. Van Nostrand Reinhold Company. New York, Copyright 1968.

12. Pleased with my little theory, I shared it with my husband, a physicist, whose mind operates in realms beyond my ken. Chuckling, he said, "That's interesting! You could say, then, that sitting on a hot stove for three seconds would seem like an hour and kissing me for an hour would seem like three seconds!" "What a clever example!" I said. "Can I use it in my book?" "Sure," he said, "But the credit's not mine—it's EINSTEIN'S!"

13. Maslow, *Motivation and Personality*, ch. 1, Harper and Row, Publishers, Inc. New York, Cambridge, Philadelphia. 1987.

14. Shakespeare, *Macbeth*, Act V, Sc. 7, ll. 18-19.

15. *The Poems of Gerard Manley Hopkins*, ed.W.H.Gardner and N.H.Mackensie. Oxford U. Press 1967. 4th edition.

16. Huxley, *Chandogya Upanishad*, p. 4.

17. *World Masterpieces*, ed. Maynard Mack, W.W. Norton and Co. Inc. N.Y. vol. 2, p. 1685.

18. *A Testament of Hope: The Essential Writings and Speeches of Martin Luther King, Jr.*, ed. James Melvin Washington. Harper San Francisco, 1986, p. 18.

19. Huxley, pp. 2, 5.
20. Da Free John, *The God in Everybody Book*, Dawn Horse Press, Clearlake, Calif., 1983, p. 27 "...no matter how many others are present, there is only One Being."
21. Sai Baba, in Sandweiss, p. 208.
22. Paramahansa Yogananda, *Autobiography of a Yogi*. Self-Realization Fellowship. p. 377.
23. Huxley, pp. 3-4, from *Chandyoga Upanishad*.
24. Sandweiss, p. 233.
25. Some notable examples from legend and mythology include Oedipus, Phaeton, Icarus, and Lucifer.
26. Sandweiss, p. 200.
27. John Donne, *Meditation XVII*. The Norton Anthology of English, vol. 1, third ed., p. 1215, l.10.
28. See note 9.
29. *Alcoholics Anonymous World Services*, Inc. Third Edition, p. 60. New York City. 1976
30. See note 5.
31. *Eighteenth-Century English Literature*. Ed. Geoffrey Tillotson, Birkbeck College, University of London; Paul Fussell, Jr., Rutgers University; Marshall Waingrove, Claremont Graduate School. Harcourt, Brace & World, Inc., 1969, p. 1506. New York/Chicago/San Francisco/Atlanta.

Notes for Appendices

Appendix I:
Codependency
1. The term "codependency" as used in this book refers not only to the "Caretaker" type with which in the public mind it has become identified and to which it has become limited, but to the three other codependent types as well, the "Clown Type," the "Forgotten Type," and the "Trouble Type."
2. This concept, central to the Freedom Process, derives from the wonderfully helpful but now rarely read work of Abraham Maslow. See *Motivation and Personality*, Harper and Row, Ind., N.Y., 3rd edition, 1970, *passim*.

3. Maslow, *Toward a Psychology of Being,* 1968, and *Religions, Values, and Peak Experiences,* 1964. Penguin Books. Published by the Penguin Group. Viking Penguin Inc., 40 West 23rd Street, New York, New York, 11010, U.S.A.

4. This refers to the theory developed by Virginia Satir of the four roles typically found in the children of dysfunctional families. The concept I present here shows the source of each of the roles, which I refer to as "types," since "role" carries the connotation of something consciously or deliberately adopted. They have also been renamed, to accord with my perception of their chief characteristics.

5. Subsequently, the Chart revealed four additional systems that correlate to the "needs" concept. They are discussed in "Discoveries and Conclusions," each in its own appendix:

    a. The sequence and nature of the components of the Chart replicate the structure and functions of the brain.

    b. The characteristics of each of the four types correlate to specific Mental Health diagnoses.

    c. The Eastern system of the Chakras correlates in very specific ways to the Hierarchy of Needs.

    d. "From Chaos to Harmony," contributed by Edward R. Pratowski, shows how certain elements of the Process can move to higher levels of intensity and meaning.

6. See Abraham Maslow, *Motivation and Personality,* 1970, pp. 18-22, which explores the relationship between needs and behavior. My debt to his work is acknowledged in the Introduction. The cycle of needs/defenses here presented is my own. Other theorists have developed similar schemes of the stages of growth. Maslow's has proved for me the most useful, effective, and accurate.

Appendix II:
Brain Structure and Functioning

    1. *The Brain: The Last Frontier.* Robert Resnack, Doubleday and Company, Inc. Garden City, N.Y., 1979, p.46, ll.20-21 "area

of the brain most concerned with emotion." Subsequent quotations of Restak will be in the text. See p. 41, Restak.

2. It is tempting to ponder the idea that something deep inside each of us knows what it is like to be snake, a fish, a cat or dog, *etc*. Indeed, we occasionally ascribe animal-like characteristics to others (sometimes derogatory, sometimes complimentary—never of course to ourselves!). The affinity we have for nature and animals is from our common origin ("we have the same Father," a friend of mine said to explain my cat's obvious affection for her upon their first meeting). The cruelty that human beings often exercise on animal beings is a hubristic denial of our common phylogenetic heritage, our essential oneness. I find comfort in reflecting on the spiritual concept found in many "primitive" religions, that animal life and nature life, as well as human life, are sacred, and are equally expressions of the divinity that abides "everywhere at the same time all the time." (Sandweiss, p.216).

3. Walt Whitman, "Song of Myself," St.1, l.13.

4. Andrew Marvell, "To His Coy Mistress," in *The Norton Anthology of English Literature*. 3rd ed. Vol. 1, p. 1288. W.W. Norton & Company, INC. New York.

5. See Clancy McKenzie, M. D., and Lance S. Wright, M.D. *Delayed Post Traumatic Stress Disorders from Infancy: The Two-Trauma Mechanism*, p. 199. Harwood Academic Publishers GMBH, 1996. American Health Association, Bala Cynwyd, Pa. The functioning of the brain actually shifts from the frontal cortex to the anterior lobe: it is darker and the frontal lobe lighter, the reverse of normal adult functioning

6. *Alcoholics Anonymous*, Step 2, altered slightly to make my point. p. 59, 3rd ed.

7. "Exploring Your Brain: Fear and Anxiety," *The Dana Alliance for Brain Initiatives*. Greater Washington Education Telecommunications Association, Inc. 1998, p. 9.

8. Researchers are fast finding evidence of the basic idea being put forth here, that stress (as they call it) in childhood affects brain development and functioning, and that the conditions the child lives in have a major shaping influence on him neurologically and therefore cognitively and limbicly (emotionally) as well.

See *Newsweek Special Edition*, Spring/Summer, 1997, pp. 28-32. See also Dr. Eric Kandel's comment, "...one of the really fascinating things that has emerged from modern studies of the brain is how much the brain is interacting with this environment *during early stages of development,* and how beneficial sensory stimulation and interaction with the mother and father are for brain development per se...an enriched environment leads to having an enriched child." "Exploring Your Memory," *The Dana Alliance for Brain Initiatives*, p. 15.

9. See McKenzie, M.D. and Wright, M.D., *Delayed Post Traumatic Stress Disorders from Infancy.* P. 63 and *passim.*

10. A phrase from the second step of AA.

Appendix III
Mental Health Correlations

1. McKenzie and Wright, 1996, p. 53 and *passim*. These two outstanding psychiatrists and I have come to virtually the same conclusion, they approaching it from the Mental Health field, I from the needs hierarchy. Briefly stated, their thesis is that mental illness in adulthood stems from early childhood trauma, which they support with extensive and convincing data from much clinical experience, research, and testing. My thesis, derived from 23 years of working with clients, is similar: growing up in a family that fails to meet the primary psychological needs is traumatic and shapes the child's persona into one of the four basic personality types, the equivalent of MacKenzie and Wright's "maladaptive defenses." The similarity of the two theories includes the concept presented above, that the earlier in childhood the needs deficit (="trauma") occurs, the more severe the illness in adulthood.

2. McKenzie and Wright put it prior to 24 months (see p. 88).

3. *Ibid.*, p. 199. PET scan showing reduction of neocortical activity and increase in limbic activity in the schizophrenic.

4. Transcript, p. 3. Wallace challenged Mrs. Kaczynski: "Wanda, back in those days—that happened to a lot of youngsters, I mean, who—whose parents couldn't see them in—in a hospital

just as with Ted...And they did not become sociopaths, if you will." She replied: "Right, but can you judge one child by another?" An additional rejoinder is that there is no reason to suppose similar results didn't occur to other children who went through similar experiences—they just haven't yet been publicly uncovered and documented.

    5. See McKenzie and Wright, pp. 25, 51.

    6. John Milton, *"Samson Agonistes,"* in the Norton Anthology of English Literature, vol. 1, p. 1526, l. 1671. 3rd ed.

    7. *"Martha, Martha, Martha,"* vol. 124, #1, p. 50. (Oct. 1996).

    8. This part was obviously written before Martha's troubles with the stock market—which, sadly, confirms my point.

    9. The frustration of those around the TC/passive aggressive can be somewhat reduced by understanding what this really means: the troublesome behavioral patterns are products of emotional/chemical encoding in the limbic system, generally from the beginning or very early in the child's life, and as such are impervious to neocortical reasoning or directives, either from self or others. All this said doesn't make unacceptable behavior acceptable, and it should not be accepted. If, however, through the Freedom Healing Process the emotional/chemical patterns are released and the limbic system reprogrammed, recovery is possible. The Trouble Child will be "transformed by the renewing of his mind."

    10. It is tempting to generalize here. If some MH conditions provably derive from unmet needs, why wouldn't others? Traumas that occur in later childhood or adulthood (*e.g.* family relocation, loss of job, severe illness, war experiences, *etc.*) also can be seen as arising from a needs deficit occurring in the present rather than the past (*e.g.* in the instances above the causes are sudden deficits in the belonging need and the security need). Not surprisingly, *most adult, present-time traumas arise from the same need deficiency as the person's childhood need.* Every present-time reactivation is an opportunity to dislodge more of the original and accumulated pain, so that eventually it dwindles away to nearly nothing.

Appendix 4
The Hierarchy of Needs and the Chakras
   1. Keith Sherwood, *Chakra Therapy: For Personal Growth and Healing*. Llewellyn Publications, St. Paul, Minnesota 55164-0383, U.S.A.
   2. John Donne, *Meditation XVII. Norton Anthology of English Literature*. Third ed. P. 1215, l.11.

Appendix 5
From Chaos to Harmony
   1. The quotation comes from the 1976 Bob Marley album, "Talkin' Blues."

Bibliography

Abrams, M.H. General Editor (1974). *The Norton Anthology of English Literature*. 3rd ed., vol.1. W.W. Norton & Company, Inc., New York.

Alcoholics Anonymous (1976), 3rd ed. Alcoholics Anonymous World Services, Inc., New York City. Third Edition, 1976.

Auden, W.H. and Norman Holmes Pearson (1965). *Romantic Poets: Blake to Poe*. New York. Copyright 1950 by the Viking Press.

Bartlett, John. (1950) Christopher Morley, ed. Louella D. Everett Assoc. Ed. *Familiar Quotations*. Little, Brown and Company, Boston. Copyright by Little, Brown and Co.

Breggin, Peter, M.D. (1991) *Toxic Psychiatry*. St. Martin's Press, New York.

Briggs, Wallace. (1936) *Great Poems of the English Language. An Anthology*. N.Y. Tudor Publishing Co.

Da Free John. (1983) *The God in Everybody Book*. Ed. Saniel Bonder and Georg Feuerstein. The Dawn Horse Press, Clearlake, Calif.

Deikman, J. Arthur, M.D. (1982) *The Observing Self: Mysticism and Psychotherapy*. Beacon Press, Boston.

Diagnostic and Statistical Manual of Mental Disorders (1987) 3rd Ed., revised. American Psychiatric Association.

Eliot, T. S. (1943*) Four Quartets: Burnt Norton*, 1.74. Copyright 1943 by T. S. Eliot. A Harvest Book. Harcourt, Inc. San Diego N.Y. London.

Gardner-Gordon, Joy. (1999) *Pocket Guide to the Chakras*. Copyright 1998 by Vybrational Healing Enterprises. The Crossing Press Pocket Ser.

Gardner, W.H. (1970) *The Poems of Gerard Manly Hopkins*. 4th ed. Oxford N.Y. Oxford U. Press.

Huxley, Aldous (1945*) The Perennial Philosophy*. Harper Colophon Books. Harper & Row, Publishers. New York, Hagerstown, San Francisco, London.

Maslow, Abraham H. *Motivation and Personality*. (1970) Harper & Row, Inc. *Toward the Psychology of Being* (1968). *Religions, Values, and Peak Experiences* (1970) Viking Penguin Inc.

McKenzie, Clancy, M.D. and Lance Wright, M.D. (1996) *Delayed Posttraumatic Stress Disorders from Infancy: The Two Trauma Mechanism*. harwood academic publishers Australia, Canada, U.K.

Pert, Candace, Ph.D. (1997) *Molecules of Emotion: Why You Feel the Way You Feel*. Scribner 1230 Avenue of the Americas. New York, N.Y. 10020.

Restak, Richard M. (1979) *The Brain: The Last Frontier*. Doubleday & Company, Inc. Garden City, N.Y.

Sandweiss, Samuel H., M.D. *Sai Baba: The Holy Man...and the Psychiatrist.* Birth Day Publishing Company, San Diego, Calif.

Schaef, Anne Wilson. (1986) *Co-Dependence: Misunderstood, Mistreated.* Llewellyn Publications. St. Paul, Minnesota. U.S.A.

Teilhard de Chardin, Pierre. (1955). *The Phenomenon of Man.* Harper Colophon Books, Harper & Row, Publishers. New York, Hagerstown, San Francisco, London.

Tillotson, Geoffrey, Paul Fussell, Jr., Marshall Waingrow, with the assistance of Brewster Fogerson (1969) *Eighteenth-Century English Literature.* Harcourt, Brace & World, Inc. New York/Chicago/San Francisco.

Wolfe, Sidney M., M.D., Rose-Ellen Hope, R.Ph. (1993) *Worst Pills Best Pills: The Older Adult's Guide to Avoiding Drug-Induced Death or Illness. Public Citizen Health Research Group. 2000 P Street NW. Suite 700 D.C. 20036.*